Lecture Notes in Artificial Intelligence   12379

Subseries of Lecture Notes in Computer Science

Luis Espinosa-Anke · Carlos Martín-Vide ·
Irena Spasić (Eds.)

Statistical Language and Speech Processing

8th International Conference, SLSP 2020
Cardiff, UK, October 14–16, 2020
Proceedings

 Springer

Editors
Luis Espinosa-Anke (ID)
Cardiff University
Cardiff, UK

Irena Spasić (ID)
Cardiff University
Cardiff, UK

Carlos Martín-Vide (ID)
Rovira i Virgili University
Tarragona, Spain

ISSN 0302-9743   ISSN 1611-3349   (electronic)
Lecture Notes in Artificial Intelligence
ISBN 978-3-030-59429-9   ISBN 978-3-030-59430-5   (eBook)
https://doi.org/10.1007/978-3-030-59430-5

LNCS Sublibrary: SL7 – Artificial Intelligence

This Springer imprint is published by the registered company Springer Nature Switzerland AG
The registered company address is: Gewerbestrasse 11, 6330 Cham, Switzerland

Preface

These proceedings contain the papers that were presented at the 8th International Conference on Statistical Language and Speech Processing (SLSP 2020), held in Cardiff, UK, during October 14–16, 2020.

The scope of SLSP deals with topics of either theoretical or applied interest, discussing the employment of statistical models (including machine learning) within language and speech processing, namely:

- Anaphora and coreference resolution
- Audio event detection
- Authorship identification, plagiarism, and spam filtering
- Biases, explainability, and interpretability in language and speech processing
- Corpora and resources for speech and language
- Data mining, term extraction, and semantic web
- Dialogue systems and spoken language understanding
- Information retrieval and information extraction
- Knowledge representation and ontologies
- Lexicons and dictionaries
- Machine translation and computer-aided translation
- Multimodal technologies
- Natural language understanding and generation
- Neural representation of speech and language
- Opinion mining and sentiment analysis
- Part-of-speech tagging, parsing, and semantic role labeling
- Question-answering systems for speech and text
- Speaker identification and verification
- Speech recognition and synthesis
- Spelling correction
- Text categorization and summarization
- Text normalization and inverted text normalization
- Text-to-speech
- User modeling
- Wake word detection

SLSP 2020 received 25 submissions. Every paper was reviewed by three Program Committee members. There were also a few external experts consulted. After a thorough and vivid discussion phase, the committee decided to accept 13 papers (which represents an acceptance rate of about 52%). The conference program included three invited talks and some poster presentations of work in progress as well.

The excellent facilities provided by the EasyChair conference management system allowed us to deal with the submissions successfully and handle the preparation of these proceedings in time.

We would like to thank all invited speakers and authors for their contributions, the Program Committee and the external reviewers for their diligent cooperation, and Springer for their very professional publishing work.

July 2020

Luis Espinosa-Anke
Carlos Martín-Vide
Irena Spasić

Organization

Program Committee

Mahmoud Al-Ayyoub	Jordan University of Science and Technology, Jordan
Chitta Baral	Arizona State University, USA
Jon Barker	The University of Sheffield, UK
Jean-François Bonastre	University of Avignon, France
Fethi Bougares	University of Le Mans, France
Felix Burkhardt	audEERING, Germany
Nicoletta Calzolari	National Research Council, Italy
Bill Campbell	Amazon, USA
Angel Chang	Simon Fraser University, Canada
Kenneth W. Church	Baidu Research, USA
Philipp Cimiano	Bielefeld University, Germany
Carol Espy-Wilson	University of Maryland, USA
Nikos Fakotakis	University of Patras, Greece
Marcello Federico	Amazon AI, USA
Robert Gaizauskas	The University of Sheffield, UK
Ondřej Glembek	Brno University of Technology, Czech Republic
Ralph Grishman	New York University, USA
Thomas Hain	The University of Sheffield, UK
Gareth Jones	Dublin City University, Ireland
Martin Karafiát	Brno University of Technology, Czech Republic
Philipp Koehn	Johns Hopkins University, USA
Haizhou Li	National University of Singapore, Singapore
Carlos Martín-Vide (Chair)	Rovira i Virgili University, Spain
Seiichi Nakagawa	Chubu University, Japan
Fuchun Peng	Facebook, USA
Stephen Pulman	University of Oxford, UK
Matthew Purver	Queen Mary University of London, UK
Paolo Rosso	Technical University of Valencia, Spain
Diana Santos	University of Oslo, Norway
Irena Spasić	Cardiff University, UK
Tomek Strzalkowski	Rensselaer Polytechnic Institute, USA
Erik Tjong Kim Sang	Netherlands eScience Center, The Netherlands
Tomoki Toda	Nagoya University, Japan
Isabel Trancoso	Instituto Superior Técnico, Portugal
K. Vijay-Shanker	University of Delaware, USA
Hsin-Min Wang	Academia Sinica, Taiwan
Andy Way	Dublin City University, Ireland
Caiming Xiong	Salesforce, USA

Steve Young   University of Cambridge, UK
Wlodek Zadrozny   University of North Carolina at Charlotte, USA
Guodong Zhou   Soochow University, China

Additional Reviewers

Baskar, Murali Karthick
Ghanem, Bilal
Krishna, Hari
Liu, Linqing
Meng, Rui
Szoke, Igor
Teixeira, Francisco
Wu, Yi-Chiao

Contents

Invited Paper

Grapheme-to-Phoneme Transduction for Cross-Language ASR   3
  Mark Hasegawa-Johnson, Leanne Rolston, Camille Goudeseune,
  Gina-Anne Levow, and Katrin Kirchhoff

Language Processing

Conditioned Text Generation with Transfer for Closed-Domain
Dialogue Systems   23
  Stéphane d'Ascoli, Alice Coucke, Francesco Caltagirone,
  Alexandre Caulier, and Marc Lelarge

FacTweet: Profiling Fake News Twitter Accounts   35
  Bilal Ghanem, Simone Paolo Ponzetto, and Paolo Rosso

Named Entity Recognition for Icelandic: Annotated Corpus and Models   46
  Svanhvít L. Ingólfsdóttir, Ásmundur A. Guðjónsson, and Hrafn Loftsson

BERT-Based Sentiment Analysis Using Distillation.   58
  Jan Lehečka, Jan Švec, Pavel Ircing, and Luboš Šmídl

A Cognitive Approach to Parsing with Neural Networks   71
  Vigneshwaran Muralidaran, Irena Spasić, and Dawn Knight

S-Capade: Spelling Correction Aimed at Particularly Deviant Errors   85
  Emma O'Neill, Robert Young, Elsa Thiaville, Muireann MacCarthy,
  Julie Carson-Berndsen, and Anthony Ventresque

Exploring Parameter Sharing Techniques for Cross-Lingual
and Cross-Task Supervision   97
  Matúš Pikuliak and Marián Šimko

A Discourse-Informed Approach for Cost-Effective
Extractive Summarization.   109
  Marta Vicente and Elena Lloret

Towards eXplainable AI in Text Features Engineering
for Concept Recognition   122
  Andreas Waldis, Luca Mazzola, and Alexander Denzler

Speech Processing

A Comparison of Metric Learning Loss Functions for End-To-End Speaker
Verification   137
  Juan M. Coria, Hervé Bredin, Sahar Ghannay, and Sophie Rosset

ANN-MLP Classifier of Native and Nonnative Speakers Using Speech
Rhythm Cues   149
  Ghania Droua-Hamdani

Deep Variational Metric Learning for Transfer of Expressivity
in Multispeaker Text to Speech.   157
  Ajinkya Kulkarni, Vincent Colotte, and Denis Jouvet

Generative Adversarial Network-Based Semi-supervised Learning
for Pathological Speech Classification   169
  Nam H. Trinh and Darragh O'Brien

Author Index   183

Invited Paper

Grapheme-to-Phoneme Transduction
for Cross-Language ASR

Mark Hasegawa-Johnson[1]([⊠]) [iD], Leanne Rolston[2], Camille Goudeseune[1] [iD],
Gina-Anne Levow[2], and Katrin Kirchhoff[3] [iD]

[1] University of Illinois, Champaign, USA
{jhasegaw,cog}@illinois.edu
[2] University of Washington, Seattle, USA
{rolston,levow}@uw.edu
[3] Amazon Alexa, Seattle, USA
katrin.kirchhoff@gmail.com

Abstract. Automatic speech recognition (ASR) can be deployed in
a previously unknown language, in less than 24 h, given just three
resources: an acoustic model trained on other languages, a set of
language-model training data, and a grapheme-to-phoneme (G2P) trans-
ducer to connect them. The LanguageNet G2Ps were created with the
goal of being small, fast, and easy to port to a previously unseen language. Data come from pronunciation lexicons if available, but if there
are no pronunciation lexicons in the target language, then data are generated from minimal resources: from a Wikipedia description of the target
language, or from a one-hour interview with a native speaker of the language. Using such methods, the LanguageNet G2Ps now include simple
models in nearly 150 languages, with trained finite state transducers in
122 languages, 59 of which are sufficiently well-resourced to permit mea-
surement of their phone error rates. This paper proposes a measure of
the distance between the G2Ps in different languages, and demonstrates
that agglomerative clustering of the LanguageNet languages bears some
resemblance to a phylogeographic language family tree. The LanguageNet G2Ps proposed in this paper have already been applied in three
cross-language ASRs, using both hybrid and end-to-end neural architectures, and further experiments are ongoing.

Keywords: Grapheme-to-phoneme transducers · Cross-language
speech recognition · Automatic speech recognition · Under-resourced
languages

1 Why IPA?

Imagine a small group of community organizers, trying to develop a spoken dialog
system for the speakers of their language, using an open-source cross-language

This research was supported by the DARPA LORELEI program. Conclusions and
findings are those of the authors, and are not endorsed by DARPA.

© Springer Nature Switzerland AG 2020
L. Espinosa-Anke et al. (Eds.): SLSP 2020, LNAI 12379, pp. 3–19, 2020.
https://doi.org/10.1007/978-3-030-59430-5_1

portability app. The first thing they might do is record examples of a few key words. If their language has a writing system (about 4000 languages do [17]), or if they have invented one [1], then they might write each word as they say it, expecting the app to use the same orthography to transcribe their speech in the future. The app creates an internal pronunciation model for each word, and reads the words back to them. After correcting its mistakes, they test it by narrating a few stories.

Such an app does not yet exist. Although the technologies necessary to create it are currently available, their error rates are still too high for casual uses. These technologies are, essentially, cross-linguistic automatic speech recognition (ASR) and cross-linguistic text-to-speech synthesis (TTS): ASR and TTS models that can be trained on several well-resourced languages, and then applied or adapted to a never-before-seen target language on the basis of one or two pronunciations, each, of a few dozen words. Every existing ASR or TTS paradigm with the potential to be applied, in such a scenario, uses the phone symbols of the international phonetic alphabet (IPA) [28] to organize the various sources of knowledge that need to be transferred from the training languages to the test language. This article discusses methods for converting text (graphemes) to phonemes (grapheme-to-phoneme transduction, or G2P) in a manner that can be extended to a previously unseen language in a few minutes using data that is usually available on Wikipedia or in elementary grammar primers.

The IPA is designed based on two key principles, which we might call the distinctive feature principle and the linguistic principle. The distinctive feature principle insists that IPA symbols should not be viewed as atomic, but rather, as "shorthand ways of indicating certain intersections of... natural classes of sounds that operate in phonological rules and historical sound changes" [34]. The interpretation of IPA phones as intersections of "distinctive features" (to use Ladefoged's term [34]) permits us to generalize from phones that we have seen (in one of the training languages) to novel phones (in the test language) by interpolating in the feature space [13], or by simply copying the acoustic parameters of an IPA phone from the training languages to the test language [51].

The linguistic principle, by contrast, limits the granularity with which the symbols of the IPA may sample distinctive feature space, by insisting that "the sounds that are represented are primarily those that distinguish one word from another" in at least one language [34]. The phonemes of any given language are the sounds that distinguish one word from another; the IPA phone symbols are intentionally designed to have only the granularity necessary so that every language's phoneme inventory can be written as a list of phones. The symbols of the IPA are therefore a "summary of agreed phonetic knowledge" [34] that can usefully prevent us from trying to model acoustic variability that is so small, or so context-dependent, that it never distinguishes words in any known language.

Because of the benefits of the distinctive feature principle and the linguistic principle, most cross-linguistic knowledge transfer, for speech technology applications, makes use of units that are indexed by IPA phones. Typically, acoustic spectra are clustered to form fenones [5], or triphone states are clustered to form senones [26] or projected onto a bottleneck feature space [21], each of which is considered to be the refinement of an IPA phone category. When speech technology needs to be rapidly developed in a previously unstudied language, some sort of knowledge-guided [51] or unsupervised [58] method is used to determine which of the IPA phones it should use. Models of those phones (including their component fenones, senones, bottleneck features, or Gaussian modes [31]) are then adapted from the training languages to the test language.

2   Related Research

Rule-based grapheme-to-phoneme transducers are as old as writing; for example, the Ashtádhyáyi of Pánini is a sequence of context-dependent rules specifying the relationship between the grapheme sequence and the phoneme sequence of Sanskrit [55]. Prior to 1960, ASR used either whole-word models [12] or isolated phone models [16]. In 1961, Hughes used a pronunciation lexicon (a table matching the graphemic form of each word to its phonemic form) to measure phone error rate [25], and Peterson proposed using a similar table to automatically map recognized phone strings to recognized words [45]. A proposal to deal with out-of-vocabulary words by decomposing them into component graphemes and digraphs was published in 1963 [33], and the name "grapheme-to-phoneme translation" was given to this process in 1969 [35]. Weighted finite state transducers (WFSTs) for grapheme-to-phoneme translation were proposed in 1991 [20]. The joint-sequence modeling approach was proposed in [6], and refined in the software toolkit Phonetisaurus [42].

G2P transducers were developed for most of the languages of Europe in the 1970s and 1980s; G2Ps for Dutch, English and German were tested in the same speech synthesis system in 1988 [53]. WFST G2Ps were trained for seven languages in 1996 [47], and for 85 languages in 2016 [14]. The latter was tested on a 292-language corpus, which was further used to train a 311-language neural sequence-to-sequence G2P [44]. Apparently none of these efforts have been released as open source, but the 61-language rule-based open-source G2P epitran [40] is available at https://github.com/dmort27/epitran.

3   Training and Testing the G2Ps

This article introduces the LanguageNet G2P transducers, available under an MIT Open Source License from https://github.com/uiuc-sst/g2ps/. At the date of this writing, lookup tables for the most common graphemes and digraphs, derived from Wikipedia descriptions, are available for 142 languages. The dataset includes WFST transducers that have been trained and tested in Phonetisaurus [42] for 122 of these languages, using additional sources of data described below.

Table 1. In languages with no available pronunciation lexicon, G2Ps were trained using descriptions of their orthography copied from Wikipedia. Left: a copy of six lines from the table on the Wikipedia page, "French orthography." Right: lines from the table at left, reformatted into a simplified partial-word pronunciation lexicon that can be used to train a G2P.

Spelling		Major value (IPA)	Examples of major value
ç		/s/	ça, garçon, reçu
c	before e, i, y	/s/	cyclone, loquace, ciel
	elsewhere	/k/	cabas, crasse, lac
cc	before e, i, y	/ks/	accès
	elsewhere	/k/	accord
ch		/ʃ/	chat, douche

ç	s
ce	s ə
ci	s i
cy	s i
c	k
cce	k s ə
cc	k
ch	ʃ

3.1 Data Collection

Three sources of data were used to train G2Ps in this article: Wikipedia symbol tables, LanguageNet open-source mined lexicons, and commercial lexicons.

The first source of data used to train the LanguageNet is a set of letter-to-sound rules, for each language, mined from Wikipedia. Wikipedia symbol tables were mined for each language by searching for entries of the form "<language> orthography" or "<language> alphabet." HTML tables on Wikipedia were reformatted into partial-word dictionaries, as shown in the last two columns of Table 1. Tables on Wikipedia do not provide information about letter-to-sound probabilities, but they often provide information about context: contexts are encoded as explicit digraphs and trigraphs (e.g., <ce,ci,cy,cce,cc,ch> in Table 1), while the unigraph entry (<c>→/k/ in Table 1) expresses the "elsewhere" case from the table on Wikipedia.

The second source of data used to train the LanguageNet is a set of pronunciation lexicons, mined incidentally during the collection of Rolston and Kirchhoff's master lexicon files (masterlex) [49]. The masterlexes are a set of bilingual translation dictionaries, mapping words from 103 non-English languages into their English near-equivalents. The data were mined semi-automatically from sources including Blench [7], Chaihana [19], Sözlük [11], IATE [27], wiktionary, ICD [48], OMWN [8], Panlex [29], TaaS [2], and a number of LDC sources. Each word, in each of the 103 source languages, is tagged with up to 11 attributes, depending on the type of information provided by the original data source: orthography, lemma, part of speech, transliteration, pronunciation, English translation, score, dialect, domain, data source, and morphological variants. Fields were populated only if a source provided the relevant information, and some fields were not usefully populated by any source. The pronunciation field was populated in about half of the available sources (40 out of 103). Entries with a pronunciation were used to train G2P transducers.

Finally, data from a number of other sources were used to train the G2P models. The Gulf Arabic model was trained using the Qatari Arabic Corpus [18], available at http://ifp-08.ifp.uiuc.edu/public/QAC/. Masterlex data on German, Dutch, and English were augmented with data from CELEX [4]. LDC corpora from BABEL and CALLHOME were also used to train G2Ps in the 24 BABEL languages, and in three of the CALLHOME languages.

3.2   Training the FSTs

Grapheme-to-phoneme finite state transducers (G2P FSTs) have been trained and tested thus far in 122 languages, using the Phonetisaurus [42] toolkit.

Phonetisaurus is based on graphone language modelling [6]. A graphone is defined to be an alignment between a sequence of graphemes and a sequence of phonemes. For example, the longest graphone in Table 1 is the trigraph-to-triphone alignment <cce>:/ksə/. Phonetisaurus does not permit 3-to-3 graphones of the form <cce>:/ksə/; instead, it requires each graphone to be either an s_1-to-1 or a 1-to-s_2 alignment, for $s_1 \leq S_1$ and $s_2 \leq S_2$, where S_1 and S_2 are user-defined parameters. Training proceeds as follows:

1. For each word in the lexicon, an initial graph of candidate alignments is created. The initial alignment graph contains all possible alignments of s_1 graphemes to one phoneme, and all alignments of one grapheme to s_2 phonemes, for $s_1 \leq S_1$ and $s_2 \leq S_2$. All such graphones are initially given equal probability.
2. Several iterations of the expectation maximization (EM) algorithm are used to re-estimate the probability of every graphone. After EM re-estimation, the Viterbi algorithm is used to compute the maximum likelihood graphone sequence for each word in the dictionary, which is printed out as training data for a graphone language model.
3. A graphone N-gram language model is trained using Kneser-Ney backoff [30], where the context length, N, is a user-specified parameter. The fully trained language model is then compiled into FST form using methods described in [3].

Language model backoff arcs prevent the FST from assigning zero probability to any sequence of known graphones. For example, if the graphone <ough>:/u/ occurs in the training lexicon only at the end of a word, then the learned lexicon can compute the test analysis <throughput>:/θrupʊt/ only by following a backoff arc from the end-of-word state to the start-of-word state, then following the unigram arc <p>:/p/. For this reason, it is possible to treat the Wikipedia symbol tables as if they were pronunciation lexicons; Phonetisaurus learns the mappings listed there, and learns backoff weights that permit them to be sequenced in any novel word.

Source data files (including Wikipedia, masterlex, and other sources) for each language were divided between training, development test, and evaluation test. Wikipedia symbol tables were assigned, in their entirety, to the training set. Other sources were divided: out of every five sequential entries, three were assigned to training, one to development, and one to evaluation. Graphone language models were trained using all hyperparameters in the range $S_1 \in \{2, 3, 4\}$, $S_2 \in \{2, 3, 4\}$, $N \in \{1, 2, 4, 8\}$. Combinations with the lowest error rate on the development test set were then evaluated using the evaluation test set. Models were also trained, but not tested, for languages with no data source other than the Wikipedia symbol table (e.g., because the masterlex file contained no pronunciations) using the hyperparameters $S_1 = 2$, $S_2 = 2$, $N = 2$.

3.3   Testing the FSTs

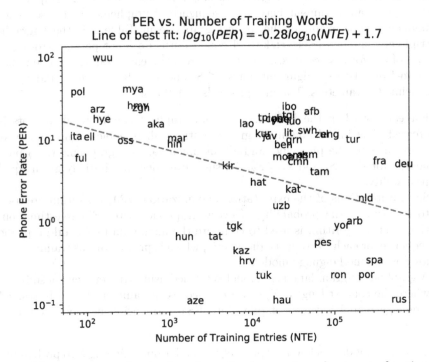

Fig. 1. Phone error rate of trained grapheme-to-phoneme transducers, as a function of the number of training words, for 59 languages. Each language is indicated by its ISO 639-3 code.

Figure 1 shows phone error rate (PER) on the evaluation test set, as a function of the number of training entries (NTE), for the 59 languages that have evaluation test data. Languages are labeled by their ISO 639-3 codes. PER is generally a decreasing function of NTE: the figure shows the line of best fit in log-log space, $\log_{10}(PER) = -0.28 \log_{10}(NTE) + 1.7$. The figure shows some languages with extremely high PER, and some with extremely low PER. Post-hoc analysis suggests that most outliers are explained by one of two causes.

First, data sparsity: some of the languages with the highest PER are languages with complex grapheme systems, whose training datasets are insufficient to represent all of the characters in the orthography. The most obvious such example is Wu Chinese (ISO 639-3: wuu), which has a 90% PER. The training data contains almost 200 Chinese characters, and their phonetic pronunciations; none of the characters in the test dataset are in the training dataset. Similarly, Tamazight (zgh) includes both Latin and Tifinagh characters, Burmese (mya) includes both Latin and Burmese characters, and Hmong Dô (hmv) includes a variety of Latin-coded lexical tones, all of which result in a low degree of overlap between the training and test datasets.

Second, label noise: some of the pronunciation lexicons used as training material were apparently created not by humans, but by rule-based G2P transducers from the provided orthography. Automatically generated reference pronunciations result in unrealistically low or unrealistically high PER, depending on whether the distributed data include just one pronunciation per word (e.g., Azerbaijani (aze), Hausa (hau), and Russian (rus)), or two to three alternate pronunciations per word (Igbo (ibo), Tok Pisin (tpi) and Tagalog (tgl)). All of these G2Ps might be useful in a real application, but there is no way to be sure, because the evaluation test corpora were apparently constructed from the same algorithms as the training corpora.

Data sparsity and label noise seem to have less influence on the languages near the regression line. There is reason to believe, therefore, that the phone error rate of a G2P is reasonably well modeled as $10^{1.7-0.28\log_{10}(NTE)} \approx 50/\sqrt[3.5]{NTE}$.

4 Applications

The LanguageNet G2Ps were designed for zero-resource speech technology applications, e.g., for the purpose of deploying automatic speech recognition in a language for which no training data exist. Sections 4.2 and 4.3 describe two such systems. Section 4.1 explores the information the G2Ps have learned, by clustering the languages of the world according to a novel G2P distance proposed here.

4.1 Clustering Languages Based on Their G2Ps

A language family is a group of languages whose "divergent development...does not completely obscure the fact that these languages are descended from a common source" [23]. Comparative linguistics attempts to reconstruct the ancestral language by the analysis of regular relationships among word forms and syntax. In particular, the pronunciations of words change gradually over time, in a manner that "is remarkably regular...This fact is, of course, a great boon to historical linguists, since it makes the job of tracing linguistic forms through history much easier" [23]. By studying sound change in particular, one can not only reconstruct the ancestral language shared by two modern languages, but also estimate how many centuries have passed since they diverged, resulting in phylogeographic language family trees that can be used to infer the movements of peoples in prehistoric times [9,32] or that, conversely, may need to be modified or dissolved in the face of new scholarship [37]. Unlike pronunciation, though, graphemes often change in step discontinuities. Often, multiple scripts co-exist, but a government decision may suddenly cause documents in one particular script to become far more common, sometimes with the intention of promoting collaboration with a specified international community. Striking recent examples include the adoption of the Latin script for Turkish [24], Malay [43], and Uzbek [52], of Cyrillic for Kazakh and Kirghiz, and of the Arabic script for Uighur [38]. These considerations suggest the following hypothesis: The G2P transducers for two languages produce similar pronunciations, for any given written form, if the two languages are part of the same language family and use the same script, or if the two languages have both recently adapted their orthography from a common international origin.

Phonetisaurus trains G2Ps so that the cost of any given path is the joint probability of the orthographic word w and its pronunciation π, so the G2P defines a joint probability mass function $p(w, \pi)$ over the set of all possible word-pronunciation pairs. The distance between two G2Ps p and q can usefully be defined as the expected distance between the pronunciations π and ρ that they produce in response to the same orthographic form w, averaged over the orthographic forms of both languages:

$$D_{G2P}(p,q) = \frac{1}{2} \mathop{\mathbb{E}}_{p(w,\pi)q(\rho|w)} [D_{PRON}(\pi, \rho)] + \frac{1}{2} \mathop{\mathbb{E}}_{q(w,\pi)p(\rho|w)} [D_{PRON}(\pi, \rho)] \quad (1)$$

The distance between two pronunciations should be proportional to the string edit distance between their phone strings $\pi = \{\pi_1, \ldots, \pi_K\}$ and $\rho = \{\rho_1, \ldots, \rho_L\}$. String edit distance is symmetric if deletion and insertion are treated identically as the pairwise phone distances $D_{PH}(\pi_k, \varnothing) = D_{PH}(\varnothing, \rho_l) = 1$ between any non-null phone symbol, π_k or ρ_l, and the null-phone symbol $\varnothing$. Let $I_M(\pi)$ be an operator that inserts $M - K$ copies of the null phone between the elements of π, resulting in a string $\tilde{\pi} = \{\tilde{\pi}_1, \ldots, \tilde{\pi}_M\}$. Then the normalized string edit distance can be written:

$$D_{PRON}(\pi, \rho) = \frac{1}{\max(K, L)} \min_M \min_{\tilde{\pi}=I_M(\pi)} \min_{\tilde{\rho}=I_M(\rho)} \sum_{m=1}^{M} D_{PH}(\tilde{\pi}_m, \tilde{\rho}_m) \quad (2)$$

Normalization by $\max(K, L)$ guarantees that $0 \leq D_{PRON}(\pi, \rho) \leq 1$ if and only if $0 \leq D_{PH}(\pi_k, \rho_l) \leq 1$ for each pair of phone symbols (π_k, ρ_l).

Ladefoged defines the distinctive features to be "natural classes of sounds that operate in phonological rules and historical sound changes" [34]; more precisely, historical sound changes tend to modify only a few of the distinctive features of a sound, while leaving the remainder unchanged. PHOIBLE [39] defines 37 distinctive features for 2908 different phones, including both simple phones (composed of a single IPA character, possibly with diacritics) and complex phones (composed of one or more IPA symbols in sequence, e.g., affricates and diphthongs). Possible values of each feature include the symbols [+], [−], blank (feature unspecified), and a variety of feature contours. For example, the dipthong /aɪ/ has the height feature [−+], meaning that the tongue moves from a [−high] position to a [+high] position. LanguageNet augments these 37 features with 8 features that can be easily specified for lexical tone sequences in all of the LanguageNet languages, and that are unspecified for all non-tonal IPA symbols: 4 tone height features (topTone, highTone, lowTone, bottomTone) and 4 tone contour features (riseTone, fallTone, hatTone, dipTone). The concatenation of the segmental and tonal features yields a total of $D = 45$ distinctive features per phone. Let each phone π_k be a vector of such feature values, $\pi_k = [f_1(\pi_k), \ldots, f_D(\pi_k)]$. Then

$$D_{PH}(\pi_k, \rho_l) = \frac{1}{D} \sum_{d=1}^{D} \mathbb{1}\left(f_d(\pi_k) \neq f_d(\rho_l)\right) \tag{3}$$

where $\mathbb{1}()$ is the unit indicator function.

The 122 Phonetisaurus G2Ps of the LanguageNet were agglomeratively clustered, using nearest-centroid agglomeration [15], resulting in a complete binary phylogenetic tree over all of the 122 languages.[1] Expectations in Eq. 1 were approximated by selecting up to 1000 orthographic words from each of the two languages. Normalizations in Eq. 2 and 3 guarantee that the distance between any pair of languages is $0 \leq D_{G2P} \leq 1$. The distance at which any pair of clusters are merged is therefore an intuitively meaningful measure of the family relationship between the two languages. If two languages use completely different character sets (for example, one uses Cyrillic characters and one uses Arabic characters), then the G2P of one language is completely unable to process words from the other language, resulting in a distance very close to $D_{G2P}(p, q) \approx 1$. On the other hand, if the two languages produce very similar pronunciations in response to the same orthographic string, then the distance between their G2Ps is $D_{G2P}(p, q) \approx 0$.

---

[1] The complete tree is at github.com/uiuc-sst/g2ps/blob/master/g2ppy/cluster/agglo merative_cluster_output_2020-07-18.txt.

Table 2. Agglomerative clustering results: Clusters with internal distance $D_{G2P} \leq$ 0.2. Numbers between rows show the distance separating the two clusters. Languages separated from the nearest cluster by $D_{G2P} > 0.2$ are not shown. Dashed horizontal lines indicate an inter-cluster distance of $D_{G2P} > 0.4$; solid horizontal lines indicate an inter-cluster distance of $D_{G2P} > 0.8$. Parentheses show the agglomerative structure within each cluster.

Malayo-Polynesian, Bantu, Indo-Aryan:	(((((((Sundanese, Malay), Indonesian), Luba-Lulua), Kongo), Shona), Rohingya), Kinyarwanda)
	0.202
Cushitic, Polynesian:	((Somali, Oromo), Fijian)
	0.311
Polynesian:	(Samoan, Tonga)
	0.441
Tahitic:	(Rarotongan, Maori)
	0.404
Finnic, Germanic:	((Estonian, Finnish), Danish)
	0.873
South Slavic:	((Serbian, Bosnian), Macedonian)
	0.958
Iranian:	(Dari, Persian)

Table 2 shows all of the clusters that were merged at levels of $D_{G2P} \leq 0.2$. Other languages that joined each of these clusters at levels of $D_{G2P} > 0.2$ are not shown in the table, but the maximum distance threshold separating each pair of clusters is shown as a three-digit floating point number separating the corresponding rows. Several observations are salient.

- Each cluster is composed primarily, but not exclusively, of members of the same language family: Sundanese, Malay, and Indonesian are members of the Malayo-Polynesian family, while Dari and Persian are members of the Iranian family.
- Neighboring clusters tend to be from related language families. For example, Malayo-Polynesian, Polynesian, and Tahitic languages are spread across the first four clusters.
- Recent history sometimes trumps family relationships: the Danish G2P is similar to those of Estonian and Finnish, despite the lack of any family relationship.
- Script differences are marked by large inter-cluster distances, of $D_{G2P} = 0.873$ between the languages that use Latin vs. Cyrillic characters, and of $D_{G2P} = 0.958$ between those that use Cyrillic vs. Arabic characters. These distances are less than 1.0 only because some of the source dictionaries, in the Slavic and Iranian clusters, include small numbers of Latin-spelled words.
- Not all cluster results are well explained by family or historical relationships among languages. The largest cluster includes three Malayo-Polynesian

languages, four Bantu languages, and an Indo-Aryan language. These three language families share no common history, except that all eight languages have, during the twentieth century, developed national standards based on the Latin alphabet.

4.2   ASR24

By converting script into IPA phone symbols, one can build an ASR in a previously unknown language in about two hours. The ASR24 [22] cross-language ASR toolkit was built and tested for a number of such experiments. It was designed to solve the problem of recognizing speech in a language for which we have monolingual speech samples, monolingual texts (usually including a highly skewed assortment of religious texts and technical manuals, quickly but incompletely normalized), but no transcribed speech.

Without transcribed speech one cannot train an acoustic model. Therefore ASR24 uses pretrained acoustic models, from the English-language ASpIRE model [54] distributed by the maintainers of the Kaldi toolkit [46]. The phone set of the ASpIRE recognizer was mapped to IPA, so that its acoustic models can be appropriated for use in any language.

The target language's G2P is created by reformatting the Wikipedia description of its alphabet, and then running Phonetisaurus, as described in Sect. 3.2. If the target language lacks a Wikipedia description (as for Ilocano, at the time of the experiments described here), then its G2P is initialized using its closest related language in LanguageNet, and then refined on the basis of one hour of interaction with a paid native speaker of the target language. If the language's character set is not in LanguageNet, and if its Wikipedia description lacks some characters (e.g., Odia), then a symbol table is created from scratch, by asking a paid native speaker consultant to read each of the characters, and by transcribing that speech into IPA.

Test data are collected from an additional five hours of interaction with a paid native speaker consultant. The native speaker is asked to read texts in the target language. Although these texts are not sufficient to train the acoustic model, they are useful for estimating word error rate (WER). Available texts are divided into those used to train the language model (LM), and those read by the native speaker consultant as test material.

Table 3. Cross-language ASR experiments on seven languages. **Models** = salient details of LM or G2P (Trigram LM = from raw text, Alt LM = includes Brown clusters, clean = remove Bible stopwords and non-standard text, better truecasing, separate language-specific apostrophized affixes, Gaz = include words from a gazetteer of relevant place names). **Train time** = time required to clean monolingual text and train a language model (2 h and 8 h were maximum permitted wall-clock times, including data cleaning; some systems required less training time). **Build time** = wall-clock time required to compose LM with acoustic model (measured only for the first LM in each language). **Transcribe speed** = minutes of transcribed speech per minute of computation (measured only for the first LM in each language). **WER** = word error rate.

Language	Models	Train Time (h)	Build Time (min)	Transcribe Speed (×RT)	WER
Somali	Trigram LM	2	90	7	93.45%
	Alt LMs, clean	8			84.58%
Hindi	Trigram+Gaz LM	2	25	20	95.09%
	Alt LMs, clean	8			93.71%
Zulu	Trigram+Gaz LM	2	60	20	108.26%
	Alt LMs, clean	8			90.22%
Sinhala	Trigram LM	2	67	25	92.4%
	Alt LMs, clean	8			93.5%
Kinyarwanda	Trigram LM	2	76	23	88.1%
	Alt LMs, clean	8			87.1%
Odia	Trigram+Gaz LM	2	20	20	98%
	Alt LMs, clean	8			106%
Ilocano	Tagalog G2P+Trigram	2	30	20	93%
	Ilocano G2P+Trigram	2			88%
	Alt LMs+Gaz, clean	8			77%

Experiments using this setup were performed for seven languages, five whose G2Ps were already in LanguageNet (Somali, Hindi, Zulu, Sinhala, and Kinyarwanda) and two that were not (Odia and Ilocano). Results are shown in Table 3. In all cases, build time (composition of the LM with the acoustic model) took 25 to 90 min, and transcription of novel audio was performed 20× faster than real time. Two checkpoints are listed. Checkpoint 1 used a trigram LM (trained in less than two hours). Checkpoint 2 used a class-based LM (if it gave lower perplexity than a trigram) trained after data cleaning (removing Bible stopwords, improved truecasing and sentence segmentation, separate language-dependent apostrophized function words from their neighbors). Word error rates (WER) are still quite high, but for the most part, they reduce substantially as a result of the six hours of extra modeling effort and data cleaning that were undertaken between checkpoints 1 and 2.

4.3   Discophone

End-to-end neural cross-language ASR experiments using LanguageNet's G2Ps were reported in [58] and [36]. In [58], speech recognizers were trained and tested using a transformer [56] sequence-to-sequence neural network implemented using the ESPnet [57] framework. In [36], speech recognizers were trained and tested using a listen, attend and spell architecture [10], implemented in the Dynet XNMT framework [41]. Speech included transcribed speech data from thirteen languages: five from the GlobalPhone distribution [50] (Czech, French, Spanish, Mandarin and Thai), and eight from the BABEL distribution (Cantonese, Bengali, Vietnamese, Lao, Zulu, Amharic, Javanese, and Georgian). The training subsets for each language varied from 11.5 h (Spanish) to 126.6 h (Cantonese). Training data transcriptions for 13 languages were converted to IPA using LanguageNet G2Ps. In [58], data were used to train three sets of speech recognizers per language: monolingual (trained and tested on the train and test subsets of the same language), multilingual (trained on all languages), and cross-lingual (trained on all languages except the test language). In [36], monolingual and multilingual systems were trained on only three tonal languages (Mandarin, Cantonese, and Vietnamese), and the cross-lingual setting used one hour of transcribed data from the test language (Lao) in order to adapt each recognizer.

An end-to-end phone recognizer, such as those trained and tested in [36,58], generates a sequence of IPA phone characters, with no further distinction between simple phones, diacritics, or complex phones. The reported error rate is therefore a new metric, which was named "phonetic token error rate" (PTER) in [58]: the string edit distance between the reference and hypothesis IPA character strings, counting the number of substitutions, deletions, and insertions of unicode IPA characters. PTER varied considerably among the 13 languages studied by [58], but in all 13 cases, the multilingual ASR was better than the monolingual ASR, and the cross-lingual ASR was worse than either. Multilingual PTER ranged from 8.1% (Czech) to 41% (Javanese). Cross-lingual PTER ranged from 61.7% (French) to 99.7% (again, Javanese).

In general, IPA tone symbols caused problems for the cross-lingual system in [58]. Mandarin had only 17.2% PTER in the multilingual setting, but had 85.9% PTER in the cross-lingual setting, because of incorrectly generated tones. Javanese is not a tone language, but most of its errors, in the cross-lingual setting, came from the incorrect insertion of IPA tone symbols. The problem of IPA tone symbols was studied in more depth by [36]. Four different models were considered. In the first model, the neural net was trained to output both phones and tones on the same output tier, as in [58]. In the second model, tones and phones were split into separate training and sequences, and the net learned to generate them on separate output tiers. The third model used all three of the tiers from models 1 and 2; the fourth model added a fourth tier, containing voice quality features. The 1-tier system was most successful if phones and tones were recombined into one stream prior to scoring. If phones and tones were scored separately, then the 4-tier model gave lowest error rates multilingually, but the 2-tier model was superior cross-lingually, suggesting that the simpler model might generalize better across language boundaries.

5 Conclusions

Creating ASR for all 7000 languages of the world requires methods that rapidly create a G2P for any new language. The methods proposed here create a G2P in about an hour, based on data from a standard alphabet table from Wikipedia or from a one-hour interview with a native speaker. Methods have also been developed to incorporate larger data sources into the G2P training pipeline, and have been applied for this purpose in 60 of the languages in the current distribution. Agglomerative clustering of the resulting G2Ps, using a novel G2P distance metric proposed here, results in clusters that tend to group together members of the same language family, with some exceptions. Cross-language ASRs using the LanguageNet G2Ps have been tested on 19 different languages: 7 using acoustic models trained on only one source language, and 13 using acoustic models each trained on 3 to 12 source languages (Zulu is in both sets). Word error rates and phonetic token error rates of cross-language ASR are high; ongoing research seeks methods that will reduce them.

References

1. Adda, G., et al.: Breaking the unwritten language barrier: the BULB project. In: Proceedings of the SLTU-2016 5th Workshop on Spoken Language Technologies for Under-resourced Languages (2016)
2. Aker, A., Paramita, M.L., Pinnis, M., Gaizauskas, R.J.: Bilingual dictionaries for all EU languages. In: Proceedings of the Conference on Language Resources and Evaluation (LREC), pp. 2839–2845 (2014)
3. Allauzen, C., Mohri, M., Roark, B.: Generalized algorithms for constructing statistical language models. In: Proceedings of the Annual Meeting of the Association for Computational Linguistics, pp. 40–47 (2003)
4. Baayen, R., Piepenbrock, R., Gulikers, L.: CELEX2. Technical report, LDC96L14, Linguistic Data Consortium (1996)
5. Bahl, L.R., Brown, P.F., de Souza, P.V., Picheny, M.A.: Acoustic Markov models used in the Tangora speech recognition system. In: Proceedings ICASSP, pp. 497–500 (1988)
6. Bisani, M., Ney, H.: Joint-sequence models for grapheme-to-phoneme conversion. Speech Commun. **50**(5), 434–451 (2008)
7. Blench, R., Nebel, A.: Dinka-English and English-Dinka dictionary (2005)
8. Bond, F., Paik, K.: A survey of wordnets and their licenses. Small **8**(4), 5 (2012)
9. Bouckaert, R., et al.: Mapping the origins and expansion of the Indo-European language family. Science **337**(6097), 957–960 (2012)
10. Chan, W., Jaitly, N., Le, Q., Vinyals, O.: Listen, attend and spell: a neural network for large vocabulary conversational speech recognition. In: Proceedings ICASSP, pp. 4960–4964 (2016). https://doi.org/10.1109/ICASSP.2016.7472621

11. Dâna, A.: Sözlük (2006). www.denizyuret.com/2006/11/turkish-resources.html. Accessed 20 July 2020
12. Davis, K., Biddulph, R., Balashek, S.: Automatic recognition of spoken digits. J. Acoust. Soc. Am. **24**(6), 637–642 (1952)
13. Deng, L.: Integrated-multilingual speech recognition using universal phonological features in a functional speech production model. In: Proceedings ICASSP (1997). https://doi.org/10.1109/ICASSP.1997.596110
14. Deri, A., Knight, K.: Grapheme-to-phoneme models for (almost) any language. In: Proceedings 54th Annual Meeting of the Association for Computational Linguistics (Volume 1: Long Papers), pp. 399–408 (2016). https://doi.org/10.18653/v1/P16-1038
15. Duda, R.O., Hart, P.E., Stork, D.G.: Pattern Classification. Wiley, New York (2001)
16. Dudley, H., Balashek, S.: Automatic recognition of phonetic patterns in speech. J. Acoust. Soc. Am. **30**, 721–732 (1958)
17. Eberhard, D.M., Simons, G.F., Fennig, C.D. (eds.): Ethnologue: Languages of the World. 23rd edn. SIL International, Dallas (2020). www.ethnologue.com
18. Elmahdy, M., Hasegawa-Johnson, M., Mustafawi, E.: Development of a TV broadcasts speech recognition system for Qatari Arabic. In: Proceedings of the Conference on Language Resources and Evaluation (LREC), pp. 3057–3061 (2014)
19. Garrett, J., Lastowka, G., et al.: Turkmen-English dictionary: a SPA project of Peace Corps Turkmenistan (1996)
20. Gilloux, M.: Automatic learning of word transducers from examples. In: Proceedings EUROSPEECH, pp. 107–112 (1991)
21. Grézl, F., Karafiaát, M., Veselý, K.: Adaptation of multilingual stacked bottle-neck neural network structure for new language. In: Proceedings ICASSP, pp. 7704–7708 (2014)
22. Hasegawa-Johnson, M., Goudeseune, C., Levow, G.A.: Fast transcription of speech in low-resource languages (2019). https://arxiv.org/abs/1909.07285
23. Hock, H.H.: Principles of Historical Linguistics. Mouton de Gruyter, Berlin (1991)
24. Howard, D.A.: The History of Turkey. Greenwood, Santa Barbara (2016)
25. Hughes, G.W.: The Recognition of Speech by Machine. Ph.D. Thesis, MIT (1961)
26. Hwang, M.Y., Huang, X.: Subphonetic modeling for speech recognition. In: Human Language Technology (HLT), pp. 174–179 (1992)
27. IATE: Interactive terminology for Europe (2020). https://iate.europa.eu. Accessed 26 July 2020
28. International Phonetic Association: Handbook of the International Phonetic Association, Cambridge (1999)
29. Kamholz, D., Pool, J., Colowick, S.M.: PanLex: building a resource for panlingual lexical translation. In: Proceedings of the Conference on Language Resources and Evaluation (LREC), pp. 3145–3150 (2014)
30. Kneser, R., Ney, H.: Improved backing-off for M-gram language modeling. In: Proc. ICASSP, pp. 181–184 (1995)
31. Köhler, J.: Comparing three methods to create multilingual phone models for vocabulary independent speech recognition tasks. In: Multi-Lingual Interoperability in Speech Technology (1999)
32. Kroeber, P.D.: The Salish Language Family: Reconstructing Syntax. University of Nebraska Press (1999)
33. Kučera, H.: Mechanical phonemic transcription and phoneme frequency count in Czech. Int. J. Slavic Linguist. Poetics **6**, 36–50 (1963)

34. Ladefoged, P.: The revised international phonetic alphabet. Language **66**(3), 550–552 (1990)
35. Lee, F.F.: Automatic grapheme-to-phoneme translation of English. J. Acoust. Soc. Am. **41**(6), 1594 (1969). https://doi.org/10.1121/1.2143635
36. Li, J., Hasegawa-Johnson, M.: Autosegmental neural nets: should phones and tones be synchronous or asynchronous? In: Proceedings Interspeech (2020)
37. Marcantonio, A.: The Uralic language family: facts, myths and statistics. Sapienza Università di Roma (2002)
38. Millward, J.: Eurasian Crossroads: A History of Xinjiang. Columbia University Press (1982)
39. Moran, S., McCloy, D. (eds.): PHOIBLE 2.0. Jena: Max Planck Institute for the Science of Human History (2019)
40. Mortensen, D.R., Dalmia, S., Littell, P.: Epitran: precision G2P for many languages. In: Proceedings of the Conference on Language Resources and Evaluation (LREC), pp. 2710–2714 (2018)
41. Neubig, G., et al.: DyNet: the dynamic neural network toolkit (2017). https://arxiv.org/pdf/1701.03980.pdf. Accessed 14 Sept 2017
42. Novak, J.R., Minematsu, N., Hirose, K.: Phonetisaurus: Exploring grapheme-to-phoneme conversion with joint n-gram models in the WFST framework. Natural Lang. Eng. **22**(6), 907–938 (2015)
43. Omar, A.H.: The Malay spelling reform. J. Simplified Spelling Soc. **1989**(2), 9–13 (1989)
44. Peters, B., Dehdari, J., van Genabith, J.: Massively multilingual neural grapheme-to-phoneme conversion. In: EMNLP 2017 Workshop on Building Linguisically Generalizable NLP Systems (2017)
45. Peterson, G.E.: Automatic speech recognition procedures. Lang. Speech **4**(4), 200–219 (1961). https://doi.org/10.1177/002383096100400403
46. Povey, D., et al.: The Kaldi speech recognition toolkit. In: IEEE 2011 Workshop on Automatic Speech Recognition and Understanding. IEEE Signal Processing Society, December 2011. IEEE Catalog No.: CFP11SRW-USB
47. Rentzepopoulos, P.A., Kokkinakis, G.K.: Efficient multilingual phoneme-to-grapheme conversion based on HMM. Comput. Linguist. **22**(3), 351–376 (1996)
48. Ritchie, M., Comrie, B. (eds.): The Intercontinental Dictionary Series. Max Planck Institute for Evolutionary Anthropology, Leipzig (2015). http://ids.clld.org. Accessed 26 July 2020
49. Rolston, L., Kirchhoff, K.: Collection of bilingual data for lexicon transfer learning. Technical report, UWEETR-2016-0000, University of Washington Department of Electrical Engineering (2016)
50. Schultz, T.: GlobalPhone: a multilingual speech and text database developed at Karlsruhe University. In: Seventh International Conference on Spoken Language Processing (2002)
51. Schultz, T., Waibel, A.: Multilingual and crosslingual speech recognition. In: Proceedings International Conference Spoken Language Processing (ICSLP), pp. 0577:1–4 (1998)
52. Uzman, M.: Romanisation in Uzbekistan past and present. J. Roy. Asiatic Soc. **20**(1), 49–60 (2010)
53. van Rijnsoever, P.: A multilingual text-to-speech system. In: IPO Annual Progress Report, pp. 34–41. Institute for Perception Research, Eindhoven (1988)
54. Varga, K.: Kaldi ASR: Extending the ASpIRE model (2017). chrisearch.wordpres s.com/2017/03/11/speech-recognition-using-kaldi-extending-and-using-the-aspire-model

55. Vasu, S.C.: The Ashtádhyáyí of Páńini. Translated into English, Sindhu Charan Bose (1897)
56. Vaswani, A., et al.: Attention is all you need. In: Guyon, I., Luxburg, U.V., Bengio, S., Wallach, H., Fergus, R., Vishwanathan, S., Garnett, R. (eds.) Advances in Neural Information Processing Systems, vol. 30, pp. 5998–6008. Curran Associates, Inc. (2017). http://papers.nips.cc/paper/7181-attention-is-all-you-need.pdf
57. Watanabe, S., et al.: ESPnet: end-to-end speech processing toolkit. In: Proceedings Interspeech, pp. 2207–2211 (2018). https://doi.org/10.21437/Interspeech.2018-1456
58. Żelasko, P., Moro-Velázquez, L., Hasegawa-Johnson, M., Scharenborg, O., Dehak, N.: That sounds familiar: an analysis of phonetic representations transfer across languages. In: Proceedings Interspeech (2020)

Language Processing

Conditioned Text Generation with Transfer for Closed-Domain Dialogue Systems

Stéphane d'Ascoli[1,2], Alice Coucke[1(✉)], Francesco Caltagirone[1],
Alexandre Caulier[1], and Marc Lelarge[2,3]

[1] Sonos Inc., Paris, France
{alice.coucke,francesco.caltagirone,alexandre.caulier}@sonos.com
[2] ENS, CNRS, PSL University, Paris, France
{stephane.dascoli,marc.lelarge}@ens.fr
[3] INRIA, Paris, France

Abstract. Scarcity of training data for task-oriented dialogue systems is a well known problem that is usually tackled with costly and time-consuming manual data annotation. An alternative solution is to rely on automatic text generation which, although less accurate than human supervision, has the advantage of being cheap and fast. Our contribution is twofold. First we show how to optimally train and control the generation of intent-specific sentences using a conditional variational autoencoder. Then we introduce a new protocol called *query transfer* that allows to leverage a large unlabelled dataset, possibly containing irrelevant queries, to extract relevant information. Comparison with two different baselines shows that this method, in the appropriate regime, consistently improves the diversity of the generated queries without compromising their quality. We also demonstrate the effectiveness of our generation method as a data augmentation technique for language modelling tasks.

Keywords: Spoken language understanding · Dialogue systems · Text generation

1 Introduction

Closed-domain dialogue systems have become ubiquitous nowadays with the rise of conversational interfaces. These systems aim at extracting relevant information from a user's spoken query, produce the appropriate response/action and, when applicable, start a new dialogue turn. The typical spoken language understanding (SLU) framework relies on a speech-recognition engine that transforms

S. d'Ascoli and A. Coucke—Both authors contributed equally.

© Springer Nature Switzerland AG 2020
L. Espinosa-Anke et al. (Eds.): SLSP 2020, LNAI 12379, pp. 23–34, 2020.
https://doi.org/10.1007/978-3-030-59430-5_2

the spoken utterance into text followed by a natural language understanding engine that extracts meaning from the text utterance.

Here we consider essentially single-turn closed-domain dialogue systems where the meaning is well summarized by an intent and its corresponding slots. As an example, the query "Play Skinny Love by Bon Iver" should be interpreted as an intent *PlayTrack* with slots *TrackTitle* "Skinny Love" and *Artist* "Bon Iver".

Training data for conversational systems consists in utterances together with their annotated intents. In order to develop a new interaction scheme with new intents, a (possibly large) representative set of manually annotated utterances needs to be produced, which is a costly and time-consuming process. It is therefore desirable to automate it as much as possible. We consider the scenario in which only a small set of annotated queries is available for all the in-domain intents, but we also have access to a large "reservoir" dataset of unannotated queries that belong to a broad spectrum of intents ranging from close to far domain. This situation is indeed very typical of conversational platforms like Google's DialogFlow or IBM Watson which offer a high degree of user customization.

1.1 Contribution and Outline

We focus on automatic generation of utterances conditioned to desired intents, aiming to alleviate the problem of training data scarcity. Using a Conditional Variational Auto-Encoder [18] (CVAE), we show how it is possible to selectively extract the valuable information from the reservoir dataset. We call this mechanism *query transfer*. We analyse the performance of this approach on the publicly-available Snips benchmark dataset [5] through both quality and diversity metrics. We also observe an improvement in the perplexity of a language model trained on data augmented with our generation scheme. This preliminary result is encouraging for future application to SLU data augmentation.

The paper is structured as follows: in Sect. 1.2, we briefly present the related literature, in Sect. 2 we introduce our approach, and in Sect. 3 we show our experimental results before concluding in Sect. 4.

1.2 Related Work

While there is a vast literature on conditional text generation, semi-supervised learning and data augmentation, there are only few existing works that combine these elements. Shortly after the Variational Autoencoder (VAE) model was introduced by [9], a conditional variation autoencoder (CVAE) model was used for semi-supervised classification tasks by [10] and later improved by [8].

[6, 7, 12] generate utterances through paraphrasing with the objective of augmenting the training set and improving slot-filling or other NLP tasks without conditioning on the intent. The data used to train the paraphrasing model is annotated and in-domain. [17] leverage a CVAE to generate queries conditioned to the presence of certain slots and observe improvements in slot-filling performance when augmenting the training set with generated data. [22] propose instead an AE that is capable of jointly generating a query together with its annotation (intent and slots) and show improvements in intent classification and slot-filling through data augmentation.

In a recent paper, semi-supervised self-learning is used to iteratively incorporate data from an unannotated set into the annotated training set [3]. Their chosen metrics are both SLU performance and query diversity. This method represents a valid alternative to our protocol and will be the object of competitive benchmarks in future work.

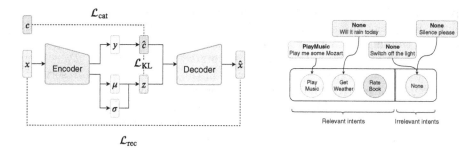

Fig. 1. Architecture of the model. (Left panel) The variational autoencoder architecture with the various losses defined in Sect. (2). (Right panel) An illustration of the categorical latent vector filtering relevant sentences

2 Approach

2.1 Conditional Variational Autoencoders

In order to generate queries conditioned to an underlying intent, we use a CVAE as depicted in Fig. 1 (left), with a continuous code z and a discrete code c thanks to the Gumbel softmax trick [8,13]. Each training sample consists in a continuous feature vector x and a categorical label expressed as a one-hot vector c. The latent code is the concatenation of a continuous latent vector z and a predicted categorical vector $\hat{c}$. The associated loss function consists of three terms: the reconstruction term, the regularization term, and the supervision term for the label:

$$\mathcal{L} = \mathcal{L}_{\text{rec}} + \gamma \mathcal{L}_{\text{KL}} + \mathcal{L}_{\text{cat}},$$

$$\mathcal{L}_{\text{rec}} = - \underset{q_\phi(z|x)}{\mathbb{E}} [\log p_\theta(x|z, \hat{c})],$$

$$\mathcal{L}_{\text{KL}} = D_{\text{KL}}(q_\phi(z|x) \| p(z)) + D_{\text{KL}}(q_\phi(\hat{c}|x) \| p(\hat{c})),$$

$$\mathcal{L}_{\text{cat}} = - \sum_{i=1}^{C} \hat{c}_i \, \alpha_i \, \log \left(q_\phi(\hat{c}_i|x) \right).$$

q_ϕ and p_θ represent the encoder and the decoder with their associated parameters, and C is the dimension of the categorical latent space. The constant γ is used to set the relative weight of the KL regularization and perform annealing during training [2,19]. The class-specific α coefficients will play a crucial role for the *query transfer* mechanism described below. In all our experiments, $p(\hat{c})$ is uniform and $p(z) = \mathcal{N}(\vec{0}, 1)$. At inference time, a sentence is generated by feeding the decoder with the concatenation of a chosen $\hat{c}$ with a sampled z and extracting greedily the most probable sequence.

2.2 Query Transfer

Approach. A CVAE can be trained on a dataset of annotated queries (x, c), where x is the sentence and c is the underlying query's intent. With too few sentences for training, a CVAE will not yield generated sentences of high enough quality and diversity. In addition to an annotated training dataset $\mathcal{D}_0$ – kept small in the data scarcity regime of interest in this paper – a large "reservoir" dataset $\mathcal{D}_r$ is considered. The latter is unannotated and contains sentences that potentially cover a larger spectrum, ranging from examples that are semantically close to the in-domain ones to completely out-of-domain examples. The categorical latent space of the CVAE contains one dimension for each intent in $\mathcal{D}_0$. The novelty in our approach is to allocate an extra dimension for irrelevant sentences coming from $\mathcal{D}_r$, namely an additional *None* intent. All sentences from $\mathcal{D}_r$ are supervised to this dimension by the cross-entropy loss, but we want the relevant ones to be allowed to transfer to one of the intents of $\mathcal{D}_0$, as illustrated in Fig. 1 (right). To control this, we adjust the amount of transfer by multiplying the supervision loss of $\mathcal{D}_r$ by a factor α (we will take $\alpha_{\text{None}} = \alpha$ and $\alpha_{i \neq None} = 1$). In the case $\alpha = 0$, the sentences from $\mathcal{D}_r$ are not supervised at all.

Illustration on Images. The transfer process and the effect of α are illustrated here in the context of computer vision. We present results on the MNIST and Fashion MNIST [21] datasets as toy examples. Here, the small annotated dataset $\mathcal{D}_0$ contains only examples from the first 6 classes of each dataset, with 10 examples per class ($0 - 5$ digits and 6 items of clothing). The larger reservoir dataset $\mathcal{D}_r$ contains examples from each of the 10 classes (half of its content being therefore irrelevant to the generative task), with 50 examples per class.

Figure 2 shows generated images obtained by training a very simple two-layer fully-connected CVAE for 200 epochs, for various values of the transfer parameter α. We see that without the reservoir dataset $\mathcal{D}_r$ (panel (a) on both figures), there is not enough training data to generate high-quality diverse images.

Using $\mathcal{D}_r$ with a too low value of α (second column) yields unwanted image transfer and corruption of the generated images (unwanted 9's corrupt the 4's in MNIST, unwanted bags corrupt the shirts in Fashion MNIST). Conversely, if α is too high (panels (d) on both figures), there is not enough transfer and the generated images do not benefit from $\mathcal{D}_r$ anymore. However, for a well-chosen value α^* (panels (c)), there is significant improvement both in quality

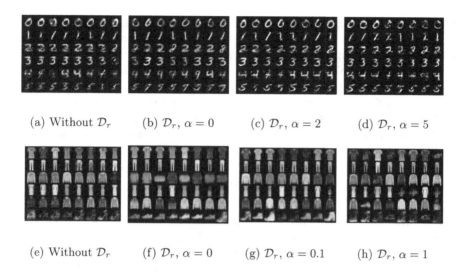

(a) Without $\mathcal{D}_r$ (b) $\mathcal{D}_r$, $\alpha = 0$ (c) $\mathcal{D}_r$, $\alpha = 2$ (d) $\mathcal{D}_r$, $\alpha = 5$

(e) Without $\mathcal{D}_r$ (f) $\mathcal{D}_r$, $\alpha = 0$ (g) $\mathcal{D}_r$, $\alpha = 0.1$ (h) $\mathcal{D}_r$, $\alpha = 1$

Fig. 2. Top row: MNIST dataset. Bottom row: Fashion MNIST dataset. In the leftmost panels, the CVAE is trained on a small labelled dataset $\mathcal{D}_0$ containing only the first 6 classes (10 images per class). In the other panels, the CVAE leverages an unlabelled reservoir dataset $\mathcal{D}_r$ containing all 10 classes (50 images per class), with a varying transfer parameter α. The best quality-diversity trade-off is reached at $\alpha = 2$ for MNIST, and $\alpha = 0.1$ for Fashion MNIST

and diversity of the generated images. As we can see here, the optimal value of α is dataset-dependent – $\alpha^\star \sim 2$ for MNIST, $\alpha^\star \sim 0.1$ for Fashion MNIST – and needs to be tuned accordingly.

2.3   Sentence Selection

To further improve the query transfer, we also introduce a sentence selection procedure in order to remove from $\mathcal{D}_r$ irrelevant data that can potentially pollute generation. In the context of natural language processing, this may be achieved by sentence embeddings. We use generalist sentence embeddings such as InferSent [4] as a first, rough, sentence selection mechanism. We first compute an "intent embedding" $\vec{I}$ for each intent of $\mathcal{D}_0$, obtained by averaging the embeddings of all the sentences of the given intent. Then we only collect the sentences from $\mathcal{D}_r$ which are "close" enough to one of the intents of $\mathcal{D}_0$, i.e. $\left\{ \vec{S} \mid \exists \vec{I}, \cos\left(\theta(\vec{I}, \vec{S})\right) > \beta \right\}$, where β is a threshold which controls selectivity.

3   Experimental Results

3.1   Experimental Setup

A PyTorch implementation of the CVAE model is publicly available on GitHub at https://github.com/snipsco/automatic-data-generation.

Datasets. We use the publicly-available Snips benchmark dataset [5], which contains user queries from 7 intents such as *PlayMusic* or *GetWeather*, with 2000 queries per intent in the training set (from which we will only keep small fractions for $\mathcal{D}_0$ to mimic scarcity) and 100 queries per intent in the test set. Each intent comes with specific slots.

As a proxy for a reservoir dataset $\mathcal{D}_r$, we use a large in-house (private) dataset which contains all sorts of queries from nearly 350 varied English intents, typical of voice assistants. Each intent comes with at least 100 examples queries. Some intents may be more or less close semantically (e.g. *RadioOn* and *MusicOn* as opposed to *SetOven*) or even duplicates with different intent names, but the only available label for $\mathcal{D}_r$ is the intent a given query belongs to.

Hyperparameters. The GloVe embedding size is set to 100. Both the encoder and the decoder of our model use one-layer GRUs, with a hidden layer of size 256 and both the continuous and categorical latent spaces are of size 8 (for the categorical one: seven intents + one *None* class). At each step of the decoding sequence, a softmax with temperature $\tau = 1$ is applied to the output of the decoder. We adopt the KL-annealing trick from [2] to avoid posterior collapse: the weight of the KL loss term is annealed from 0 to 1 using the logistic function, at a time and a rate given by two hyper-parameters t_{KL} and r_{KL}. The hyper-parameters were chosen to ensure satisfactory intent conditioning: $t_{KL} = 300$ and $r_{KL} = 0.01$, but were not optimized in any particular way since model selection is not particularly meaningful outside of a specific task.

The *Adam* optimizer is used and we train for 50 epochs at a learning rate of 0.01 with a batch size of 128. Depending on the size of $\mathcal{D}_0$, it takes a few dozens of minutes per experiment on a laptop. No word or embedding dropout is applied. Note that we draw a fixed number of samples from both $\mathcal{D}_0$ and $\mathcal{D}_r$, however since we are in a data scarcity regime and only consider small $\mathcal{D}_0$, this draw entails high variability. Hence all results presented are averaged over five random seeds. For all of the experiments described in Sect. 3.3, the size of the dataset is set to $|\mathcal{D}_0| = 200$ and the sentence selection threshold to $\beta = 0.9$. The α parameter allows to control the amount of transfer between $\mathcal{D}_0$ and the reservoir $\mathcal{D}_r$.

Delexicalization Procedure. The word embeddings fed to the encoder are pre-trained GloVe embeddings [15]. We use a delexicalization procedure similar to that used in [6] for Seq2Seq models. First, slot values are replaced a placeholder and stored in a dictionary ("Weather in Paris" → "Weather in [City]"). The model is then trained on these delexicalized sentences and new delexicalized sentences are generated. The last step is to relexicalize the generated sentences: abstract slot names are replaced by stored slot values. The effort is indeed put on generating new contexts, rather than just shuffling slot values.

We tried various strategies for the initialization of slot-embeddings (e.g. the average of all slot values) and found that it had no impact in our experiments. We therefore initialize them with random embeddings.

3.2 Generation Metrics

Our generation task must optimize a trade-off between quality and diversity: the generated sentences need to be consistent with the original dataset and to bring novelty. To account for quality, we first consider the **intent conditioning** accuracy. The generated sentences need to be well-conditioned to the intent imposed. We train an intent classifier on the full Snips training set, which reaches near-perfect accuracy on the test set, and use it as an "oracle" to evaluate intent conditioning accuracy, independently of the the generation mechanism. We then assess the semantic quality of the generated sentences by considering the **BLEU-quality**, namely the forward Perplexity [23], or the BLEU score [14] computed against the reference sentences of the given intent.

To account for diversity, we consider the **BLEU-diversity** defined as $1 - $ self-BLEU where self-BLEU is merely the BLEU score of the generated sentences of a given intent computed against the other generated sentences of the same intent [24]. However, enforcing high BLEU-diversity does not ensure that we are not just reproducing the training examples. Therefore, we also consider **originality**, defined as the fraction of generated sentences that are not present in the training set under their delexicalized form.

These four metrics take values in $[0, 1]$. The three last metrics are evaluated intent-wise, which may be problematic if the intent conditioning of the generated sentences is poor. For example, if we condition to *PlayMusic* and the generated sentence is "What is the weather ?", the diversity metrics of the *PlayMusic* intent would be over-estimated while the quality would be under-estimated. To reduce this effect as much as possible, the computation of these metrics is therefore restricted to generated sentences for which the oracle classifier (used for the intent conditioning accuracy metric) agrees with the conditioning intent.

3.3 Generation Results

Quality-Diversity Trade-Off. Figure 3 shows that α (left panel) and β (right panel) are useful cursors to control the diversty-quality tradeoff. Increasing them yields generated sentences of higher quality (both in terms of intent conditioning and BLEU-quality) but lower diversity (in terms of BLEU-diversity and originality). A satisfying tradeoff seems to be found for $\alpha = 0.2$ and $\beta = 0.9$, which will be used in the results that follow.

Both parameters determine the amount of transfer which occurs. However, they intervene in different ways. The parameter β acts as a first rough pre-selection, and completely discards irrelevant sentences. Instead, α determines how strongly the queries from the reservoir are encouraged to be classified as a *None* intent. Those which are classified as *None* can nonetheless benefit the CVAE, as explained below.

Efficiency of Query Transfer. To test the efficiency of the query transfer, we compare it to two baselines. The first one is simply a CVAE trained only on

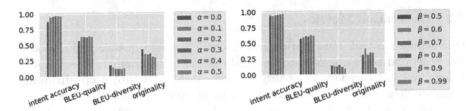

Fig. 3. (Left Panel) Evolution of the generation metrics as a function of the transfer parameter α for $|\mathcal{D}_0| = |\mathcal{D}_r|$ and $\beta = 0.9$. (Right Panel) Evolution of the generation metrics as a function of the transfer parameter β for $|\mathcal{D}_0| = |\mathcal{D}_r|$ and $\alpha = 0.2$ (Color figure online)

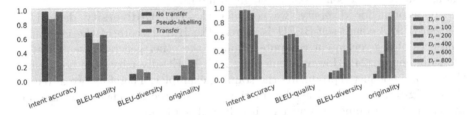

Fig. 4. Generation metrics. (Left Panel) Comparison of our query transfer method with two baselines: one without any transfer and one with InferSent pseudo-labelling. (Right Panel) Effect of the size of the reservoir $\mathcal{D}_r$ on the generation metrics. We set $|D_0| = 200$, $\alpha = 0.2$, $\beta = 0.9$ (Color figure online)

$\mathcal{D}_0$ (in blue on the left panel of Fig. 4). The second one, referred to as *pseudo-labelling* (in orange on the figure), leverages queries from $\mathcal{D}_r$ directly associated to intents of $\mathcal{D}_0$ using InferSent-based similarity scores (the CVAE is trained without a *None* class and a sentence in $\mathcal{D}_r$ is mapped to its closest intent as defined in Sect. 2.3). For this second baseline, when the measured similarity exceeds a certain threshold for a given intent, the sentence from $\mathcal{D}_r$ is directly added to the corresponding intent in $\mathcal{D}_0$, on which the CVAE is trained.

The left panel of Fig. 4 shows that the proposed query transfer method improves the diversity metrics (especially the originality) of the generated sentences, with hardly any deterioration in quality. In comparison, the pseudo-labelling approach significantly deteriorates the quality of generated sentences. This means that the proposed mechanism does more than extracting relevant queries from the reservoir: the underlying intuition is that the CVAE benefits from the irrelevant intents by improving its language modelling abilities, without corrupting the generation task thanks to the extra *None* class.

Finally, the right panel of Fig. 4 shows a remarkable improvement of the diversity metrics when the number of sentences injected from the reservoir $\mathcal{D}_r$ increases, without any loss in quality up to a certain point at which the quality degrades strongly. This is due to the important imbalance introduced in the conditioning mechanism of the CVAE, too much irrelevant content being passed onto the intent classes. A satisfying trade-off is found for $|\mathcal{D}_r| = |\mathcal{D}_0|$.

3.4   Results on Data Augmentation for Language Models

In this section, we show that our query transfer mechanism can effectively be used as data augmentation technique for language modeling tasks. Indeed, leveraging in-domain language models – trained for a specific use case rather than in a large vocabulary setting – allows to both reduce their size and increase their in-domain accuracy [16]. We compare the perplexity [1] of Language Models (LM) trained on three datasets: (i) $\mathcal{D}_0$, the initial dataset; (ii) $\mathcal{D}_{\text{aug}}$, containing $\mathcal{D}_0$ augmented by sentences generated by the CVAE model trained on $\mathcal{D}_0$ with query transfer; (iii) $\mathcal{D}_{\text{ref}}$, containing $\mathcal{D}_0$ augmented by "real" sentences from the original dataset as a reference point.

Augmentation Setup. This experiment is done on the publicly-available Snips benchmark dataset [5]. The different training sets $\mathcal{D}_0$ are drawn from the original set of 2000 queries per intent (files denoted `train_IntentName_full.json` in the dataset GitHub repository[1]. The test set $\mathcal{D}_{\text{test}}$ used to evaluate language model perplexities (see next section) consists in the validation sets of the Snips benchmark dataset (`validate_IntentName.json` files).

Four different data regimes are explored for training (i.e. $|\mathcal{D}_0|$ taking values in $[125, 250, 500, 1000]$). For each data regime, a CVAE is trained with 5 initialization seeds and a hyperparameter search on the embedding dimension and the encoder and decoder hidden sizes. In this experiment, we set $\alpha = 0.2$, $\beta = 0.9$ and $|\mathcal{D}_r| = |\mathcal{D}_0|$, consistently with results displayed in Sect. 3.3. Three models are then selected based on the four metrics defined above, yielding 3 models per size of $\mathcal{D}_0$. Each model is used to generate a set of 1000 new queries used to augment the training set – the newly formed training set being denoted $\mathcal{D}_{\text{aug}}$. We consider two augmentation ratios: +50% ($|\mathcal{D}_{\text{aug}}| = 1.5 \times |\mathcal{D}_0|$) and +100% ($|\mathcal{D}_{\text{aug}}| = 2 \times |\mathcal{D}_0|$).

Perplexity Computation. The SRILM toolkit [20] is used to train 4-grams language models with Kneser-Ney Smoothing [11] on $\mathcal{D}_0$, $\mathcal{D}_{\text{aug}}$, and $\mathcal{D}_{\text{ref}}$ respectively, when varying the size of $\mathcal{D}_0$ and the augmentation ratio. Perplexities are only comparable if the vocabulary supported by the various models is the same. To fix this issue, the words contained in at least $\mathcal{D}_0$, $\mathcal{D}_{\text{aug}}$ and $\mathcal{D}_{\text{ref}}$ are added as unigrams with a count 1 in every LM. The CVAE might generate sentences already present in $\mathcal{D}_0$ but every sentence is kept only once. The perplexity – averaged over the 3 experiments – is then evaluated on a pool $\mathcal{D}_{\text{test}}$ of 700 test sentences.

Results. Table 1 shows the results when varying the size of $\mathcal{D}_0$ and the number of sentences generated by the augmentation process (augmentation ratios of 50% and 100%). The perplexity computed on the test set of the Snips dataset is

---

[1] https://github.com/snipsco/nlu-benchmark/tree/master/2017-06-custom-intent-engines.

Table 1. Relative loss of perplexity (%) with respect to LM trained on the original dataset $\mathcal{D}_0$, when varying the size of $\mathcal{D}_0$ and the augmentation ratio. Results can only be compared row-wise because of the vocabulary restriction

$|\mathcal{D}_0|$	Augmentation ratio	PPL(%) $\mathcal{D}_{aug}$	PPL(%) $\mathcal{D}_{ref}$
125	+50%	−2.322	−17.73
	+100%	−5.909	−28.62
250	+50%	−1.756	−17.72
	+100%	−3.755	−22.85
500	+50%	−3.335	−12.34
	+100%	−4.046	−18.55
1000	+50%	−1.031	−9.278
	+100%	−0.511	−13.62

consistently lower when the LM is trained on $\mathcal{D}_{aug}$ rather than on $\mathcal{D}_0$ (though it does not reach the performance of augmentation with real data $\mathcal{D}_{ref}$). The improvement is less significant as the dataset size increases, illustrating that most phrasings of the various intents are already covered in this data regime. These results are encouraging in the low data regime and we will evaluate our query transfer as a data augmentation process for SLU tasks in a future work.

3.5   Examples of Generated Samples

In this section, we display examples of sentences generated with a CVAE trained on 250 queries (approximately 36 examples per intent). This trained model is used to generate 1000 new sentences, some of which are displayed in Table 2 for the *GetWeather* intent. The presented approach is able to generate patterns that were not present in the training set – as underlined by the "originality" metrics – but also patterns that are never seen in the full Snips benchmark dataset (14000 queries). Interestingly, the number of occurrences of patterns among all generated examples does not seem to be related to their prevalence in the training set, or even in the full Snips benchmark dataset.

Table 2. Examples of generated delexicalized sentences (patterns) obtained with a CVAE trained on 250 examples, along with the corresponding occurrences among the 1000 generated sentences (leftmost column), the 250 training utterances (middle column) and the 14000 queries of the full Snips dataset (rightmost column). We used $\alpha = 0.2$, $\beta = 0.9$

# generated	# in train	# total	Generated pattern
13	1	8	Is it [ConditionDescription] in [City]
21	1	13	What is the weather forecast for [City]
17	0	10	What's the weather forecast for [City]
14	0	2	Tell me the weather forecast for [City]
8	0	0	How's the weather supposed to be on [TimeRange]

4   Conclusion

We introduce a transfer method to alleviate data scarcity in conditional generation tasks where one has access to a large unlabelled dataset containing some potentially useful information. We use conditional variational autoencoders with a transfer parameter α and a selectivity threshold β which are both used to control the trade-off between quality and diversity of the data augmentation. We choose to focus on the low data regime, as it is the most relevant for customized closed-domain dialogue systems, where gathering manually annotated datasets is cumbersome.

Transferring knowledge from the large reservoir dataset $\mathcal{D}_r$ to the original dataset $\mathcal{D}_0$ comes with the risk of introducing unwanted information which may corrupt the generative model. However, this risk may be controlled by adjusting two parameters. First, we consider a selectivity threshold β to adjust how much irrelevant data is discarded from $\mathcal{D}_r$ during a pre-processing step. Second, we introduce a transfer parameter α, adjusting the supervision of unlabelled examples from $\mathcal{D}_r$, low values of α facilitating transfer from the reservoir.

While we assess the performance of the proposed generation technique by both introducing *quality* and *diversity* metrics and showing how the introduced parameters may help choosing the best trade-off, we also apply it as a data augmentation technique on a small language modelling task. The full potentiality of this method for more complex SLU tasks still needs to be explored and will be the subject of a future work.

References

1. Bahl, L.R., Jelinek, F., Mercer, R.L.: A maximum likelihood approach to continuous speech recognition. IEEE Trans. Pattern Anal. Mach. Intell. **5**(2), 179–190 (1983)
2. Bowman, S.R., Vilnis, L., Vinyals, O., Dai, A.M., Jozefowicz, R., Bengio, S.: Generating sentences from a continuous space (2015). arXiv preprint arXiv:1511.06349
3. Cho, E., Xie, H., Lalor, J., Kumar, V., Campbell, W.: Efficient semi-supervised learning for natural language understanding by optimizing diversity. CoRR (2019)
4. Conneau, A., Kiela, D., Schwenk, H., Barrault, L., Bordes, A.: Supervised learning of universal sentence representations from natural language inference data (2017). arXiv preprint arXiv:1705.02364
5. Coucke, A., et al.: Snips voice platform: an embedded spoken language understanding system for private-by-design voice interfaces (2018). arXiv preprint arXiv:1805.10190
6. Hou, Y., Liu, Y., Che, W., Liu, T.: Sequence-to-sequence data augmentation for dialogue language understanding. In: Proceedings of the 27th International Conference on Computational Linguistics, pp. 1234–1245. Association for Computational Linguistics, Santa Fe (2018)
7. Hu, Z., Yang, Z., Liang, X., Salakhutdinov, R., Xing, E.P.: Toward controlled generation of text. In: Proceedings of the 34th International Conference on Machine Learning, vol. 70, pp. 1587–1596. JMLR. org (2017)

8. Jang, E., Gu, S., Poole, B.: Categorical reparameterization with gumbel-softmax (2016). arXiv preprint arXiv:1611.01144

9. Kingma, D.P., Welling, M.: Auto-encoding variational bayes (2013). arXiv preprint arXiv:1312.6114

10. Kingma, D.P., Mohamed, S., Rezende, D.J., Welling, M.: Semi-supervised learning with deep generative models. In: Advances in Neural Information Processing Systems, pp. 3581–3589 (2014)

11. Kneser, R., Ney, H.: Improved backing-off for m-gram language modeling. In: 1995 International Conference on Acoustics, Speech, and Signal Processing, vol. 1, pp. 181–184. IEEE (1995)

12. Kurata, G., Xiang, B., Zhou, B.: Labeled data generation with encoder-decoder LSTM for semantic slot filling. In: INTERSPEECH (2016)

13. Maddison, C.J., Mnih, A., Teh, Y.W.: The concrete distribution: a continuous relaxation of discrete random variables (2016). arXiv preprint arXiv:1611.00712

14. Papineni, K., Roukos, S., Ward, T., Zhu, W.J.: Bleu: a method for automatic evaluation of machine translation. In: Proceedings of the 40th Annual Meeting on Association for Computational Linguistics, ACL '02, pp. 311–318. Association for Computational Linguistics, Stroudsburg (2002)

15. Pennington, J., Socher, R., Manning, C.D.: Glove: global vectors for word representation. In: EMNLP (2014)

16. Saade, A., et al.: Spoken language understanding on the edge (2018). CoRR abs/1810.12735

17. Shin, Y., Yoo, K., Lee, S.G.: Utterance generation with variational auto-encoder for slot filling in spoken language understanding. IEEE Signal Process. Lett. **26**, 1–1 (2019)

18. Sohn, K., Lee, H., Yan, X.: Learning structured output representation using deep conditional generative models. In: Cortes, C., Lawrence, N.D., Lee, D.D., Sugiyama, M., Garnett, R. (eds.) Advances in Neural Information Processing Systems, vol. 28, pp. 3483–3491. Curran Associates Inc., New York (2015)

19. Sønderby, C.K., Raiko, T., Maaløe, L., Sønderby, S.K., Winther, O.: How to train deep variational autoencoders and probabilistic ladder networks. In: 33rd International Conference on Machine Learning (ICML 2016) (2016)

20. Stolcke, A.: Srilm-an extensible language modeling toolkit. In: Seventh International Conference on Spoken Language Processing (2002)

21. Xiao, H., Rasul, K., Vollgraf, R.: Fashion-mnist: a novel image dataset for benchmarking machine learning algorithms (2017). arXiv preprint arXiv:1708.07747

22. Yoo, K.M., Shin, Y., Lee, S.: Data augmentation for spoken language understanding via joint variational generation. In: Proceedings of the Thirty-Third AAAI Conference on Artificial Intelligence (2019)

23. Zhao, J., Kim, Y., Zhang, K., Rush, A., LeCun, Y.: Adversarially regularized autoencoders. In: Dy, J., Krause, A. (eds.) Proceedings of the 35th International Conference on Machine Learning, Proceedings of Machine Learning Research, 10–15 Jul 2018, vol. 80, pp. 5902–5911. PMLR, Stockholmsmässan (2018)

24. Zhu, Y., et al.: Texygen: a benchmarking platform for text generation models. In: The 41st International ACM SIGIR Conference on Research & #38; Development in Information Retrieval, SIGIR '18, pp. 1097–1100. ACM, New York (2018)

FacTweet: Profiling Fake News Twitter Accounts

Bilal Ghanem[1]([⊠]), Simone Paolo Ponzetto[2], and Paolo Rosso[1]

[1] Universitat Politècnica de València, Valencia, Spain
bigha@doctor.upv.es, prosso@dsic.upv.es
[2] University of Mannheim, Mannheim, Germany
simone@informatik.uni-mannheim.de

Abstract. We present an approach to detect fake news in Twitter at the account level using a neural recurrent model and a variety of different semantic and stylistic features. Our method extracts a set of features from the timelines of news Twitter accounts by reading their posts as chunks, rather than dealing with each tweet independently. We show the experimental benefits of modeling latent stylistic signatures of mixed fake and real news with a sequential model over a wide range of strong baselines.

Keywords: Fake news · Twitter accounts · Factual accounts

1 Introduction

Social media platforms have made the spreading of fake news easier, faster as well as able to reach a wider audience. Social media offer another feature which is the anonymity for the authors, and this opens the door to many suspicious individuals or organizations to utilize these platforms. Recently, there has been an increased number of spreading fake news and rumors over the web and social media [23]. Fake news in social media vary considering the intention to mislead. Some of these news are spread with the intention to be ironic or to deliver the news in an ironic way (satirical news). Others, such as propaganda, hoaxes, and clickbaits, are spread to mislead the audience or to manipulate their opinions. In the case of Twitter, suspicious news annotations should be done on a tweet rather than an account level, since some accounts mix fake with real news. However, these annotations are extremely costly and time consuming – i.e., due to high volume of available tweets. Consequently, a first step in this direction, e.g., as a pre-filtering step, is the task of detecting fake news at the account level. The main obstacle for detecting suspicious Twitter accounts is due to the behavior of mixing some real news with the misleading ones. Consequently, we investigate a way to detect suspicious accounts by considering their tweets in groups (chunks). Our hypothesis is that suspicious accounts have a unique pattern in posting tweet sequences. Since their intention is to mislead, the way they transition from one set of tweets to the next has a hidden signature, biased by their intentions. Therefore,

© Springer Nature Switzerland AG 2020
L. Espinosa-Anke et al. (Eds.): SLSP 2020, LNAI 12379, pp. 35–45, 2020.
https://doi.org/10.1007/978-3-030-59430-5_3

reading these tweets in chunks has the potential to improve the detection of the fake news accounts.

In this work, we investigate the problem of discriminating between factual and non-factual accounts in Twitter. To this end, we collect a dataset of tweets using a list of *propaganda*, *hoax* and *clickbait* accounts and compare different versions of sequential chunk-based approaches using a variety of feature sets against several baselines. Several approaches have been proposed for news verification, whether in social media (rumors detection) [22,23], or in news claims [4]. The main line of research of previous works is to verify the textual tweets but not their sources. Another existing direction in the literature is the detection of online trolls or bots [21]. This is different from our setting, since online trolls are less formal and try to imitate individuals by spreading a mixed content, e.g., social media funneling [6], news, personal opinions [8], etc. On the other hand, the content of fake news Twitter accounts is formal, objective, and focused on spreading news content only. To the best of our knowledge, this is the first work aiming to detect factuality at account level, specifically from a textual perspective. The contributions of this work are the following ones:

- We propose an approach to detect non-factual Twitter accounts by treating post streams as a sequence of tweets' chunks. We test several semantic and dictionary-based features together with a neural sequential approach, and apply an ablation test to investigate their contribution.
- We benchmark our approach against other approaches that discard the chronological order of the tweets or read the tweets individually. The results show that our approach produces superior results at detecting non-factual accounts.

The rest of the paper is structured as follows. In the following section, we present an overview on the related work. In Sect. 3, we present the methodology of our approach. Section 4 describes the collected dataset, the experiments, and the results. Finally, we draw some conclusions and discuss possible future works.

2   Related Work

Fake news detection has gained a lot of attention and has been approached from several perspectives in both social media and online news sites. Our work is closely related to the following areas.

2.1   Fake News Sources

Previous works focuses on approaching and analyzing online news texts or claims [15,16]. Instead, the work in [4] looks at characterizing entire news media. The authors propose a set of features for the detection of low-factual news media. They use features based on Wikipedia pages and Twitter accounts, like *Does it have Wikipedia page?*, *Is the Twitter account verified?*, etc. Also, they use manual features to identify the low-factual media using their malicious URLs, a set of features to capture the reporting language of the news articles, and the *Alexa Rank* metric to model the web traffic over the news media. The system shows a macro-F1 value of ~0.6 over 3 classes, low, mixed, and high factuality. Another work [5] approaches the problem of detecting the trustworthiness of news media by combining the factuality with bias in a multi-task ordinal regression framework that models the two problems jointly. The authors use the same feature set that was proposed in [4] and show that their system can generate a good result using the Mean Absolute Error metric with a value of ~0.53. In the direction of understanding the characteristics of not credible news sources, the work [1] studied the correlation of a set of features with credible and transparent news media. And in [2], the same authors propose a regression task for source credibility assessment using a set of features like *Google page rank, Alexa rank, Spam score, etc.*, and achieve a value of ~17.7 using RMSE (Root Mean Squared Error).

2.2 Fishy Twitter Accounts

Suspicious accounts in social media play a key role in spreading fake news and deceiving other online users. A set of works has been done to detect bots or trolls accounts. Many works [3,6,12,18] propose a set of features to detect online trolls, starting from textual features such as *the existence of hashtags and URLs in the trolls tweets, bag-of-words, part-of-speech features* or with including more sophisticated features such as *bot likelihood, topic-based information, and activity-related account metadata*. The majority of these works focus on online Russian trolls that were spreading fake news during the US 2016 elections, and produced superior results comparing to baselines.

The work in [9] propose a bots detection system called *BotorNot*[1] to detect bots in Twitter. The system uses content, sentiment, friend, network, temporal, and user features. The authors use a dataset of Twitter accounts – collected previously in another work – that spread tweets about online products (advertisements), duplicate others' tweets, etc. The system obtained an Area Under ROC Curve (AUC) value of 0.95. In a similar attempt, the authors of [11] propose *SentiBot* to detect online bots in the context of the 2014 Indian election. The system uses a large combination of features that contain sentiment, topic, network, and syntax features. The proposed model obtains Receiver Operating Characteristic Curve (ROC) value of ~0.73 on a dataset collected within a year from Twitter.

3 Methodology

Given a news Twitter account, we read its tweets from the account's timeline. Then we sort the tweets by the posting date in ascending way and we split them

---

[1] Later on, the authors created an online API for the system called Botometer in: https://botometer.iuni.iu.edu.

into N chunks. Each chunk consists of a sorted sequence of tweets labeled by the label of its corresponding account. We extract a set of features from each chunk and we feed them into a recurrent neural network to model the sequential flow of the chunks' tweets. We use an attention layer with dropout to attend over the most important tweets in each chunk. Finally, the representation is fed into a softmax layer to produce a probability distribution over the account types and thus predict the factuality of the accounts. Since we have many chunks for each account, the label for an account is obtained by taking the majority class of the account's chunks.

Input Representation. Let t be a Twitter account that contains m tweets. These tweets are sorted by date and split into a sequence of chunks $ck = \langle ck_1, \ldots, ck_n \rangle$, where each ck_i contains s tweets. Each tweet in ck_i is represented by a vector $v \in \mathbb{R}^d$, where v is the concatenation of a set of features' vectors, that is $v = \langle f_1, \ldots, f_n \rangle$. Each feature vector f_i is built by counting the presence of tweet's words in a set of lexical lists.

Features. We argue that different kinds of features like the sentiment of the text, morality, and other text-based features are critical to detect the nonfactual Twitter accounts by utilizing their occurrence during reporting the news in an account's timeline. We employ a rich set of features borrowed from previous works in fake news, bias, and rumors detection [4,22,23].

- **Emotion:** We build an emotions vector using word occurrences of 8 emotion types from the NRC lexicon [20], which contains ~14K words labeled using the eight Plutchik's emotions. The emotions feature can detect if an account is frequently triggering negative emotions like fear, anger, etc.
- **Sentiment:** We extract the sentiment of the tweets by employing Effect-WordNet [7], SenticNet[2], NRC [20][3], and subj_lexicon [24], where each has the two sentiment classes, *positive* and *negative*. The sentiment feature can highlight the polarity in a more abstract level than emotions.
- **Morality:** Features based on morality foundation theory [17] where words are labeled in one of the following 10 categories (*care, harm, fairness, cheating, loyalty, betrayal, authority, subversion, sanctity,* and *degradation*). Using the morality features, we can highlight if some Twitter fake news accounts are posting more frequently news about harmful, subversion, or degradation events. It has been proved that fake news accounts usually post messages about very negative events to catch the readers' eyes [15].
- **Style:** We use canonical stylistic features, such as the count of question marks, exclamation marks, consecutive characters and letters[4], links, hashtags, users' mentions. In addition, we extract the uppercase ratio and the tweet length. We aim to detect if a specific account uses a fixed language style.

---

[2] https://sentic.net/.

[3] NRC has also two sentiment categories, positive and negative.

[4] We considered 2 or more consecutive characters, and 3 or more consecutive letters.

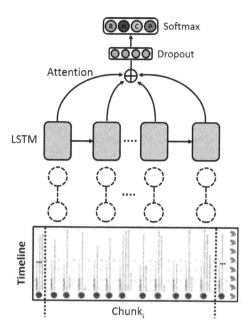

Fig. 1. The FacTweet's architecture.

- **Words embeddings**: We extract words embeddings of the tweets' words using $Glove840B - 300d$[5] pretrained model[6]. The tweet final representation is obtained by averaging its words embeddings. The word embeddings is important to extract the topic information from the messages. Fake news accounts usually post news about specific topics. Also, this feature is complementary to the previous ones where, for an example, detecting a negative sentiment without knowing the topic of the messages would not be useful.

Model. To account for chunk sequences we make use of a *de facto* standard approach and opt for a recurrent neural model using long short-term memory (LSTM). In our model, the sequence consists of a sequence of tweets belonging to one chunk (Fig. 1). The LSTM learns the hidden state h_t by capturing the sequential changes in the timesteps. The produced hidden state h_t at each time step is passed to the attention layer which computes a 'context' vector c_t as the weighted mean of the state sequence h by: $c_t = \sum_{j=1}^{T} \alpha_{tj} h_j$, Where T is the total number of timesteps in the input sequence and α_{tj} is a weight computed at each time step j for each state h_j.

---

[5] https://nlp.stanford.edu/projects/glove/.

[6] Experimentally, we found that the *GloVe* model achieves better results than *Google News word2vec* or *fastText* models.

Table 1. Statistics on the data with respect to each account type: propaganda (**P**), clickbait (**C**), hoax (**H**), and real news (**R**).

	Accounts types			
	P	C	H	R
# of accounts	96	36	7	32
Max # of tweets/account	3,250	3,246	3,250	3,250
Min # of tweets/account	33	877	453	212
Avg # of tweets/account	2,978	3,112	2,723	3,124
Total # of tweets	291,885	112,050	19,065	99,967

4   Experiments and Results

Data. We build a dataset of Twitter accounts based on two lists annotated by professional journalists. For the non-factual accounts, we rely on a list of approximately 180 Twitter accounts from [22][7]. This list was created based on public resources[8] where suspicious Twitter accounts were annotated with the main fake news types (clickbait, propaganda, satire, and hoax). We discard the satire labeled accounts since their intention is not to mislead or deceive. On the other hand, for the factual accounts, we use a list with another 32 Twitter accounts from [19] that are considered trustworthy by independent third parties[9]. We discard accounts that publish news in languages other than English (e.g., Russian or Arabic). Moreover, to ensure the quality of the data, we remove the duplicate, media-based, and link-only tweets. For each account, we collect the maximum amount of tweets allowed by Twitter API. Table 1 presents statistics on our dataset.

Baselines. We compare our approach (FacTweet) to the following baselines:

- **LR + Bag-of-words**: We aggregate the tweets of a feed and we use a bag-of-words representation with a logistic regression (LR) classifier.
- **Tweet2vec**: We use the model proposed in [10] which is a Bidirectional Gated recurrent neural network to predict the tweets based on their hashtags. Their model converts the tweets into character one-hot encoding and feed them to the model. We used our collected dataset which consists of ∼0.5M tweets to train this model. We keep the default parameters that were provided with the implementation. To represent the tweets, we use the decoded embedding produced by the model. With this baseline we aim at assessing if the tweets' hashtags may help detecting the non-factual accounts.

---

[7] Many of the accounts were deactivated during the collecting process, consequently only 144 accounts were used.
[8] http://www.propornot.com/p/the-list.html.
[9] https://tinyurl.com/yctvve9h.

- **LR + All Features (tweet-level)**: We extract all our features from each tweet and feed them into a LR classifier. Here, we do not aggregate over tweets and thus view each tweet independently.
- **LR + All Features (chunk-level)**: We concatenate the features' vectors of the tweets in a chunk and feed them into a LR classifier.
- **FacTweet (tweet-level)**: Similar to the FacTweet approach, but at tweet-level; the sequential flow of the tweets is not utilized. We aim at investigating the importance of the sequential flow of tweets.
- **Botometer**: We use Botometer [9], a state-of-the-art Twitter bots detection system. Botometer uses Network, User, Friends, Temporal, Content, and Sentiment features for bots detection. We aim at checking whether we can detect the Twitter fake news accounts using a bots detection system, where such accounts might have employed automated softwares to release fake news. Also, with this baseline, we assess the performance of the state-of-the-art bots detection system in our task. We fed the Botometer generated predictions to a Random Forest (RF) classifier. We chose RF after testing several classifiers, e.g., Logistic Regression, Support Vector Machine, Naive Bayes, and Feed Forward Neural Network.
- **Top-k replies, likes, or re-tweets**: Some approaches in rumors detection use the number of replies, likes, and re-tweets to detect rumors [13]. Thus, we extract top k replied, liked or re-tweeted tweets from each account to assess the accounts factuality. We tested different k values between 10 tweets to the max number of tweets from each account. Figure 2 shows the macro-F1 values for different k values. It seems that $k = 500$ for the top *replied* tweets achieves the highest result. Therefore, we consider this as a baseline.

Experimental Setup. We report the results using accuracy and macro F1. We experiment with 25% of the accounts for validation and parameters selection, and we apply 5 cross-validation on the rest of the data (75%). The validation split is extracted on the class level using stratified sampling: for this, we take a random 25% of the accounts from each class since the dataset is unbalanced. Discarding the classes' size in the splitting process may affect the minority classes (e.g., hoax). We use hyperopt library[10] to select the hyper-parameters on the following values: LSTM layer size (16, 32, 64), dropout (0.0–0.9), activation function (*relu, selu, tanh*), optimizer (*sgd, adam, rmsprop*) with varying the value of the learning rate (1e−1, .., 1e−5), and batch size (4, 8, 16). To reduce the effect of overfitting in FacTweet, we use the early stopping technique. For the baselines' classifier, we tested many classifiers and the LR showed the best overall performance.

Results. Table 2 presents the results. We present the results using a chunk size of 20, which was found to be the best size using the validation set. Figure 3 shows the results of different chunks sizes.

FacTweet performs better than the proposed baselines and obtains the highest macro-F1 value of 0.565. Our results indicate the importance of taking into

---

[10] https://github.com/hyperopt.

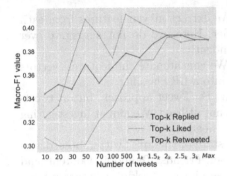

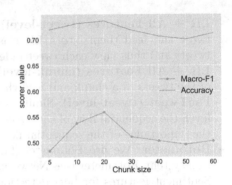

Fig. 2. Results on the top-K replied, linked or re-tweeted tweets.

Fig. 3. The FacTweet performance on difference chunk sizes.

Table 2. Results on accounts classification.

Methods	A	P	R	F1
Baselines				
Majority class	0.563	0.141	0.251	0.18
Random class	0.252	0.21	0.21	0.209
Bag-of-Words	0.601	0.252	0.327	0.284
Tweet2vec	0.558	0.157	0.213	0.181
Botometer	0.512	0.356	0.371	0.363
Tweet-level approaches				
LR + All	0.671	0.378	0.411	0.393
LR + All (top-500 replied)	0.443	0.368	0.467	0.411
LR + FacTweet	0.651	0.34	0.37	0.351
Chunk-level approaches				
LR + All	0.737	0.603	0.552	0.559
FacTweet	**0.74**	**0.549**	**0.582**	**0.565**

account the sequence of the tweets in the accounts' timelines. The sequence of these tweets is better captured by our proposed model sequence-agnostic or non-neural classifiers. Moreover, the results demonstrate that the features at tweet-level do not perform well to detect the Twitter accounts factuality, since they obtain a result near to the majority class (0.18). Another finding from our experiments shows that the performance of the Tweet2vec is weak. This demonstrates that tweets' hashtags are not informative to detect non-factual accounts. Furthermore, the results show that the performance of the Botometer system is weak comparing to the other models, and this emphasizes that fake news accounts use more advanced techniques to spread fake news comparing to the more basic bots techniques. Also, we argue that the low performance of Botometer is due to the different nature of our task. Bots and trolls spread mixed information that contains advertisements and opinions, where the proposed bots detection systems, like Botometer, utilize features that give importance to such information in tweets. Also, bots accounts usually are not well connected with other users accounts (considering the network features e.g. number of followers), and such features are important to detect these accounts but not fake news accounts that gained the trust of many followers. In Table 3, we present ablation tests so as to quantify the contribution of subset of features. The results indicate that most performance gains come from words embeddings, style, and morality features. Other features (emotion and sentiment) show lower importance: nevertheless, they still improve the overall system performance (on average 0.35% macro-F_1 improvement). These performance figures suggest that non-factual accounts use semantic and stylistic hidden signatures mostly while tweeting news, so as to be able to mislead the readers and behave as reputable (i.e., factual) sources.

Table 3. Ablation tests.

Methods	Accuracy	Precision	Recall	F1
LR + All	0.737	0.603	0.552	0.559
− Emotion	0.731	0.581	0.535	0.557
− Sentiment	0.731	0.535	0.575	0.554
− Morality	0.725	0.554	0.542	0.548
− Style	0.737	0.521	0.508	0.514
− Words embeddings	0.678	0.43	0.444	0.437

Since the dataset is highly imbalanced, we apply upsampling by replicating the minority classes. In Table 4 we present the results. For the model (LR + All) that is applied on the chunk-level, we do not get any improvement. For the FacTweet, we notice a small improvement in terms of F1 score. We leave a more fine-grained, diachronic analysis of semantic and stylistic features – how semantic and stylistic signature evolve across time and change across the accounts' timelines – for future work.

Table 4. Up-sampling (Up-s).

Methods	Accuracy	$F1_{macro}$
LR + All	0.737	0.559
LR + All + Up-s	0.737	0.559
FacTweet	0.74	0.565
FacTweet + Up-s	0.74	0.571

5   Conclusions and Future Work

In this paper, we proposed a model that utilizes chunked timelines of tweets and a recurrent neural model in order to infer the factuality of a Twitter news account. Our experimental results indicate the importance of analyzing tweet stream into chunks, as well as the benefits of heterogeneous knowledge source (i.e., lexica as well as text) in order to capture factuality. In future work, we would like to extend this line of research with further in-depth analysis to understand the flow change of the used features in the accounts' streams. Moreover, we would like to take our approach one step further incorporating explicit temporal information, e.g., using timestamps. Crucially, we are also interested in developing a multilingual version of our approach, for instance by leveraging the now ubiquitous cross-lingual embeddings [14]. Finally, we will investigate the potential of applying transfer learning from social media posts. As transfer learning models are starving for data, we will work on extending the used dataset with further social media accounts to enable more accurate fine-tuning process.

Acknowledgment. The work of Paolo Rosso was partially funded by the Spanish MICINN under the research project MISMIS-FAKEnHATE on Misinformation and Miscommunication in social media: FAKE news and HATE speech (PGC2018-096212-B-C31).

References

1. Aker, A., Kevin, V., Bontcheva, K.: Credibility and transparency of news sources: data collection and feature analysis. arXiv (2019)
2. Aker, A., Kevin, V., Bontcheva, K.: Predicting news source credibility. arXiv (2019)
3. Badawy, A., Lerman, K., Ferrara, E.: Who falls for online political manipulation? In: Companion Proceedings of the 2019 World Wide Web Conference, pp. 162–168. ACM (2019)
4. Baly, R., Karadzhov, G., Alexandrov, D., Glass, J., Nakov, P.: Predicting factuality of reporting and bias of news media sources. In: Proceedings of the 2018 Conference on Empirical Methods in Natural Language Processing (EMNLP), pp. 3528–3539 (2018)
5. Baly, R., Karadzhov, G., Saleh, A., Glass, J., Nakov, P.: Multi-task ordinal regression for jointly predicting the trustworthiness and the leading political ideology of news media. In: Proceedings of the 2019 Conference of the North American Chapter of the Association for Computational Linguistics: Human Language Technologies, Volume 1 (Long and Short Papers), pp. 2109–2116 (2019)
6. Boyd, R.L., et al.: Characterizing the Internet Research Agency's Social Media Operations During the 2016 US Presidential Election using Linguistic Analyses. PsyArXiv (2018)
7. Choi, Y., Wiebe, J.: +/-EffectWordNet: sense-level lexicon acquisition for opinion inference. In: Proceedings of the 2014 Conference on Empirical Methods in Natural Language Processing (EMNLP), pp. 1181–1191 (2014)
8. Clark, E.M., Williams, J.R., Jones, C.A., Galbraith, R.A., Danforth, C.M., Dodds, P.S.: Sifting robotic from organic text: a natural language approach for detecting automation on Twitter. J. Comput. Sci. **16**, 1–7 (2016)

9. Davis, C.A., Varol, O., Ferrara, E., Flammini, A., Menczer, F.: BotOrNot: a system to evaluate social bots. In: Proceedings of the 25th International Conference Companion on World Wide Web, pp. 273–274. International World Wide Web Conferences Steering Committee (2016)

10. Dhingra, B., Zhou, Z., Fitzpatrick, D., Muehl, M., Cohen, W.W.: Tweet2Vec: character-based distributed representations for social media. In: The 54th Annual Meeting of the Association for Computational Linguistics (ACL), p. 269 (2016)

11. Dickerson, J.P., Kagan, V., Subrahmanian, V.: Using sentiment to detect bots on Twitter: are humans more opinionated than bots? In: 2014 IEEE/ACM International Conference on Advances in Social Networks Analysis and Mining (ASONAM 2014), pp. 620–627. IEEE (2014)

12. Ghanem, B., Buscaldi, D., Rosso, P.: TexTrolls: identifying Russian trolls on Twitter from a textual perspective. arXiv preprint arXiv:1910.01340 (2019)

13. Ghanem, B., Cignarella, A.T., Bosco, C., Rosso, P., Rangel, F.: UPV-28-UNITO at SemEval-2019 Task 7: exploiting post's nesting and syntax information for rumor stance classification. In: Proceedings of the 13th International Workshop on Semantic Evaluation (SemEval), pp. 1125–1131 (2019)

14. Ghanem, B., Glavas, G., Giachanou, A., Ponzetto, S.P., Rosso, P., Pardo, F.M.R.: UPV-UMA at CheckThat! Lab: verifying Arabic claims using a cross lingual approach. In: Working Notes of CLEF 2019 - Conference and Labs of the Evaluation Forum, Lugano, Switzerland, 9–12 September 2019 (2019)

15. Ghanem, B., Rosso, P., Rangel, F.: An emotional analysis of false information in social media and news articles. ACM Trans. Internet Technol. (TOIT) **20**(2), 1–18 (2020)

16. Giachanou, A., Rosso, P., Crestani, F.: Leveraging emotional signals for credibility detection. In: Proceedings of the 42nd International ACM SIGIR Conference on Research and Development in Information Retrieval, pp. 877–880 (2019)

17. Graham, J., Haidt, J., Nosek, B.A.: Liberals and conservatives rely on different sets of moral foundations. J. Pers. Soc. Psychol. **96**(5), 1029 (2009)

18. Im, J., et al.: Still out there: modeling and identifying Russian troll accounts on Twitter. arXiv preprint arXiv:1901.11162 (2019)

19. Karduni, A., et al.: Can you verifi this? Studying uncertainty and decision-making about misinformation using visual analytics. In: Twelfth International AAAI Conference on Web and Social Media (ICWSM) (2018)

20. Mohammad, S.M., Turney, P.D.: Emotions evoked by common words and phrases: using mechanical turk to create an emotion lexicon. In: Proceedings of the NAACL HLT 2010 Workshop on Computational Approaches to Analysis and Generation of Emotion in Text, pp. 26–34 (2010)

21. Shao, C., Ciampaglia, G.L., Varol, O., Flammini, A., Menczer, F.: The spread of fake news by social bots. arXiv preprint arXiv:1707.07592, pp. 96–104 (2017)

22. Volkova, S., Shaffer, K., Jang, J.Y., Hodas, N.: Separating facts from fiction: linguistic models to classify suspicious and trusted news posts on Twitter. In: Proceedings of the 55th Annual Meeting of the Association for Computational Linguistics (ACL) (Volume 2: Short Papers), vol. 2, pp. 647–653 (2017)

23. Vosoughi, S., Roy, D., Aral, S.: The spread of true and false news online. Science **359**(6380), 1146–1151 (2018)

24. Wilson, T., Wiebe, J., Hoffmann, P.: Recognizing contextual polarity in phrase-level sentiment analysis. In: Proceedings of Human Language Technology Conference and Conference on Empirical Methods in Natural Language Processing (EMNLP) (2005)

Named Entity Recognition for Icelandic: Annotated Corpus and Models

Svanhvít L. Ingólfsdóttir(✉) , Ásmundur A. Guðjónsson ,
and Hrafn Loftsson

Language and Voice Lab, Reykjavik University, Menntavegur 1,
101 Reykjavík, Iceland
svanhviti16@ru.is, asmundur10@ru.is, hrafn@ru.is
https://lvl.ru.is

Abstract. Named entity recognition (NER) can be a challenging task, especially in highly inflected languages where each entity can have many different surface forms. We have created the first NER corpus for Icelandic by annotating 48,371 named entities (NEs) using eight NE types, in a text corpus of 1 million tokens. Furthermore, we have used the corpus to train three machine learning models: first, a CRF model that makes use of shallow word features and a gazetteer function; second, a perceptron model with shallow word features and externally trained word clusters; and third, a BiLSTM model with external word embeddings. Finally, we applied simple voting to combine the model outputs. The voting method obtains an F_1 score of 85.79, gaining 1.89 points compared to the best performing individual model. The corpus and the models are publicly available.

Keywords: Named entity recognition · Corpus annotation ·
BiLSTM · CRF · Clustering · Machine learning

1 Introduction

Since the integration of named entity recognition (NER) into the sixth Message Understanding Conference (MUC) in 1995 [16], NER has become recognized as an important task in natural language processing (NLP), and NER datasets and methods have been developed for many languages. Detecting and recognizing named entities (NEs) in text is not a trivial task, as various patterns need to be learned, and new proper names appear frequently. Furthermore, in highly inflected languages, such as Icelandic, each proper name can have many different surface forms, which further complicates the task.

No NER corpus was available for the Icelandic language before the work introduced in [18], where a sample of 200,000 tokens, from the MIM-GOLD corpus of 1 million tokens [23], was annotated with four NE types and used for training a NER prototype. In this paper, we describe the completion of the

L. Espinosa-Anke et al. (Eds.): SLSP 2020, LNAI 12379, pp. 46–57, 2020.
https://doi.org/10.1007/978-3-030-59430-5_4

annotation of the whole corpus, using eight NE types, which has resulted in 48,371 NEs. The corpus, MIM-GOLD-NER, is available online[1]. Furthermore, we describe the evaluation of three different models trained on the corpus: first, a Conditional Random Field (CRF) model that makes use of shallow word features and a gazetteer function; second, a perceptron model with shallow word features and externally trained word clusters; and third, a bidirectional long short-term memory (BiLSTM) model with external word embeddings. Finally, we have combined our model outputs using a simple voting method, obtaining an F_1 score of 85.79 and gaining 1.89 points compared to the best performing individual model. The code for our models is available online[2].

2   Related Work

The most commonly annotated entity types in NER corpora in the general domain are PERSON, LOCATION and ORGANIZATION, both due to the fact that these entities are very common in general texts and newswire texts, which are often the source of NER corpora, and that they contain information that may be valuable for a variety of purposes. The three generic NE types were first proposed for the MUC-6 event as a subtask called ENAMEX [16]. The other subtasks in MUC-6 are named TIMEX (dates and times) and NUMEX (monetary values and percentages). In the CoNLL shared task, a fourth category, MISCELLANEOUS was introduced, which covers proper names that fall outside of the three classic categories, PERSON, LOCATION and ORGANIZATION [31].

While rule-based methods for NER can be highly efficient, especially in a well-defined domain [10], machine learning (ML) methods took over from rule-based method as the main approach to NER as the field developed and data became more readily available. These range from unsupervised to fully supervised methods (e.g. [3,25,35]), as well as hybrid systems, combining various supervised and unsupervised methods and carefully engineered features, e.g. [2].

Although the majority of the early work on NER was conducted on the English language, NER corpora and published work is now available for various different languages. This is an important development, because of the many structural, morphological, and orthographic features that characterize different languages. Enriching the input representation with pre-trained word embeddings has, for example, proven useful for NER in languages such as Turkish [12] and Arabic [21], as have the larger and more complex language models that have recently become popular, such as the Finnish [33] and Slavic [4] BERT models.

Various published work exists for the languages most related to Icelandic, i.e. the Scandinavian languages. The most recent work for Swedish includes a BiLSTM model [34]. A Danish NER corpus is presented in [13], but some of the latest research for Danish NER focuses on cross-lingual transfer, to make up for the limited data available [27]. For Norwegian, the most recent work includes [19], which involves new annotated NER datasets for the two written

---

[1] http://hdl.handle.net/20.500.12537/42.
[2] http://github.com/cadia-lvl/NER.

forms of Norwegian, Bokmål and Nynorsk, and BiLSTM models enriched with pre-trained word embeddings.

Limited work exists on NER for the Icelandic language, most likely due to the lack of an annotated NER corpus. IceNER, a rule-based NER system is part of the IceNLP toolkit [22]. It has been reported to reach an F_1 score of 71.5 without querying a gazetteer, and 79.3 with a gazetteer lookup [32].

3   Corpus Annotation

As a basis for our NER corpus, we used MIM-GOLD, the Icelandic Gold Standard corpus [23], a balanced text corpus of approximately 1 million tokens, tagged with part-of-speech (PoS). All the texts are from the years 2000–2009 and are sourced from thirteen text types, including news texts, books, blogs, websites, laws, adjudications, school essays, scripted radio news, web media texts and emails. For most languages, this variety of text genres is not common in NER corpora, which are often centered on newswire texts (with some exceptions, such as the Portuguese HAREM NER contests [28,29]). Nevertheless, our corpus, MIM-GOLD-NER, is heavy on news-related content, as newspaper articles, web media, and radio news account for 36% of the tokens.

3.1   Annotation Process

Eight NE types are tagged in MIM-GOLD-NER: PERSON, LOCATION, ORGANIZATION, MISCELLANEOUS, DATE, TIME, MONEY and PERCENTAGE. The first four entity types are the same as used in the CoNLL shared tasks. The last four NE types were adapted from the NUMEX and TIMEX types in the MUC events.

We applied a semiautomatic approach when annotating the corpus, using gazetteers and regular expressions to extract as many entities as possible before reviewing and correcting the corpus manually.

Preprocessing. Gazetteers were collected from official Icelandic resources. For extracting the person names, we used the Database of Modern Icelandic Inflections (DMII) [6]. Additionally, we collected lists of place names and addresses, as well as company names. In the end, we had gazetteers with 15,000 person names, 97,000 location names, and 90,000 organization names. Since the original MIM-GOLD is PoS-tagged, we were able to use the PoS tags to filter out likely proper nouns and match them with our gazetteers, to produce NE candidates. Heuristics and knowledge of the language were used to resolve doubts and ambiguities and to try to determine NE boundaries. Remaining ambiguities were registered to be resolved manually. Regular expressions were used for automatically extracting the numerical entities, taking care to match entities regardless of how they are written out in the corpus, whether numerically or alphabetically.

Manual Review. After the automatic preprocessing step, the next task was reviewing the resulting annotations, fixing errors and picking up any remaining NEs missed in the previous step, since some inaccuracies were bound to appear, both in the classification and the span (boundaries) of the entities.

Guidelines were constructed regarding the taxonomy used for the annotation of the corpus. For the four NE types adapted from CoNLL, we mostly relied on the CoNLL guidelines for each entity type [9], though with some modifications to fit Icelandic settings and writing conventions. The four numerical and temporal entity types, DATE, TIME, MONEY, and PERCENT, appeared less commonly in the corpus, and were easier to find using regular expressions. The MUC guidelines were followed as closely as possible when annotating these entities.

One implication of using a balanced corpus such as MIM-GOLD, is that only parts of it have been reviewed/edited, so the texts vary quite a lot in writing quality; some have been thoroughly proofread (published books, laws and adjudications), some have undergone some editing (news articles, some web content, scripted texts for radio), and some have not been edited at all (blogs, emails, web content, classified newspaper ads). The corpus contained many problematic NE candidates, for which annotation was not clear. These were marked specially during the annotation and resolved at the end, to keep consistency within the corpus. In some parts of the corpus, such as laws and regulatory texts, NEs are sparsely distributed, but we have nonetheless opted for annotating the whole corpus without removing sentences unlikely to contain NEs. This was done both to keep the organic distribution of NEs in the corpus and to ensure compatibility with the original MIM-GOLD corpus.

One annotator (the first author of this paper) was in charge of defining the annotation task and labeling the bulk of the corpus. This was done part-time in the course of a year. A second annotator (the second author) stepped in to help in the last weeks, and reviewed around 8% of the corpus. We estimate that 150–200 h went into the manual annotation stage. The annotation resulted in 48,371 NEs, split between the eight entity types as shown in Table 1.

Table 1. NE split in the MIM-GOLD-NER corpus.

Entity type	Total NE count	Percentage
Person	15,599	32.25%
Location	9,011	18.63%
Organization	8,966	18.54%
Miscellaneous	6,264	12.95%
Date	5,529	11.43%
Time	1,214	2.51%
Money	1,050	2.17%
Percent	738	1.53%
Total	48,371	

Once the annotation was finished, an external linguist reviewed a randomly chosen 10% sample of the corpus, to estimate the accuracy of the annotation. The corpus sample contained a total of 4,527 NEs. The reviewer was presented with the same instructions and guidelines as annotator 1 and annotator 2, and was asked to mark any doubts or errors spotted in the corpus sample. Annotator 1 then reviewed this list of error candidates and, in accordance with the guidelines, evaluated which of them were true positives, i.e. real errors that should be fixed. In the end, 250 error candidates were found, out of which 180 were marked as false positives by annotator 1. These false positives were due to either doubts that the reviewer had on how to annotate or lack of detail in the annotation guidelines. Thus, the total number of real errors was 70, which is equivalent to an accuracy of 98.45% for this corpus sample.

4 Models

Until recently, the main approach for NER has been the application of BiLSTM models, along with the best hybrid feature-engineered ML systems [36]. Even though these methods have mostly fallen in the shadow of state-of-the-art transformer models [5,15], they do a good job of solving problems where the input is sequential data, such as in NER. Since a transformer model does not yet exist for Icelandic, we opted for these tried and tested methods for the first experiments with our new corpus.

Three different methods were chosen for the experiments: a CRF model, a perceptron model, and a BiLSTM model. The three models were then combined into one ensemble NER tagger using simple voting. Before presenting our results, we will briefly describe each method.

4.1 Conditional Random Field (CRF)

CRF is a conditional probabilistic modeling method, which can take context into account [20]. Passos et al. [25] implemented a stacked linear-chain CRF system for NER that makes use of shallow word features in their baseline model, along with gazetteers, and then compared the results when adding Word2Vec embeddings [24] and Brown clusters [8], among other things. Their best performing model achieved an F_1 score of 90.9 on the English CoNLL-03 test set.

We implemented a model inspired by this baseline system. Our model uses the following word features:

- the word lower-cased
- word suffixes, length 1 to 4
- a boolean for whether the word is all in uppercase letters
- a boolean for whether the first letter of the word is in uppercase
- a boolean for whether the word is a digit
- all the character n-grams within the word, of length 2 to 5
- the four words prior to the word
- the four words after the word

These parameters were mostly found by trial and error. If a parameter did not improve the model, or if removing a parameter made no difference on the validation set, it was discarded. As an example, suffixes are used, but not prefixes, since the prefixes did not contribute any difference. The gazetteers used for the corpus annotation stage were reused for this model, and each list had its own boolean parameter for whether the word appeared in the list.

4.2   IXA-pipe-nerc

In a survey on different NER architectures [36], the best performing non-neural model was *IXA-pipe-nerc*, a NER module which is a part of the IXA pipes NLP tool [1]. IXA-pipe-nerc is based on a perceptron model and utilizes both shallow local word features and semi-supervised word clusters [2]. It supports including PoS tags as features, as well as a gazetteer lookup. The clustering features used were Brown [8], Clark [11], and Word2Vec [24] clusters. The software is open source and language-independent, making it straightforward to train a model for a new language. The supported local word features are:

- current lower-cased token
- token shape
- the previous prediction for the word
- whether it is the first token in the sentence
- both the prefixes and suffixes of the token, with default of length 4
- word bigrams and trigrams, which both include the current token and the token shape
- all the character n-grams within the word, with default of length 2 to 5

Evaluation shows that the biggest performance boost comes from the word clusters. The best model in [2] achieved an F_1 score of 91.36 on the English CoNLL-03 test set.

The configuration for our model was chosen by experimenting on the validation set, selecting the features that gave the best results. In our model, we used the default values for the features enumerated above, except we used character n-grams of length 1 up to 11, as well as the word trigrams, which are disabled by default. We trained the three types of word clusters on the Icelandic Gigaword Corpus (IGC) [30], a corpus of around 1.4 billion words of Icelandic texts from various sources.

4.3   BiLSTM with Pre-trained Word Embeddings

For the BiLSTM experiments, we used a program called *NeuroNER* [14]. NeuroNER is described as an easy-to-use program for training models to recognize and classify NEs. It uses TensorFlow[3] for training the neural networks and has been reported to reach an F_1 of 90.5 on the English CoNLL-03 dataset. NeuroNER is divided into three layers. First, a BiLSTM layer maps each token to

---

[3] https://www.tensorflow.org/.

a vector representation using two types of embeddings: a word embedding and a character-level token embedding. The resulting embeddings are fed into the second layer, a BiLSTM which outputs the sequence of vectors containing the probability of each label for each corresponding token. Finally, a CRF decoding layer outputs the most likely sequence of predicted labels based on the output from the previous label prediction layer.

Instead of implicitly learning the word embeddings, NeuroNER offers the possibility to incorporate external word embeddings, pre-trained on a larger dataset. We have provided external word embeddings, trained on the 2018 version of the IGC. For the sake of comparison, Word2Vec [24], GloVe [26], as well as Fast-Text [7] embeddings were tested. GloVe embeddings turned out to give slightly better results than the other two, so they were used in the models presented in our results. For the GloVe embeddings, dimensions were set at 300, window size at 10, and the minimum term count at 5. NeuroNER was configured with the following main parameters:

- character embedding dimension = 25
- character lstm dimension = 25
- dropout = 0.5
- patience = 10
- maximum number of epochs = 100
- optimizer = stochastic gradient descent
- learning rate = 0.005

4.4   CombiTagger

Different ML models may have different strengths and weaknesses depending on the methods used to train them. For NER, some may, for example, work better on the more regular numerical entities, while others may be better at overcoming misspellings in the text. One way of leveraging the strengths of different models, for an increased overall performance, is using a voting system for the output tags. CombiTagger [17], a system originally developed for combining different PoS taggers, offers simple and weighted voting. In our work, we fed our three best NER model outputs into CombiTagger and applied simple voting.

5   Results and Discussion

In this section, we present and discuss the results from training on MIM-GOLD-NER using the methods described in Sect. 4.

For the total corpus of 1 million tokens, the split between training, validation and test sets was 80%, 10% and 10%, respectively, which gave a training set of around 800,000 tokens, and validation and test sets of around 100,000 tokens each. We also trained on five different sizes of the corpus, keeping the test set intact in all experiments to maintain consistency in the evaluation. The CoNLL-03 evaluation metrics are used, meaning that both the type and the boundaries of a predicted NE need to match the gold label for it to count as correct.

Table 2. F_1 for the different models, in addition to CombiTagger, which combines the output from the three best models.

	Overall	PER	LOC	ORG	MISC	DATE	TIME	MON	PERC
BiLSTM-internal	73.60	80.11	74.98	65.82	44.10	86.73	91.83	81.86	92.73
CRF	82.24	87.18	86.04	77.02	53.87	90.90	94.46	84.30	98.21
IXA-pipe-nerc	83.10	87.90	85.54	77.02	61.57	91.96	94.29	85.59	97.35
BiLSTM-GloVE	83.90	89.53	85.45	79.03	61.77	90.60	94.78	89.45	95.54
CombiTagger	**85.79**	90.19	88.21	81.23	64.27	93.13	96.41	86.58	98.65

In Table 2, the results from training the different models on the whole corpus are presented. Before considering the best performing method, CombiTagger, we will discuss how the CRF, IXA-pipe-nerc, and BiLSTM models performed overall, and on each NE type.

It is not surprising that the most advanced model, BiLSTM, outperforms the other two in overall score, but it is interesting to see how close behind the IXA-pipe-nerc model comes – by only 0.80 points. Furthermore, IXA-pipe-nerc, which uses externally trained (semi-supervised) word clusters, only improves from the CRF by 0.86 points. In [36], the IXA-pipe-nerc model also obtained marginally better scores (0.46 points) than a CRF model, when evaluated on English.

Looking at the individual entity types, we see that the BiLSTM outperforms the other two in five out of eight types, which should not come as a surprise. What was more unexpected, however, is that the CRF, despite scoring somewhat worse overall, outperforms the IXA-pipe-nerc model in two categories, LOCATION and PERCENT. The reason for the high-scoring LOCATION type may be the gazetteer lookup, implemented as part of the CRF model, since the place names gazetteer was quite exhaustive. The IXA-pipe-nerc model, however, gives the best results for DATE, outperforming the others by over 1% point.

Note the effect of using pre-trained word embeddings as external input into the BiLSTM. BiLSTM-internal was trained without these external word embeddings, i.e. word and character embeddings were trained internally using the training data itself. In contrast, BiLSTM-GloVe uses externally trained GloVe embeddings. We attribute this gain from using the pre-trained word vectors to the fact that Icelandic, being a highly inflected language, has so many surface forms for any lemma, that even though during training the network has seen one surface form of a word, it doesn't know the next time it sees a different surface form that it is the same word. Incorporating a pool of word vectors trained from a corpus of 1.4 billion tokens gives the network access to information on many different word forms.

The CombiTagger ensemble method improves the overall results, with an F_1 score of 85.79, which is better than any of the individual models. When it is compared with our best NER model, we see a 1.89 points improvement in overall F_1, and 2.69 points when compared with the second best model. The observed results show that while the three different models are not equal in quality, each one of them is better than the other two at predicting some particular NE type.

The different models thus tend to produce different (complementary) errors and the differences can be exploited to yield better results. Therefore, CombiTagger outperforms all the others on all but one NE types.

Table 3 shows that training on increasing sizes of the data gradually improves the performance. However, even with a dataset of 540,000 tokens, the overall F_1 is 82.37, and 85.17 in the 720,000 token dataset, which is not far behind from the result obtained on the whole corpus. Furthermore, preliminary experiments with training on a subset of the text types, containing only news texts, indicate that this may be a viable approach, especially if the intended use is within a particular domain.

Table 3. F_1 scores for CombiTagger on different sizes of the data. For clarification of the model names, CombiTagger-180K stands for a corpus size of around 180,000 tokens, with a training data size of around 160,000 tokens, validation set size of approximately 20,000 tokens, and the consistent test set size of 100,693 tokens (10% of each corpus size was reserved for the test set).

	Overall	PER	LOC	ORG	MISC	DATE	TIME	MON	PERC
CombiTagger-180K	76.67	85.50	81.87	69.18	46.34	79.60	89.75	71.50	96.46
CombiTagger-360K	79.14	88.24	82.13	71.59	54.11	84.34	86.89	78.10	97.78
CombiTagger-540K	82.37	89.23	83.75	76.00	58.92	89.77	91.97	87.67	98.20
CombiTagger-720K	85.16	89.19	87.19	81.96	61.16	92.59	95.40	90.35	97.78
CombiTagger-900K	85.79	90.19	88.21	81.23	64.27	93.13	96.41	86.58	98.65

6   Conclusion

We have described the annotation of the first NER corpus for Icelandic and the initial experiments on using the data for training and evaluating Icelandic NER models. This corpus, with 48,371 NEs tagged in 1 million tokens, is one of the largest manually annotated NER corpora we have come across in the literature, and includes a variety of text types that have been annotated for eight common entity types.

Several different model architectures and training set sizes were tested on the data, and an ensemble method using simple voting from three models was shown to perform considerably better than any individual model. These results are presented without any post-processing, such as a gazetteer lookup, commonly used to boost NER results. The morphological intricacies of Icelandic make NER a nuanced problem, but based on these first results we are optimistic about obtaining higher scores with more advanced models in the future, e.g. by using BERT-type models.

Acknowledgments. This work was funded by the Icelandic Strategic Research and Development Programme for Language Technology 2019, grant no. 180027-5301.

References

1. Agerri, R., Bermudez, J., Rigau, G.: IXA pipeline: efficient and ready to use multilingual NLP tools. In: Proceedings of the Ninth International Conference on Language Resources and Evaluation, LREC 2014, Reykjavik, Iceland (2014)
2. Agerri, R., Rigau, G.: Robust Multilingual Named Entity Recognition with Shallow Semi-Supervised Features (2017). arXiv e-prints arXiv:1701.09123
3. Ahmed, I., Sathyaraj, R.: Named entity recognition by using maximum entropy. Int. J. Database Appl. Theory **8**, 43–50 (2015). https://doi.org/10.14257/ijdta.2015.8.2.05
4. Arkhipov, M., Trofimova, M., Kuratov, Y., Sorokin, A.: Tuning multilingual transformers for language-specific named entity recognition. In: Proceedings of the 7th Workshop on Balto-Slavic Natural Language Processing, Florence, Italy (2019). https://doi.org/10.18653/v1/W19-3712
5. Baevski, A., Edunov, S., Liu, Y., Zettlemoyer, L., Auli, M.: Cloze-driven pretraining of self-attention networks. In: Proceedings of the 2019 Conference on Empirical Methods in Natural Language Processing and the 9th International Joint Conference on Natural Language Processing. EMNLP/IJCNLP, Hong Kong, China (2019). https://doi.org/10.18653/v1/D19-1539
6. Bjarnadóttir, K.: The database of modern Icelandic inflection. In: Proceedings of the "Language Technology for Normalisation of Less-Resourced Languages" (SaLTMiL 8 - AfLaT2012), Workshop at the 8th International Conference on Language Resources and Evaluation. LREC 2012, Istanbul, Turkey (2012)
7. Bojanowski, P., Grave, E., Joulin, A., Mikolov, T.: Enriching word vectors with subword information. Trans. Assoc. Comput. Linguist. **5**, 135–146 (2017). https://doi.org/10.1162/tacl_a_00051
8. Brown, P.F., deSouza, P.V., Mercer, R.L., Pietra, V.J.D., Lai, J.C.: Class-based n-gram models of natural language. Comput. Linguist. **18**(4), 467–479 (1992). https://www.aclweb.org/anthology/J92-4003
9. Chinchor, N., Brown, E., Ferro, L., Robinson, P.: Named entity recognition task definition. Technical report Version 1.4, The MITRE Corporation and SAIC (1999)
10. Chiticariu, L., Krishnamurthy, R., Li, Y., Reiss, F., Vaithyanathan, S.: Domain adaptation of rule-based annotators for named-entity recognition tasks. In: Proceedings of the Conference on Empirical Methods in Natural Language Processing, EMNLP 2010, Cambridge, MA, USA (2010). http://aclweb.org/anthology/D10-1098
11. Clark, A.: Combining distributional and morphological information for part of speech induction. In: Proceedings of the 10th Conference of the European Chapter of the Association for Computational Linguistics, EACL 2003, Budapest, Hungary (2003). https://www.aclweb.org/anthology/E03-1009
12. Demir, H., Özgür, A.: Improving named entity recognition for morphologically rich languages using word embeddings. In: Proceedings of the 13th International Conference on Machine Learning and Applications, ICMLA 2013, Miami, FL, USA (2014). https://doi.org/10.1109/ICMLA.2014.24

13. Derczynski, L., Field, C.V., Bøgh, K.S.: DKIE: open source information extraction for Danish. In: Proceedings of the Demonstrations at the 14th Conference of the European Chapter of the Association for Computational Linguistics, EACL 2014, Gothenburg, Sweden (2014). https://doi.org/10.3115/v1/E14-2016

14. Dernoncourt, F., Lee, J.Y., Szolovits, P.: NeuroNER: an easy-to-use program for named-entity recognition based on neural networks. In: Proceedings of the Conference on Empirical Methods in Natural Language Processing, EMNLP 2017, Copenhagen, Denmark (2017)

15. Devlin, J., Chang, M.W., Lee, K., Toutanova, K.: BERT: pre-training of deep bidirectional transformers for language understanding. In: Proceedings of the 2019 Conference of the North American Chapter of the Association for Computational Linguistics: Human Language Technologies, Volume 1 (Long and Short Papers), NAACL, Minneapolis, MN, USA (2019). https://doi.org/10.18653/v1/N19-1423

16. Grishman, R., Sundheim, B.: Message understanding conference-6: a brief history. In: Proceedings of the 16th Conference on Computational Linguistics - Volume 1, COLING 1996, Copenhagen, Denmark (1996). https://www.aclweb.org/anthology/C96-1079/

17. Henrich, V., Reuter, T., Loftsson, H.: CombiTagger: a system for developing combined taggers. In: Proceedings of the 22nd International FLAIRS Conference, Special Track: "Applied Natural Language Processing". Sanibel Island, FL, USA (2009). https://www.aaai.org/ocs/index.php/FLAIRS/2009/paper/viewFile/67/296

18. Ingólfsdóttir, S.L., Þorsteinsson, S., Loftsson, H.: Towards high accuracy named entity recognition for Icelandic. In: Proceedings of the 22nd Nordic Conference on Computational Linguistics, NoDaLiDa 2019, Turku, Finland (2019). https://www.aclweb.org/anthology/W19-6142

19. Johansen, B.: Named-entity recognition for Norwegian. In: Proceedings of the 22nd Nordic Conference on Computational Linguistics, NoDaLiDa 2019, Turku, Finland (2019). https://www.aclweb.org/anthology/W19-6123

20. Lafferty, J.D., McCallum, A.K., Pereira, F.C.N.: Conditional random fields: probabilistic models for segmenting and labeling sequence data. In: Proceedings of the Eighteenth International Conference on Machine Learning, ICML 2001, Williamstown, MA, USA (2001)

21. Liu, L., Shang, J., Han, J.: Arabic named entity recognition: what works and what's next. In: Proceedings of the Fourth Arabic Natural Language Processing Workshop. Florence, Italy (2019). https://doi.org/10.18653/v1/W19-4607

22. Loftsson, H., Rögnvaldsson, E.: IceNLP: a natural language processing toolkit for Icelandic. In: Proceedings of the Annual Conference of the International Speech Communication Association, Antwerp, Belgium (2007)

23. Loftsson, H., Yngvason, J.H., Helgadóttir, S., Rögnvaldsson, E.: Developing a PoS-tagged corpus using existing tools. In: Proceedings of "Creation and use of basic lexical resources for less-resourced languages", workshop at the 7th International Conference on Language Resources and Evaluation, LREC 2010, Valetta, Malta (2010)

24. Mikolov, T., Chen, K., Corrado, G., Dean, J.: Efficient Estimation of Word Representations in Vector Space (2013). arXiv e-prints arXiv:1301.3781

25. Passos, A., Kumar, V., McCallum, A.: Lexicon infused phrase embeddings for named entity resolution. In: Proceedings of the Eighteenth Conference on Computational Natural Language Learning, CoNLL 2014, Ann Arbor, Michigan (2014). https://doi.org/10.3115/v1/W14-1609

26. Pennington, J., Socher, R., Manning, C.: Glove: global vectors for word representation. In: Proceedings of the Conference on Empirical Methods in Natural Language Processing, EMNLP 2014, Doha, Qatar (2014). https://www.aclweb.org/anthology/D14-1162/

27. Plank, B.: Neural cross-lingual transfer and limited annotated data for named entity recognition in Danish. In: Proceedings of the 22nd Nordic Conference on Computational Linguistics, NoDaLiDa 2019, Turku, Finland (2019). https://www.aclweb.org/anthology/W19-6143

28. Santos, D., Freitas, C., Gonçalo Oliveira, H., Carvalho, P.: Second HAREM: New Challenges and Old Wisdom. In: Computational Processing of the Portuguese Language, 8th International Conference, Proceedings, PROPOR 2008, Aveiro, Portugal (2008), https://doi.org/10.1007/978-3-540-85980-2_22

29. Santos, D., Seco, N., Cardoso, N., Vilela, R.: HAREM: an advanced NER evaluation contest for Portuguese. In: Proceedings of the Fifth International Conference on Language Resources and Evaluation, LREC 2006, Genoa, Italy (2006). http://www.lrec-conf.org/proceedings/lrec2006/pdf/59_pdf.pdf

30. Steingrímsson, S., Helgadóttir, S., Rögnvaldsson, E., Barkarson, S., Gudnason, J.: Risamálheild: A very large Icelandic text corpus. In: Proceedings of the Eleventh International Conference on Language Resources and Evaluation, LREC 2018, Miyazaki, Japan (2018). https://www.aclweb.org/anthology/L18-1690

31. Tjong Kim Sang, E.F., De Meulder, F.: Introduction to the CoNLL-2003 shared task: language-independent named entity recognition. In: Proceedings of the Conference on Computational Natural Language Learning, CoNLL 2003, Edmonton, Canada (2003). https://www.aclweb.org/anthology/W03-0419

32. Tryggvason, A.: Named Entity Recognition for Icelandic. Research report, Reykjavik University (2009)

33. Virtanen, A., et al.: Multilingual is not enough: BERT for Finnish (2019). arXiv e-prints arXiv:1912.07076

34. Weegar, R., Pérez, A., Casillas, A., Oronoz, M.: Recent advances in Swedish and Spanish medical entity recognition in clinical texts using deep neural approaches. BMC Med. Inf. Decis. Making **19**, 274 (2019)

35. Wu, Y.-C., Fan, T.-K., Lee, Y.-S., Yen, S.-J.: Extracting named entities using support vector machines. In: Bremer, E.G., Hakenberg, J., Han, E.-H.S., Berrar, D., Dubitzky, W. (eds.) KDLL 2006. LNCS, vol. 3886, pp. 91–103. Springer, Heidelberg (2006). https://doi.org/10.1007/11683568_8

36. Yadav, V., Bethard, S.: A survey on recent advances in named entity recognition from deep learning models. In: Proceedings of the 27th International Conference on Computational Linguistics, COLING 2018, Santa Fe, NM, USA (2018). https://www.aclweb.org/anthology/C18-1182.pdf

BERT-Based Sentiment Analysis Using Distillation

Jan Lehečka[✉][iD], Jan Švec[iD], Pavel Ircing[iD], and Luboš Šmídl[iD]

Department of Cybernetics,
University of West Bohemia in Pilsen,
Univerzitní 2732/8, 301 00 Pilsen, Czech Republic
{jlehecka,honzas,ircing,smidl}@kky.zcu.cz

Abstract. In this paper, we present our experiments with BERT (Bidirectional Encoder Representations from Transformers) models in the task of sentiment analysis, which aims to predict the sentiment polarity for the given text. We trained an ensemble of BERT models from a large self-collected movie reviews dataset and distilled the knowledge into a single production model. Moreover, we proposed an improved BERT's pooling layer architecture, which outperforms standard classification layer while enables per-token sentiment predictions. We demonstrate our improvements on a publicly available dataset with Czech movie reviews.

Keywords: Sentiment analysis · BERT · Knowledge distillation

1 Introduction

In present days, Sentiment Analysis (SA) is one of the most active research fields in Natural Language Processing (NLP) [9]. The goal of SA is to automatically extract the sentiment from a given piece of text (e.g. sentence, document) and thus reveal the emotions the author was experiencing at the time of writing.

The basic type of SA is to detect the overall polarity of the text, i.e. decide if the text has positive, negative or neutral sentiment. Such type of SA can be useful for example to see if people like some product or not. If the main polarity categories are expanded to cover a wider range of sentiment categories (e.g. "very negative", "negative", "neutral", "positive" and "very positive"), the SA task is known as *Fine-grained Sentiment Analysis*. Another widely-studied type of SA is *Aspect-based Sentiment Analysis* (ABSA), which aims to capture the sentiment about specific entities mentioned in the text (e.g. mobile phone) and their aspects (e.g. display, battery).

During the last two decades, the paradigm of models used for solving SA problems has moved from lexicon-based models across shallow machine learning classifiers (mainly Naive Bayes, SVMs and Maximum Entropy classifiers) to deep neural networks using transfer learning [20]. The current paradigm is to learn complex language representations from huge unlabelled text corpora and transfer this knowledge to downstream NLP tasks, such as SA.

© Springer Nature Switzerland AG 2020
L. Espinosa-Anke et al. (Eds.): SLSP 2020, LNAI 12379, pp. 58–70, 2020.
https://doi.org/10.1007/978-3-030-59430-5_5

The significant milestone in the NLP history was the release of pre-trained BERT models [3] and corresponding source codes[1]. BERT models eschew recurrence and convolutions and instead rely entirely on an attention mechanism [29]. They are trained in two phases. In the first phase, the model learns general language representations from huge unlabelled text corpora. This pre-training phase is computationally very expensive but it is a one-time procedure for each language. The second phase, fine-tuning to a target task, is inexpensive as it can be typically done in a few hours on a single GPU using smaller labelled dataset. BERT models achieved amazing results in many NLP tasks (including SA) and thus they established a new paradigm.

Although huge neural networks (even huge ensembles) are achieving tremendous results in many NLP tasks, they are hard to deploy on resource-restricted production devices. An elegant approach of how to transfer the knowledge from huge cumbersome models into a single small production model is *distillation* [6], which is designed to reduce the model size and shorten the inference time while retaining the performances of the huge model. The main idea behind distillation is to train a distilled model on soft targets predicted from the huge model as they provide much more information per training case than hard targets.

This paper is focused on training a single production model for the basic type of SA (i.e. polarity detection). We collected a large Czech movie reviews dataset, trained a large ensemble of BERT models and distilled the knowledge into a single production model. The paper is organized as follows. Section 2 describes related work we are aware of. In Sect. 3, we formalize the BERT-based sentiment analysis task and propose an innovative pooling scheme. The process of knowledge distillation is described in detail in Sect. 4. Section 5 offers details about our experimental setup. Our results are summarized in Sect. 6 and in Sect. 7, we discuss achieved results.

2   Related Work

The majority of the SA-related research in the literature is devoted to English. However, with an increasing volume of online data available for languages with less native speakers, more and more research attention is focused also on SA in other languages. The target language of this paper is Czech, for which several SA-related works have been already published. The initial research was presented in [24,30]. In [4], authors introduced three labelled datasets (10k Facebook posts, 90k movie reviews, and 130k product reviews) and reported results using three classifiers (Naive Bayes, SVM, Maximum Entropy). The SA for the movie dataset was further improved in [1] and [11]. The first attempt at using neural networks for SA in Czech was presented in [14]. A systematic survey of lexical, morphosyntactic, semantic and pragmatic aspects of SA in Czech can be found in the book [31]. Also, the task of ABSA in Czech was addressed by several papers [5,23,27].

---

[1] https://github.com/google-research/bert.

After establishing pre-trained BERT models as a new paradigm in NLP, there have been published many works applying BERT models on SA task, e.g. [7,15,19,25]. The majority of published works use BERT with default pooling layer, i.e. the classification is based only on the final hidden state of the special classification token denoted as [CLS]. In [17], the effect of different pooling layers on top of BERT models was studied. The mean-pooling of hidden states performed the best in this paper experiments. In [22], another two effective pooling strategies have been proposed. The idea here was to pool all intermediate representations of the [CLS] token. In [13], we proposed a new pooling layer architecture, which improves the quality of classification by using information from the [CLS] token in combination with pooled sequence output.

The idea of distilling knowledge from BERT models is also not new in the literature. Several models have been proposed in order to reduce the size of BERT models while retaining the performance, namely DistilBERT [21], TinyBERT [10] and a self-distilling FastBERT [16]. In [28], authors showed that it is even possible to distil the knowledge from BERT into a simple BiLSTM model.

In this paper, we further develop our pooling layer architecture and apply it on the SA task. Moreover, we use distillation from an ensemble of BERT models to train a production model. To the best of our knowledge, no similar approach has been introduced for the SA task yet.

3   BERT-Based Sentiment Analysis

As mentioned in the previous section, the standard BERT-based classification is based on the final hidden state of the special classification token denoted as [CLS]. Such classification is easy to implement and trainable without the use of any metaparameters. But we found in [13] that the more careful processing of the BERT output could bring some improvements in the classification accuracy.

The processing exploits the fact that the BERT-based model outputs the context-dependent embedding for each token of the input, not only the [CLS] token. Based on this fact, we can use common pooling schemes to combine the token predictions into a single sentiment prediction for the whole input. There are many options, but the most common pooling schemes are average and max pooling. The observation from [18] states that the sum of average and max pooling outputs provides a consistent improvement in the model performance. So in [13], we experimented with the pooling scheme consisting of the sum of the predictions for the [CLS] token, the average of token predictions and the maximum prediction with equal weights. We further develop this idea.

First, we introduce the notation used. Lets denote the sequence of the N input tokens to the BERT-based model as $X = \{x_0, x_1, \ldots x_N\}$ where x_0 is the index of a [CLS] token and x_i are indices of the tokens of the original input, generally $x_i \in \mathbb{Z}$. The BERT maps the input indices ($BERT(\cdot) : \mathbb{Z} \to \mathbb{R}^M$) into a context-dependent embeddings $B = \{b_0, b_1, \ldots b_N\}$ with a given dimensionality M. In addition we can use some non-linearities stacked on top of the BERT output to reduce the dimensionality M into a dimensionality of the outputs K (the number of target classes). Lets denote such non-linearities as a function $g(.) : \mathbb{R}^M \rightarrow \mathbb{R}^K$ which maps the sequence B into a sequence $Y = \{g(b_0), g(b_1), \ldots g(b_N)\} = \{y_0, y_1 \ldots y_N\}$. We implemented $g(.)$ as a cascade of three time-distributed dense layers with decaying number of neurons (256, 128, 2) and ReLU activation as it gave us the best results. The non-linearity outputs Y are then pooled using the pooling scheme $pool(\cdot) : \{\mathbb{R}^K\}_0^N \rightarrow \mathbb{R}^K$ to form the vector of logits $L = pool(Y) = [l_1, l_2, \ldots l_K]$. Then the softmax activation with temperature T is applied to the logits to predict the vector of class probabilities $Q = softmax(L) = [q_1, q_2, \ldots q_K] \in [0; 1]^K$. The scheme of described model is depicted in Fig. 1. Summary of the notation:

– *Network input*

$$X = \{x_0, x_1, \ldots x_N\}, \quad x_i \in \mathbb{Z} \tag{1}$$

– *BERT output*

$$B = \{b_0, b_1, \ldots b_N\}, \quad b_i = BERT(x_i) \in \mathbb{R}^M \tag{2}$$

– *Non-linearity output*

$$Y = \{y_0, y_1 \ldots y_N\}, \quad y_i = g(b_i) \in \mathbb{R}^K \tag{3}$$

– *Pooling output (logits)*

$$L = pool(Y) = [l_1, l_2, \ldots l_K] \in \mathbb{R}^K \tag{4}$$

– *Softmax output (class probabilities) with temperature T*

$$Q = softmax(L, T) = [q_1, q_2, \ldots q_K] \in [0; 1]^K \tag{5}$$

$$q_i = \frac{\exp(l_i/T)}{\sum_{k=1}^{K} \exp(l_k/T)}, \quad T \in \mathbb{R} \tag{6}$$

3.1 Pooling Scheme

As we stated above, the goal of the pooling scheme $pool(\cdot) : \{\mathbb{R}^K\}_0^N \rightarrow \mathbb{R}^K$ is to compress the information from the level of N tokens (assuming that the x_0 is the [CLS] token) into a single vector of K logits l_k. We further define the following pooling schemes:

1. *CLS pooling* uses only the prediction for the [CLS] token:

$$pool_{\text{CLS}}(Y) = y_0 \tag{7}$$

2. *Average pooling*:

$$pool_{\text{avg}}(Y) = \left[\frac{1}{N} \sum_{i=1}^{N} y_i^{(k)} \right]_{k=1}^{K} \tag{8}$$

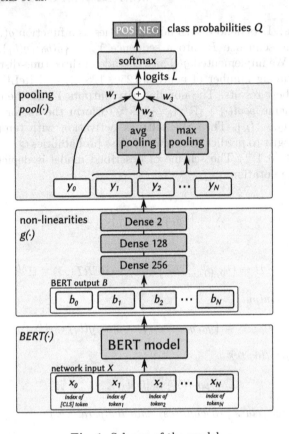

Fig. 1. Scheme of the model

3. *Maximum pooling*:

$$pool_{\max}(Y) = \left[\max_{i \in \{1,2,\dots N\}} y_i^{(k)} \right]_{k=1}^{K} \tag{9}$$

The different pooling schemes express different properties of the input sequence – the CLS pooling gives the overall prediction of the BERT model, the average pooling adds the predictions per each token and the maximum pooling favors the most expressive tokens of the input. To combine the different pooling, we can use a simple sum as in [13]. In this paper, we used the weighted sum with trainable weights:

$$pool(Y) = w_1 \cdot pool_{\mathrm{CLS}}(Y) + w_2 \cdot pool_{\mathrm{avg}}(Y) + w_3 \cdot pool_{\max}(Y) \tag{10}$$

where $w_i \in [0; 1]$ and $\sum_i w_i = 1$. The weighted sum was implemented as Keras [2] layer with a weights trained as part of a stochastic gradient descent and with the constrained values of the parameters.

Explainable Output of Sentiment Analysis. A large advantage of the proposed model for sentiment analysis is an inherent explainability of the model predictions. The sentiment could be tracked back to the token level logits and from such logits, the class probabilities could be generated for any sub-sequence of tokens. This can be useful e.g. for tracking the changes of the sentiment in long text inputs (such as output of an automatic speech recognizer) or for generating word-based sentiment heat maps.

4   Distillation of Knowledge

To benefit from the huge number of training data while keeping the size of the model suitable for production, we employed the method which is called *distillation of knowledge* [6]. The method first trains the detailed model with a huge number of parameters. Then this huge model is used to predict the *soft-targets* (i.e. the class probabilities) on some transfer training set. Finally, the method trains a smaller model suitable for production on the transfer set using the soft-targets and (optionally) the original targets of the transfer set. The use of soft-targets brings additional improvements in the model performance if compared with the model trained only from the transfer set.

Since the description of distillation in [6] is not very formal, we will describe our training and distillation procedure in more detail.

The first step of the distillation method is to train the huge BERT-based model, in our case the model $\bar{M} : \mathbb{Z} \to \mathbb{R}^K$ which maps the input sequence of tokens X into a sequence of logits L and subsequently into a class probabilities Q. The huge model $\bar{M}$ is trained from the set of $\mathbf{N}$ training samples $\{\mathbf{X}, \mathbf{O}\}$ where $\mathbf{O} = \{O_i\}_{i=1}^{\mathbf{N}}, O_i = [o_i]_1^K \in \{0,1\}^K$ are the target labels for inputs X_i.

To perform distillation of knowledge, we employ the so called *transfer training set* $(\bar{\mathbf{X}}, \bar{\mathbf{O}})$ consisting of $\bar{\mathbf{N}}$ samples, where $\bar{\mathbf{X}} = \{\bar{X}_i\}_{i=1}^{\bar{\mathbf{N}}}$ and $\bar{\mathbf{O}} = \{\bar{O}_i\}_{i=1}^{\bar{\mathbf{N}}}, \bar{O}_i \in \{0,1\}^K$. The pair $(\bar{X}_i, \bar{O}_i)$ is the input sequence of tokens and the corresponding one-hot target vector for the i-th example in the transfer training set. Given the transfer training set, the model $\bar{M}$ is used to map the inputs $\bar{\mathbf{X}}$ into the logits $\bar{\mathbf{L}} = \{\bar{L}_i\}_{i=1}^{\bar{\mathbf{N}}}$ where the logits for i-th example $\bar{L}_i$ are obtained from input sequences $\bar{X}_i$ by applying the Eqs. (1)–(4). The logits $\bar{\mathbf{L}}$ are the only intermediate link between the huge model $\bar{M}$ and the final production model M.

The smaller production model M is trained from the transfer training set enriched with the logits predicted by $\bar{M}$. The paper [6] suggests to train the model M using the combination of two target losses:

- *soft-target loss*$_{\text{soft}}(M|\bar{\mathbf{X}}, \bar{\mathbf{Q}}, T)$: For the fixed temperature T, the loss is computed as categorical cross-entropy of the probabilistic outputs of the model $\bar{M}$ computed using the temperature T from logits $\bar{L}$ on the transfer training set and the probabilistic outputs of the model M computed from the input $\bar{X}$ using the same temperature T.
- *hard-target loss*$_{\text{hard}}(M|\bar{\mathbf{X}}, \bar{\mathbf{O}})$: The loss is computed as categorical cross-entropy of the one-hot targets $\bar{O}$ and the probabilistic outputs of the model M for inputs $\bar{X}$ using the temperature $T = 1$.

The overall loss function is combined as linear combination of soft-target loss and hard-target loss:

$$loss(M|\bar{\mathbf{X}}, \bar{\mathbf{O}}, \bar{M}, T) = \alpha \cdot loss_{\text{soft}}(M|\bar{\mathbf{X}}, \bar{\mathbf{Q}}, T) + \beta \cdot loss_{\text{hard}}(M|\bar{\mathbf{X}}, \bar{\mathbf{O}}) \quad (11)$$

where α and β are weights of the soft- and hard-target loss respectively. Both losses are defined as categorical cross-entropy of model M outputs with respect to target observations $\bar{\mathbf{O}}$ or soft-targets $\bar{\mathbf{Q}}$, given input token sequences and the temperature T. According to [6] we used a much higher weight for the soft-target loss than the hard-target loss. The concrete values for T and combination coefficients are provided in Sect. 5. The scheme of our distillation method is depicted in Fig. 2.

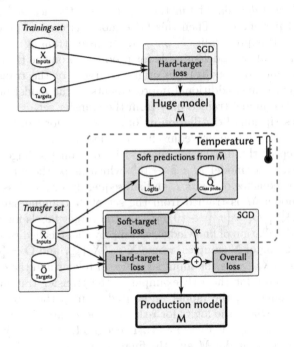

Fig. 2. Scheme of the distillation

5   Experimental Setup

In all our experiments, we decided to use only two sentiment categories: positive and negative class. In consequence, we ignored all data samples with a neutral sentiment as we had large amount of training examples and we found neutral labels to be unreliable[2]. In this way, the model does not get confused during the training, while the predictions could still be extended to more fine-grained categories e.g. by adding a very simple softmax layer on top of the model and estimating several corresponding parameters.

5.1 BERT Model

In our experiments, we set the architecture of all used BERT models in the same way as in Google's BERT-base model, i.e. 12 transformation blocks, 12 attention heads, 110 million trainable parameters and the hidden size of 768 neurons.

Although we were experimenting also with multi-lingual pre-trained model released by Google, which was trained for many languages including Czech, we decided to pre-train our own BERT model from the scratch. Since our model was pre-trained specifically for Czech from a large collection of thoroughly pre-processed text data, we achieved significantly better results with this model.

Vocabulary. First, we had to create the vocabulary, i.e. the list of all possible tokens in the language. Since source codes for WordPiece tokenization (which was used to create vocabularies for original Google's BERT models) are not publicly available, we decided to use a similar approach known as SentencePiece tokenization [12]. The open-source `SentencePiece` tool[3] provides language-independent subword tokenizer. The tokenization is lossless, i.e. the tokenized text could be transformed into a sequence of tokens and back without any loss of characters or punctuation and spacing. The only parameter needed to train the SentencePiece model is the size of the vocabulary. In our experiments, we set the vocabulary size to 100 thousand. We trained uncased BERT model, so we converted all input texts into lower case. Since the SentencePiece model was trained from a large text corpus, it easily deduced basic morphological analysis of Czech language and so it can be used also for tasks like spelling correction [32].

Pre-training. The pre-training phase of BERT model requires a large unlabelled text corpus. We used the collection of web data processed in our web mining tool [26]. Our text corpus for pre-training consists of more than 8 million documents harvested during the last decade from Czech news servers. With a total word count exceeding 2.75 billion words and vocabulary size 6.4 million words, this corpus provides a rich data source for pre-training Czech BERT models.

---

[2] For example, when rating a movie, 3 stars out of 5 does not usually mean that the reviewer had a neutral opinion about the movie. More often, the emotions are bipolar (e.g. the reviewer likes the story but dislikes the main actor) or the review is rather negative, but the reviewer tends to be generous in his ratings. Also, switching to ABSA task was not an option for us because we didn't have any manual annotations for downloaded reviews.

[3] https://github.com/google/sentencepiece.

We pre-trained the BERT model in 5 million gradient steps. For about 90% of the training steps, we used sequences with a maximum length of 128 tokens, batch size 256 and the learning rate warmed up over the first $10\,000$ steps to a peak value at 1×10^{-4}. For the remaining 10% updates, we tuned positional embeddings by feeding sequences with a maximum length of 512 tokens and batch size 64. The whole pre-training took approximately 4 weeks on one 8-core TPU with 128 GB of memory.

Fine-Tuning. We run fine-tuning on single GPUs using the `keras-bert` library[4]. During the fine-tuning, we used adapters [8] and updated only about 3% of BERT's parameters, namely self-attention normalization layers, feed forward normalization layers, multi-headed self-attention of the last layer and the adapter layers. We trained all models for 10 epochs, batch size 48 and maximum sequence length of 128 tokens.

5.2   Sentiment Analysis Dataset

We decided to experiment with the movie reviews domain which is very popular among SA researchers. The largest available dataset for SA in Czech we are aware of was created in [4]. It consists of 90k text reviews from Czech-Slovak movie database (ČSFD)[5]. Since this dataset has been already studied in several papers [1,4,11], we decided to use it as our test data. However, our results cannot be directly compared with results in other papers because we did not train models to predict neutral sentiment and we used also large amount of external data.

Since training of huge neural networks requires large labelled dataset, we crawled our own (as large as possible) dataset from ČSFD web. We crawled 840 thousand movie pages and extracted all reviews and corresponding ratings. In ČSFD reviews, there are 6 possible ratings: 0–5 stars[6]. To narrow these fine-grained categories into sentiment polarity, we mapped 0–2 stars to negative sentiment, 3 stars to neutral sentiment and 4–5 stars to positive sentiment. In sum, we collected 4 million reviews (2.1M positive, 1M neutral and 0.9M negative).

As mentioned before, in our experiments, we ignored all reviews with the neutral sentiment, so our final training dataset consisted of 3 million movie reviews (2.1M positive, 0.9M negative) containing 188 million words in total. The test dataset (from [4]) consisted of 60k reviews (30k positive, 30k negative) with almost 3 million words in total. Since there was a large overlap between train and test data, we removed all test reviews from the training dataset.

5.3   Distillation

We used the general distillation procedure described in Sect. 4. In our experiments, the structure of the huge model, from which the knowledge was distilled,

---

[4] https://github.com/CyberZHG/keras-bert.
[5] https://www.csfd.cz.
[6] The 0-star rating is displayed as "odpad!" meaning "trash!" in English.

was an ensemble of 11 BERT classifiers. Since we collected a large dataset and training each classifier from all data would consume a very long time, each BERT classifier was trained only from 1/11th of the training data (so the training process could be easily parallelized on a computing cluster) and subsequently used in an ensemble, which predicted the soft-targets on the whole training set. This way the whole training set is used as a transfer training set and also it is ensured that each sample in the training set was not seen by a majority of ensemble members during its training, i.e. only 1 of 11 ensemble members was trained using each training sample.

In the experiments we used the following meta-parameter values which were chosen according to [6]: temperature $T = 5$, weight of soft-target loss $\alpha = 0.95$ and weight of hard-target loss $\beta = 0.05$.

Table 1. Experimental results (k stands for thousands, M for millions)

Model type	Trainable params	Accuracy [%]
MaxEnt classifier	1M	90.24
SVM classifier	1M	90.59
Naive Bayes classifier	1M	90.62
[CLS]-based BERT classifier	315k	91.08
Single BERT classifier from ensemble	543k	92.70 ± 0.23
Ensemble of BERT classifiers	$11 \times 543k$	93.80
Distilled BERT classifier	543k	93.65

5.4 Evaluation

Our models have softmax activation in their final layer, so the predictions are in the form of probability distributions over classes. We mapped these soft predictions into hard predictions by assigning the most probable label for each tested review. After that, we evaluated our experiments in terms of accuracy, i.e. the percentage of correctly classified reviews. There is no need to report also F-scores because we have only two target classes (positive and negative sentiment) and equally balanced test dataset.

6 Results

Our achieved results are summarized in Table 1. In the first three rows, we show results for classifiers from the pre-BERT era to picture the difference. These results were computed from all training data encoded as TF-IDF and the vocabulary limited to 1 million words. The next row corresponds to our baseline model, i.e. the BERT model trained from all data with [CLS]-based predictions.

The second part of the table shows results for the ensemble of BERT models with our improved pooling layer, where each member was trained only from 1/11 of the training dataset. As can be seen, the model distilled from this ensemble is much better than individual ensemble members while preserving the same size of the model.

7 Conclusion

In this paper, we presented our experiments with BERT models in the task of sentiment analysis. We collected a large movie reviews dataset and trained an ensemble of BERT models with a special pooling classification layer. This pooling layer outperforms standard [CLS]-based classification approach while enabling per-token sentiment predictions, which can be very useful in order to track down the distribution of the sentiment in the text to individual words or tokens. Since a large ensemble of BERT models is not very practical in the production, we distilled the knowledge into a single BERT-base model with only a modest deterioration of the accuracy.

Acknowledgments. This research was supported by the Technology Agency of the Czech Republic, project No. TN01000024.

References

1. Brychcín, T., Habernal, I.: Unsupervised improving of sentiment analysis using global target context. In: Proceedings of the International Conference Recent Advances in Natural Language Processing RANLP 2013, pp. 122–128 (2013)
2. Chollet, F., et al.: Keras (2015). https://keras.io
3. Devlin, J., Chang, M.W., Lee, K., Toutanova, K.: BERT: pre-training of deep bidirectional transformers for language understanding. arXiv preprint arXiv:1810.04805 (2018)
4. Habernal, I., Ptáček, T., Steinberger, J.: Sentiment analysis in Czech social media using supervised machine learning. In: Proceedings of the 4th Workshop on Computational Approaches to Subjectivity, Sentiment and Social Media Analysis, pp. 65–74 (2013)
5. Hercig, T., Brychcín, T., Svoboda, L., Konkol, M., Steinberger, J.: Unsupervised methods to improve aspect-based sentiment analysis in Czech. Computación y Sistemas **20**(3), 365–375 (2016)
6. Hinton, G., Vinyals, O., Dean, J.: Distilling the knowledge in a neural network. arXiv preprint arXiv:1503.02531 (2015)
7. Hoang, M., Bihorac, O.A., Rouces, J.: Aspect-based sentiment analysis using BERT. In: Proceedings of the 22nd Nordic Conference on Computational Linguistics, pp. 187–196. Linköping University Electronic Press, Turku, September–October 2019. https://www.aclweb.org/anthology/W19-6120
8. Houlsby, N., et al.: Parameter-efficient transfer learning for NLP. arXiv preprint arXiv:1902.00751 (2019)
9. Hussein, D.M.E.D.M.: A survey on sentiment analysis challenges. J. King Saud Univ. Eng. Sci. **30**(4), 330–338 (2018)

10. Jiao, X., et al.: TinyBERT: distilling BERT for natural language understanding. arXiv preprint arXiv:1909.10351 (2019)

11. Kincl, T., Novák, M., Přibil, J.: Improving sentiment analysis performance on morphologically rich languages: language and domain independent approach. Comput. Speech Lang. **56**, 36–51 (2019)

12. Kudo, T., Richardson, J.: SentencePiece: a simple and language independent subword tokenizer and detokenizer for neural text processing. arXiv preprint arXiv:1808.06226 (2018)

13. Lehečka, J., Švec, J., Ircing, P., Šmídl, L.: Adjusting BERT's pooling layer for large-scale multi-label text classification. In: Sojka, P., Kopeček, I., Pala, K., Horák, A. (eds.) TSD 2020. LNCS (LNAI), vol. 12284, pp. 214–221. Springer, Cham (2020). https://doi.org/10.1007/978-3-030-58323-1_23

14. Lenc, L., Hercig, T.: Neural networks for sentiment analysis in Czech. In: ITAT, pp. 48–55 (2016)

15. Li, X., et al.: Enhancing BERT representation with context-aware embedding for aspect-based sentiment analysis. IEEE Access **8**, 46868–46876 (2020)

16. Liu, W., Zhou, P., Zhao, Z., Wang, Z., Deng, H., Ju, Q.: FastBERT: a self-distilling BERT with adaptive inference time. arXiv preprint arXiv:2004.02178 (2020)

17. Ma, X., Xu, P., Wang, Z., Nallapati, R., Xiang, B.: Universal text representation from BERT: an empirical study. arXiv preprint arXiv:1910.07973 (2019)

18. Mishkin, D., Sergievskiy, N., Matas, J.: Systematic evaluation of convolution neural network advances on the Imagenet. Comput. Vis. Image Underst. **161**, 11–19 (2017). https://doi.org/10.1016/j.cviu.2017.05.007. http://www.sciencedirect.com/science/article/pii/S1077314217300814

19. Rietzler, A., Stabinger, S., Opitz, P., Engl, S.: Adapt or get left behind: domain adaptation through BERT language model finetuning for aspect-target sentiment classification. arXiv preprint arXiv:1908.11860 (2019)

20. Salloum, S.A., Khan, R., Shaalan, K.: A survey of semantic analysis approaches. In: Hassanien, A.-E., Azar, A.T., Gaber, T., Oliva, D., Tolba, F.M. (eds.) AICV 2020. AISC, vol. 1153, pp. 61–70. Springer, Cham (2020). https://doi.org/10.1007/978-3-030-44289-7_6

21. Sanh, V., Debut, L., Chaumond, J., Wolf, T.: DistilBERT, a distilled version of BERT: smaller, faster, cheaper and lighter. arXiv preprint arXiv:1910.01108 (2019)

22. Song, Y., Wang, J., Liang, Z., Liu, Z., Jiang, T.: Utilizing BERT intermediate layers for aspect based sentiment analysis and natural language inference. arXiv preprint arXiv:2002.04815 (2020)

23. Steinberger, J., Brychcín, T., Konkol, M.: Aspect-level sentiment analysis in Czech. In: Proceedings of the 5th Workshop on Computational Approaches to Subjectivity, Sentiment and Social Media Analysis, pp. 24–30 (2014)

24. Steinberger, J., et al.: Creating sentiment dictionaries via triangulation. Decis. Support Syst. **53**(4), 689–694 (2012)

25. Sun, C., Huang, L., Qiu, X.: Utilizing BERT for aspect-based sentiment analysis via constructing auxiliary sentence. arXiv preprint arXiv:1903.09588 (2019)

26. Švec, J., et al.: General framework for mining, processing and storing large amounts of electronic texts for language modeling purposes. Lang. Resour. Eval. **48**(2), 227–248 (2013). https://doi.org/10.1007/s10579-013-9246-z

27. Tamchyna, A., Fiala, O., Veselovská, K.: Czech aspect-based sentiment analysis: a new dataset and preliminary results. In: ITAT, pp. 95–99 (2015)

28. Tang, R., Lu, Y., Liu, L., Mou, L., Vechtomova, O., Lin, J.: Distilling task-specific knowledge from BERT into simple neural networks. arXiv preprint arXiv:1903.12136 (2019)

29. Vaswani, A., et al.: Attention is all you need. In: Advances in Neural Information Processing Systems, pp. 5998–6008 (2017)
30. Veselovská, K.: Sentence-level sentiment analysis in Czech. In: Proceedings of the 2nd International Conference on Web Intelligence, Mining and Semantics, pp. 1–4 (2012)
31. Veselovská, K.: Sentiment analysis in Czech. Studies in Computational and Theoretical Linguistics, vol. 16. ÚFAL, Praha, Czechia (2017)
32. Švec, J., Lehečka, J., Šmídl, L., Ircing, P.: Automatic correction of i/y spelling in Czech ASR output. In: Sojka, P., Kopeček, I., Pala, K., Horák, A. (eds.) TSD 2020. LNCS (LNAI), vol. 12284, pp. 321–330. Springer, Cham (2020). https://doi.org/10.1007/978-3-030-58323-1_35

A Cognitive Approach to Parsing with Neural Networks

Vigneshwaran Muralidaran[1(✉)], Irena Spasić[1], and Dawn Knight[2]

[1] School of Computer Science and Informatics, Cardiff University, Queen's Buildings,
5 The Parade, Roath, Cardiff CF24 3AA, UK
{MuralidaranV,SpasicI}@cardiff.ac.uk
[2] School of English, Communication and Philosophy, Cardiff University,
John Percival Building, Colum Drive, Cardiff CF10 3EU, UK
KnightD5@cardiff.ac.uk

Abstract. According to Cognitive Grammar (CG) theory, the overall structure of a natural language is motivated by a relatively small set of domain-independent cognitive abilities. In this paper, we draw insights from CG to propose an approach to natural language parsing with little syntactic annotation. A sentence functions as a cohesive whole because its parts are meaningfully linked. We propose that every part of a sentence can be analysed along three axes: composition, interaction and autonomy. When two expressions semantically correspond in all the three axes we call them cohesive. We present an algorithm that reads parts of sentences incrementally, recognises their construction schemas along the three axes, assembles any two component schemas into one composite schema if they are cohesive, parses a span of text as incrementally successive assembly of components into composites, retains multiple running parses within the span and chooses the best parse. The basic construction schema definitions and their patterns of assembly are implemented as dictionary-cum-rules because they are fewer in number, largely language-independent and can be extended to handle language-specific variations. A basic feedforward neural network component was trained to learn all valid patterns of assemblies possible in a span of text and to choose the best parse. A successful parse exhausts all the words in the sentence and ensures local cohesion and assembly at every stage of analysis. We present our approach, parser implementation and evaluation results in Welsh and English. By adding WordNet synsets we are able to show improvements in parser performance.

Keywords: Parsing · Natural language processing · Cognitive grammar · Neural networks

1 Introduction

Syntactic parsing is the task of analysing the grammatical structure of natural language sentences. As one of the fundamental steps in natural language processing (NLP), it is used in various information retrieval tasks such as document

© Springer Nature Switzerland AG 2020
L. Espinosa-Anke et al. (Eds.): SLSP 2020, LNAI 12379, pp. 71–84, 2020.
https://doi.org/10.1007/978-3-030-59430-5_6

summarisation [10,12], sentiment analysis [2,20], machine translation [4] and search engines [16]. With advancements in supervised machine learning techniques and the availability of large annotated treebanks for many languages, the performance of state-of-the-art parsers are comparable to humans. However, such treebanks may not be available for many languages. In fact, few languages have more than 10,000 sentences annotated for syntactic structure. This poses challenges in developing a parser for less-resourced, minoritised languages. Moreover, there is no single, standard framework for grammatical analysis and the corresponding annotation scheme. Therefore, there has been a shift from supervised to unsupervised approaches to parsing in an attempt to harness computational power to decode the grammar of natural languages. These approaches are based on an assumption that the probabilistic patterns of a language are generated by simple, hidden models of syntactic structure. Their implementation is concerned with defining the model space, estimator function and the search approach with the aim of estimating the probability of a grammatical structure. Most approaches learn the syntactic structure in the form of constituency or dependency trees and evaluate their output against a gold standard created manually by linguists. Despite sophisticated inferencing approaches, the performance of unsupervised parsers is still considerably lower than that of supervised counterparts [21].

In this paper, we present our approach to parsing based on insights from cognitive grammar (CG) [9]. According to CG, grammar is entirely symbolic i.e. a mapping between form and function. No sharp difference can be maintained between lexicon, morphology and syntax since they form a continuum along the spectrum of symbolic complexity. Grammatical organisation is understood in terms of general cognitive abilities such as categorisation, focus, comparison, schematisation, grouping, reification and so on. These abilities, typically used for non-linguistic purposes, are now repurposed to support linguistic processing. In this study, we explored the idea that a sentence can be seen as a miniature version of a text. By doing so, we were able to recognise that local cohesion plays a significant role in how the grammatical structure of a text is organised. We identified that every expression can be analysed along three axes: composition, interaction and autonomy. If two expressions meaningfully correspond in all the three axes, they can be assembled into a composite expression. The two component expressions are said to be locally cohesive. The patterns of cohesion along the three axes are defined as basic construction schemas. We propose seven basic schemas along the composition axis, six along the interaction axis and two along the autonomous axis. More specific usages patterns can be treated as extensions of one or more of these basic schemas. Incremental assembly of partial structures of a sentence into locally cohesive schemas successively results in the final parse. In Sect. 2, we present the background and related work. Subsection 3.1 presents the concepts involved in our approach, Subsect. 3.2 lays out the algorithm for an incremental cognitive parsing, Subsect. 3.3 describes the implementation and results. The paper ends with final remarks and directions for future research in Sect. 4.

2   Background and Related Work

Different theoretical frameworks have been proposed to study grammatical structures in linguistics, e.g. generative grammar [1], constraint-based grammar, structuralist theory, construction grammar [6], cognitive approaches, quantitative linguistics, etc. [13]. These diverse approaches can be classified broadly into two schools of thought: *generative-formal* and *functional-cognitive*. In generative-formal approaches, a grammar is treated as an autonomous system independent of meaning. Another related idea is that there are innate, universal principles of grammar encoded in the human brain with abstract properties such as distinguishing a noun from a verb, a content word from a function word and so on. Variations found in human languages are seen as parametric variations of the universal grammar principles. In contrast, the functional-cognitive approaches hold that a grammatical structure cannot be analysed without reference to meaning, conceptualisation is the basis of all language phenomena and grammar is not an independent mental faculty, but is instead connected to general cognitive processes and structures. The generative-formal school has had a significant influence on the mainstream ideas about language and grammar. The idea that an abstract, formal set of rules define and constrain the way words are arranged into well-formed sentences has found appeal in various disciplines such as compiling and interpreting programming languages, psycholinguistic studies, music theory [11], computational linguistics and NLP. Earlier implementations of parsers defined a grammar manually in the form of context-free rules or dependency rules. With the emergence of data-driven methods, the phrase structures and dependency structures were learned from large annotated corpora by exploiting their statistical properties. However, due to the lack of large training datasets, unsupervised approaches to induce parsers from raw text alone have been growing since 2004 [8].

Our research goal was to develop an unsupervised parsing approach suitable for minoritised languages, with lesser NLP resources. We wanted to explore how to adapt functional-cognitive ideas for parsing such languages with minimal annotation. We conducted a systematic literature review on unsupervised approaches to grammar induction to understand the influence of theory of grammar, methodologies used in implementation, features for learning, output representation, sentence processing strategy used in various studies. We identified that most unsupervised grammar induction systems treated a grammar as a generative-formal system independent of meaning and conceptualisation. Parsers were decoded in a non-incremental, head-driven manner by assuming that all words of a sentence were available for the parsing model. Output representations were hierarchical structures, typically a constituency or dependency tree. However, the theoretical and psycholinguistic studies in our review suggested that a usage-based, incremental, sequential approach that takes discourse information and local dependencies can model parsing better [5,7,18]. This gap between the theoretical studies and the prevalent trends in parsing should be addressed to enable further progress in unsupervised parsing. We previousuly used ideas from cognitive and construction grammar to understand the syntax of Dravidian languages and developed the corresponding annotation framework. A full parser was created for Tamil through supervised learning from a manually annotated corpus [19]. We were able to explain the morphosyntactic properties of Dravidian languages by explicitly defining 29 construction schemas. This was specific to the given language family. The present work is an attempt to generalise the previous understanding to make it applicable to other languages and develop a parsing strategy without explicit annotation.

3   Methods

3.1   Conceptualisation

The intuition behind our approach is that self-similar cognitive construals occur at different levels of syntactic organisation. Construal is our ability to conceive and portray the same situation in alternative ways. Profile is one of the many aspects relevant to an expression's construal. For example, 'he', 'the boy', 'the one who came to school', 'the fact that the boy came to school' occur at different levels of grammatical organisation with formally different syntactic properties. However they all profile a THING construal irrespectively of their internal complexity. This explains their occurrence in similar construction patterns - such as being an argument of a verb: '*He* says', '*The boy* says', '*The one who came to school* says the truth', '*The fact that the boy came to school* says a lot'. In other words, all these expressions function as a THING and, therefore, can PARTICIPATE in a PROCESS even though one is a simple pronoun and another one is a noun phrase modified by a relative clause. Recognising that they share the profile of a THING does not mean that they are one and the same. For example, the word 'boy' (THING) can assemble with an adjective to form an expression 'good boy', but the noun phrase 'the boy' (THING) cannot assemble with adjective to form '*good the boy'. This is because the profile determinant is just one aspect of an expression's construal. There are other aspects that determine how an entity is construed either by itself and in the context of other entities. For a cognitive parsing of grammatical structure, we should delineate what aspects of linguistic construals are relevant for syntactic organisation. In our earlier work, although 29 construction schemas were defined explicitly to capture the morphosyntax of Tamil, they only tacitly embodied the general aspects relevant for syntactic organisation [14]. Now, we have attempted to bring those tacit aspects explicitly so that a more general approach to parsing can be developed.

In CG the boundaries between grammar, discourse and pragmatics are not discrete, but lie on a continuum. Many properties which make a larger piece of text meaningful are applicable to a sentence that is organised grammatically. A sentence can be treated as a smaller text sharing with it a few important properties: it is relatively independent, internally structured, displays cohesion in how parts are arranged as a whole, has specific communicative intention. We recognise that local cohesion plays a very crucial role in the production and parsing of grammatical structures. Every linguistic expression can be analysed along three axes: composition, interaction and autonomy. Composition refers to those aspects of an expression's construal which are in focus and which determine the expression's profile. Interaction refers to those aspects which are not in focus but which function as sites of elaboration. Autonomy refers to the aspect of whether an expression necessarily requires some other entity for its characterisation. If so, it is said to be dependent, otherwise it is autonomous.

We will illustrate these notions using an example. On seeing the word 'slow' we construe an ATEMPORAL RELATIONSHIP/STATUS of 'being slow' that is attributed to an unknown THING. The focus is on the ATEMPORAL RELATION-SHIP/STATUS and the THING slot is out of focus. We say that 'slow' instantiates ATEMPORAL RELATIONSHIP/STATUS schema along its composition axis. This is shown in Fig. 1[1]. The unknown THING functions as the elaboration site, which means that when a noun, e.g. 'transition', is encountered, it semantically corresponds to this site. The STATUS ('being slow') qualifies its attribute on the THING ('transition'). We say that 'slow' instantiates QUALIFIER schema along its interaction axis. This again is shown in Fig. 1. How do we determine if the expression 'slow' is construed as AUTONOMOUS or DEPENDENT along the autonomy axis? In certain expressions like 'the' it is clear that its construal necessarily depends on a THING and so it always instantiates DEPENDENT schema along the autonomy axis. However 'slow' can be conceived autonomously or dependently based on the difference in usage. When used in attribute

Adjective 'slow' - Composition axis: Status

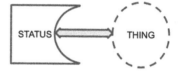

Adjective 'slow' - Interaction axis: Qualifier

Fig. 1. Composition and interaction axes

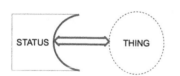

Adjective 'slow' - Autonomy axis: Dependent

Adjective 'slow' - Autonomy axis: Autonomous

Fig. 2. Autonomy axis

---

[1] Conventions of image schema used in CG are more detailed and specific than what is used here. The figures used here do not share those conventions. This is just our own rough sketch for the sake of illustration. Conventions used: circle - THING, rectangle - RELATIONSHIP, rectangle with right side curved - any RELATIONSHIP which anticipates a THING, double arrow - assembly of two entities, dotted - unknown entity waiting elaboration, colour-filled - focussed entity, colour border - portions scanned for construing along an axis.

adjective constructions ('slow transition'), the focus is on the STATUS slot and the unknown THING slot is focussed, not on its composition, but on for its interaction. So in an attribute adjective construction, it is construed as DEPENDENT. However, in predicate adjective constructions ('the transition is slow'), the focus is both on the STATUS as well as unknown THING. Thus as a predicate adjective, it is construed as AUTONOMOUS. The construals of attribute and predicate adjectives and the difference in their autonomy is shown in Fig. 2. Based on the discussion above we can say that the adjective in the phrase 'slow transition' instantiates 'STATUS_QUALIFIER_DEPENDENT' schema. Every expression at any syntactic level - such as words, phrases and clauses - can be analysed along these three axes and their construction schema can be identified. There are seven basic construals along composition axis: THING, RELATIONSHIP, PRONOUN, PROCESS, STATUS, OPERATOR, EVENT, six basic construals along interaction axis: CONTINUATIVE, COMBINATIVE, PARTICIPANT, DESCRIPTIVE, QUALIFIER, CLOSED and two basic schemas along autonomy axis: AUTONOMOUS, DEPENDENT. These are fundamental for schematising any linguistic expression along the three axes of local cohesion. More specific constructions in the language inherit the basic properties of these construals and add more specific construals to characterise their construction schema. The definitions of these basic schemas are in Table 1.

Table 1. Basic construals along the three axes of local cohesion

Construal	Definition
Construals along composition axis	
THING	A product of grouping and reification
RELATIONSHIP	Viewing an entity not in isolation but in its overall arrangement/configuration
PRONOUN	A THING which is least specific in a discourse
PROCESS	A RELATIONSHIP that is mentally scanned through time (sequential scanning)
STATUS	A RELATIONSHIP that is scanned holistically at an instant (summary scanning)
OPERATOR	A STATUS, which takes one or more entities and changes the nature of their relationship with other entities
EVENT	Construing a PROCESS summarily after all its elaboration sites are fully elaborated
Construals along interaction axis	
CONTINUATIVE	When a RELATIONSHIP is expected in the discourse for interaction
COMBINATIVE	When a THING is expected in the discourse for interaction
PARTICIPANT	When a THING is construed as a part of a PROCESS's profile
DESCRIPTIVE	When a RELATIONSHIP is construed as a part of a PROCESS's profile
QUALIFIER	When a RELATIONSHIP is construed as part of a PROCESS's profile
CLOSED	When an entity is AUTONOMOUS and construed as nuclear entity in discourse
Construals along autonomy axis	
AUTONOMOUS	The profile of an entity can be construed independently of another entity at the same functional level
DEPENDENT	The profile of an entity can be construed only by construing another entity at the same functional level

Just like linguistic expressions organise into formal categories at different syntactic levels, the construals behind them also organise into different construction schemas at different functional levels. We observed that self-similar construction patterns recur at each of these functional levels. There are three functional levels that are relevant for parsing a sentence: Basic level, Process level and Event level. Table 2 defines the full list of schemas at all these three levels to parse English sentences. Construction schemas relevant for every level are defined in terms of how they pattern with other schemas at the same level or at the lower levels. The schemas mentioned in Table 2 inherit the basic construals from Table 1 and make them more specific by tailoring them for usage patterns in English language. A detailed theoretical discussion on how the contents of Table 2 are able to capture the grammatical structures in English is beyond the scope of this paper. For now, we will point out a few examples to illustrate how this is possible. Consider auxiliary verb constructions such as 'has come (POS tags: VBZ VBN), would have given (MD VB VBN), are doing (VB VBG), must have been going on (MD VB VBN VBG PRT)'. They are all recognised by the definitions of PROCESS_CLOSED-AUTONOMOUS. For instance, the expression 'has come' is recognised as: has come < VBZ VBN < PROCESS_CLOSED--AUTONOMOUS <=> STATUS_CLOSED-DEPENDENT < PROCESS_CLOSED-AUTONOMOUS. However the definitions of the same schema can recognise self-similar structure at a higher level of organisation as well. Consider the expression 'He felt broken' captured by the same schema: felt broken < VBD VBN < PROCESS_CLOSED-AUTONOMOUS <=> STATUS_CLOSED -DEPENDENT < PROCESS_CLOSED -AUTONOMOUS. Constructions which can be schematised in similar ways at different levels of usage are identified as manifestations of the same construals. These definitions were suitably modified before using them to parse Welsh sentences. For example, STATUS_ QUALIFIER <==> THING_CONTINUATIVE is a valid assembly in English. But THING_CONTINUATIVE <==> STATUS_QUALIFIER is the valid assembly in Welsh because the adjectives follow the nouns in attribute adjective constructions in Welsh.

So far we have discussed schema definitions. There are other two parts relevant for parsing a text: patterns of how any two components will assemble to form a composite schema and what will be the profile determinant of the composite assembly. The valid patterns of assembly and the profile determinant of the assembly can be obtained from the definitions in Table 1 and stored in a dictionary. When parsing a sentence incrementally, the words already observed and parsed interact with new words. If the interaction axess of the already parsed words and the composition axis of the new word correspond semantically, they will be assembled together. Adding each possible sequence of assemblies as a potential parse, we have multiple running parses as more and more words are read. The algorithm presented in Sect. 3.2 describes a procedure that uses these concepts for parsing.

Table 2. List of construction schemas

Construction schema	Patterns with
Defining THINGS	
THING_PARTICIPANT	NOUN_CONTINUATIVE, STATUS_CLOSED-AUTONOMOUS, NUM_CONTINUATIVE, DET_CONTINUATIVE, THING_PARTICIPANT< − >STATUS_CLOSED-DEPENDENT
PRON_PARTICIPANT	PRON_CONTINUATIVE, EVENT_PARTICIPANT, (THING_PARTICIPANT)< − >EVENT_QUALIFIER
THING_COMBINATIVE	NOUN_COMBINATIVE, PRON_COMBINATIVE
THING_CLOSED-AUTONOMOUS	PROCESS_CONTINUATIVE-AUTONOMOUS, STATUS_CLOSED-AUTONOMOUS, EVENT_CLOSED-DEPENDENT
Defining PROCESS relationships	
PROCESS_CONTINUATIVE-AUTONOMOUS	TO< − >VB, VBG
PROCESS_CLOSED-DEPENDENT	MD
PROCESS_CLOSED-AUTONOMOUS	VB, VBZ, VBD, PROCESS_CLOSED-AUTONOMOUS< − >PRT, PROCESS_CLOSED-AUTONOMOUS< − >PROCESS_CONTINUATIVE-AUTONOMOUS, PROCESS_CLOSED-AUTONOMOUS< − >STATUS_CLOSED-DEPENDENT, PROCESS_CLOSED-DEPENDENT< − >PROCESS_CLOSED-AUTONOMOUS
Defining STATUS/ATEMPORAL relationships	
STATUS_PARTICIPANT	STATUS_CONTINUATIVE-DEPENDENT< − >THING_PARTICIPANT, STATUS_CONTINUATIVE-DEPENDENT< − >PRON_PARTICIPANT, STATUS_CONTINUATIVE-DEPENDENT< − >THING_CLOSED-AUTONOMOUS
STATUS_DESCRIPTIVE	ADV
STATUS_CONTINUATIVE-DEPENDENT	ADP
STATUS_QUALIFIER	ADJ, VBN, NUM, ADP
STATUS_COMBINATIVE	PRP$, DET
STATUS_CLOSED-AUTONOMOUS	VBN, ADV, ADJ
STATUS_CLOSED-DEPENDENT	ADJ, VBN
Defining OPERATORS	
OPERATOR_DESCRIPTIVE	CONJ
OPERATOR_JOIN	CONJ,
OPERATOR_CLOSED	.
Defining EVENTS	
EVENT_CONTINUATIVE-AUTONOMOUS	EVENT_CONTINUATIVE-DEPENDENT< − >EVENT_CLOSED-AUTONOMOUS, EVENT_CONTINUATIVE-DEPENDENT< − >STATUS_CLOSED-DEPENDENT, EVENT_CONTINUATIVE-DEPENDENT< − >THING_CLOSED-AUTONOMOUS
EVENT_CONTINUATIVE-DEPENDENT	ADP, ADV, DET
EVENT_COMBINATIVE-DEPENDENT	DET, PRON, ADV
EVENT_QUALIFIER	EVENT_COMBINATIVEDEPENDENT< − >PROCESS_CLOSED-AUTONOMOUS, EVENT_COMBINATIVE-DEPENDENT< − >EVENT_CLOSED-AUTONOMOUS
EVENT_CLOSED-AUTONOMOUS	(PARTICIPANT)< − >PROCESS_CLOSED-AUTONOMOUS, (DESCRIPTIVE)< − >PROCESS_CLOSED-AUTONOMOUS
EVENT_CLOSED-DEPENDENT	EVENT_CONTINUATIVE-DEPENDENT< − >EVENT_CLOSED-AUTONOMOUS

3.2   Algorithm

After preprocessing, the original sequence of tokens is converted into a sequence of POS tags. Each POS tag can be mapped to multiple local cohesion schemas defined in Table 2. Before the parsing procedure begins, we have a sequence of a list of possible schemas corresponding to each POS tag. Parsing a sentence becomes the task identifying a procedure to implement the following goals:

1. Process a sentence incrementally. This means that as the words in a sentence are read one by one, each word is added to parse memory and assembled with all possible parses obtained from previous words. Thus all the possible parses are continuously updated.
2. Retain all possible parses in the parse memory until a particular span of words are processed. Call this the 'retain span' of the parse. This could be a function of number of words or number of phrases or some other criterion.
3. After each retain span, choose the best parse out of all possible parses stored in the memory.
4. Repeat the procedure until all words in the sentence are read and all the components are integrated into one CLOSED schema (Table 1).

---

input : *corpus, schema_definitions, assembly_definitions*
output: Every sentence is assembled into one CLOSED schema
STEP 1 - PREPROCESSING STAGE;
for *sentence in corpus* **do**
  pos_sequence←POS-TAGGER(*sentence*);
  for *current_pos in pos_sequence* **do**
    list_cx_schemas←ALL-POSSIBLE-SCHEMAS(*current_pos*) FROM *schema_definitions*;
  end
  cx_schema_list_sequence ← Sentence stored as a sequence of list of all schemas for each word;
end
retain_span ← 0 ;
STEP 2 - PROCESSING STAGE;
for *(pos_tag, list_schema) in (pos_sequence, list_cx_schemas)* **do**
  running_parse ← ADD-TO-RUNNING-PARSE (*pos_tag, list_schema*);
  if *CHECK-LANDING-POINT (list_schema)* **then**
    retain_span ← *retain_span* +1;
    GET-VALID-ASSEMBLIES (*running_parse, assembly_definitions*);
    multiple_running_parses ← RETAIN-MULTIPLE-RUNNING-PARSES (*running_parse*);
    if *retain_span* > 2 **then**
      STEP 3 - PREDICTION AND FEEDBACK STAGE;
      for *possible_parse in multiple_running_parses* **do**
        for *assembly_pattern in possible_parse* **do**
          assembly_pattern is of the form *schema1 <=>schema2 =schema3*;
          head_predicted ← PREDICT-ASSEMBLY-HEAD-ANN (*schema1 <=>schema2*);
          LEARN-ASSEMBLY-ANN(*schema1<=>schema2=schema3*);
        end
        - Collect the total error for each assembly prediction inside every possible parse.
      end
      - Choose the best parse as the one whose total error is minimum - Remove all other possible parses in *multiple_running_parses* and update it with the best parse chosen
    end
  end
end

Algorithm 1: Procedure for incremental cognitive parsing

Algorithm 1 describes the parsing procedure which involves three stages. In the preprocessing stage, the sentences are POS tagged, each POS tag is mapped to a list of construction schemas as per the definitions in Table 2. Next in the processing step, as we read each word, we add to the parse memory all combinations of interactions possible between the words and their schemas encountered so far. At this stage we do not determine if the interaction results in a cohesive assembly as per the definitions in Tables 1 and 2. We simply add all possible interactions to the parse memory. There is also a possibility that the interaction cannot be determined correctly until more context is available. For example when we see two NOUNs one after another there are ambiguous interactions: (a) They may form a noun compound with the second word as the head (b) Both the words may expect another noun and together they might form a noun compound (c) They do not interact with each other but the second noun is going to interact with an upcoming word, and so on. Therefore individual words and their schemas are just added to the running parse without assuming their interaction, hoping to deal with them later. We identified certain schemas as landing points. After encountering these landing points, all such ambiguous interactions can be deterministically found (e.g. When we see a comma after a noun, the possibility that it is a part of a single noun compound is shut. So PUNCT is a landing point). PROCESS', 'CLOSED', 'EVENT', 'THING', 'QUALIFIER', 'COMBINATIVE', 'PUNCT' were treated as landing points. After seeing the landing point, we validate the interactions in parse memory to retain only cohesive ones and discard all others. For words seen until landing point, all cohesive interactions are assembled and composite schemas are found. The parse memory is updated with multiple assembly sequences. Each sequence schematises the assembly of words seen so far and each can be treated as possible parses of the words. In this way, all possible parses are stored in *multiple_running_parses*. For example, after seeing two words 'The' (DET), 'asbestos' (NOUN) in a sentence we have the items stored in the running parse RUNNING_PARSE in Fig. 4.

We continue to retain all possible assemblies for a span of two landing points - the retain span. It is intended to ensure that sufficient span of text is seen before choosing the best parse while preventing the number of possible parses from increasing exponentially. We experimentally changed this span and found that a span of two landing points was optimal. The third stage uses a neural network to carry out two functions: (a) to predict the composite schema given the component schemas of an assembly and (b) to learn all valid assemblies from every possible parse. The best parse is chosen as the one that minimises the total loss in predicting all the composite schemas within a parse. The basic idea is to train a neural network to predict the composite schema given the components and feedback the correct composite schema learned from local cohesion rules. By feeding locally cohesive assemblies within the retain span and minimising the prediction loss, a globally cohesive parse can be obtained for the same span of text. Our hypothesis is that a globally cohesive parse can be discovered by repeating the prediction and feedback stage for all retained spans from a large corpus of sentences.

3.3   Implementation and Results

Figure 3 shows the overview of the system. The system has four components -
schema definition, preprocessing stage, processing stage, prediction and feedback
stage. The schema definition component is implemented as a dictionary and a
list. The preprocessing stage uses the parts of speech tags from Wall Street
Journal (WSJ) corpus for English [17] and from Cronfa Electroneg o Gymraeg
(CEG) corpus for Welsh [3]. The other mappings in the preprocessing stage and
the steps in the processing stage are implemented according to Algorithm 1. A
feedforward neural network with one hidden layer was implemented with DyNet
toolkit [15]. We initialised a SimpleGSDTrainer with a learning rate of 0.1. The
dimensions of the input, hidden layer are fixed at 128. The assembling words,
POS tags and the construction schemas are initialised as model parameters and
are updated during training. The construction assembly head is predicted as the
output. Optionally, the synset information from the WordNet could be given to
improve the learning by adding semantics to the parsing process.

We trained the system using a total of 3,912 sentences from a freely available
portion of the WSJ corpus for English and 3,000 sentences from a portion of the

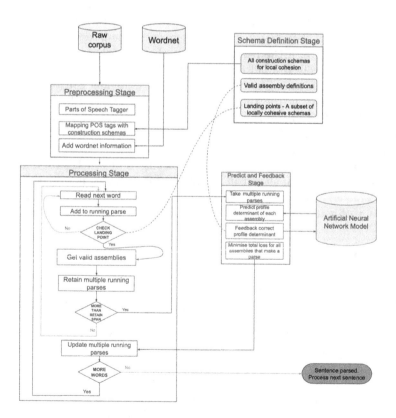

Fig. 3. System overview

```
Words      : {  <['The'], ['asbestos']> ,
                  <['The asbestos']>
            }
Assemblies : {  <['STATUS_COMBINATIVE', 'EVENT_CONTINUATIVE-DEPENDENT', 'EVENT_COMBINATIVE-DEPENDENT'] ,
                  ['THING_COMBINATIVE', 'THING_CONTINUATIVE']> ,

                <['STATUS_COMBINATIVE<=>THING_COMBINATIVE=THING_COMBINATIVE'] ,
                  ['STATUS_COMBINATIVE<=>THING_CONTINUATIVE=THING_CONTINUATIVE'] >
            }
```

Fig. 4. Multiple running parses

Table 3. Evaluation results

Language	Accuracy	Condition
English	83.46%	Without synsets
Welsh	76.51%	Without synsets
English	87.19%	With synsets
Welsh	78.85%	With synsets

CEG corpus for Welsh. Only sentences of length greater than 3 and less than 20 were selected. All sentences were used for schema prediction and feedback. But only the parses chosen from the final 50 sentences (in both English and Welsh) were considered for evaluation because it represents the latest state of learning by the neural network. If the parse chosen by the network is correct, the words and the schemas involved in all the assemblies that make up a parse should be a valid constituent in the constituency tree. The matching constituent should not be the leaf nodes in the tree because those are just words. When all the assembly heads of the network's parse match at some constituency level in a constituency, we consider it to be correct and otherwise incorrect. We annotated the constituency representation of 50 sentences in English and 50 sentences in Welsh. The accuracy of predicting assembly heads all of which have a match in the constituency tree are shown in Table 3. Adding synset information to the model parameters along with POS tags and the construction schemas improves the accuracy of getting a correct parse.

4   Conclusion

We presented a cognitive approach to parsing grammatical structures from Welsh and English corpus without explicit linguistic annotation. One obvious difficulty that we faced was in output evaluation. The parsed output does not follow traditional representation such as constituency or dependency tree, but the sequence in which locally cohesive schemas were assembled into self-similar schemas at a higher level of organisation. Therefore, we were not able to re-use existing treebanks as a gold standard directly. Instead, we assumed that if the assembly heads predicted by the system are correct, the text within the span must match the constituents in the standard phrase structure tree. A baseline result for parsing by applying the theoretical insights from Cognitive Grammar has been presented. In future work, the optimisation of neural network models and a more effective evaluation strategy can be formulated.

References

1. Chomsky, N., Lightfoot, D.W.: Syntactic Structures. Walter de Gruyter, Berlin (2002)
2. Di Caro, L., Grella, M.: Sentiment analysis via dependency parsing. Comput. Stand. Interfaces **35**(5), 442–453 (2013)
3. Ellis, N.C., O'Dochartaigh, C., Hicks, W., Morgan, M., Laporte, N.: Cronfa electroneg o gymraeg (CEG): a 1 million word lexical database and frequency count for welsh (2001). http://corpws.cymru/ceg
4. Eriguchi, A., Tsuruoka, Y., Cho, K.: Learning to parse and translate improves neural machine translation. arXiv preprint arXiv:1702.03525 (2017)
5. Frank, S.L., Bod, R., Christiansen, M.H.: How hierarchical is language use? Proc. R. Soc. B Biol. Sci. **279**(1747), 4522–4531 (2012)
6. Goldberg, A.E.: Constructions at Work: The Nature of Generalization in Language. Oxford University Press, Oxford (2006)
7. Kaiser, E., Trueswell, J.C.: The role of discourse context in the processing of a flexible word-order language. Cognition **94**(2), 113–147 (2004)
8. Klein, D., Manning, C.D.: Corpus-based induction of syntactic structure: models of dependency and constituency. In: Proceedings of the 42nd Annual Meeting on Association for Computational Linguistics, p. 478. Association for Computational Linguistics (2004)
9. Langacker, R.W., Langacker, R.: Cognitive Grammar: A Basic Introduction. OUP, Oxford (2008)
10. Lapata, M.: Probabilistic text structuring: experiments with sentence ordering. In: Proceedings of the 41st Annual Meeting on Association for Computational Linguistics-Volume 1, pp. 545–552. Association for Computational Linguistics (2003)
11. Lerdahl, F., Jackendoff, R.S.: A Generative Theory of Tonal Music. MIT Press, Cambridge (1996)
12. Li, C., Liu, Y., Liu, F., Zhao, L., Weng, F.: Improving multi-documents summarization by sentence compression based on expanded constituent parse trees. In: Proceedings of the 2014 Conference on Empirical Methods in Natural Language Processing (EMNLP), pp. 691–701 (2014)
13. Müller, S.: Grammatical Theory: From Transformational Grammar to Constraint-Based Approaches. Language Science Press, Berlin (2019)
14. Muralidaran, V., Misra Sharma, D.: Construction grammar based annotation framework for parsing Tamil. In: Gelbukh, A. (ed.) CICLing 2016. LNCS, vol. 9623, pp. 378–396. Springer, Cham (2018). https://doi.org/10.1007/978-3-319-75477-2_27
15. Neubig, G., et al.: DyNet: the dynamic neural network toolkit. arXiv preprint arXiv:1701.03980 (2017)
16. Ohta, T., et al.: An intelligent search engine and GUI-based efficient MEDLINE search tool based on deep syntactic parsing. In: Proceedings of the COLING/ACL 2006 Interactive Presentation Sessions, pp. 17–20 (2006)
17. Paul, D.B., Baker, J.M.: The design for the wall street journal-based CSR corpus. In: Proceedings of the Workshop on Speech and Natural Language, pp. 357–362. Association for Computational Linguistics (1992)

18. Saffran, J.R.: The use of predictive dependencies in language learning. J. Mem. Lang. **44**(4), 493–515 (2001)

19. Vigneshwaran, M.: Construction grammar approach for Tamil dependency parsing. Ph.D. thesis, International Institute of Information Technology Hyderabad (2016)

20. Wilson, T., Wiebe, J., Hoffmann, P.: Recognizing contextual polarity in phrase-level sentiment analysis. In: Proceedings of Human Language Technology Conference and Conference on Empirical Methods in Natural Language Processing, pp. 347–354 (2005)

21. Yu, J., Chen, W., Li, Z., Zhang, M.: Building powerful dependency parsers for resource-poor languages. In: Lin, C.-Y., Xue, N., Zhao, D., Huang, X., Feng, Y. (eds.) ICCPOL/NLPCC -2016. LNCS (LNAI), vol. 10102, pp. 27–38. Springer, Cham (2016). https://doi.org/10.1007/978-3-319-50496-4_3

S-Capade: Spelling Correction Aimed at Particularly Deviant Errors

Emma O'Neill[1]($\boxtimes$), Robert Young[2], Elsa Thiaville[2], Muireann MacCarthy[2], Julie Carson-Berndsen[1], and Anthony Ventresque[2]

[1] ADAPT Centre, School of Computer Science,
University College Dublin, Dublin, Ireland
emma.1.oneill@ucdconnect.ie, julie.berndsen@ucd.ie
[2] Lero Research Centre, School of Computer Science, University College Dublin,
Dublin, Ireland
{robert.young2,elsa.thiaville,
muireann.maccarthy}@ucdconnect.ie,anthony.ventresque@ucd.ie

Abstract. S-capade (spelling correction aimed at particularly deviant errors) is a phonemic distance based spellchecking tool (Source code repository may be found in the references section [35].) intended for the correction of misspellings made by children. Whilst typographic misspellings typically deviate from the target by only one or two characters, children's misspellings tend to be more phonetic. They are influenced both by how the child perceives the pronunciation of a word and by the letters they choose to represent that pronunciation. As such, these misspellings are particularly deviant from the target and can negatively impact the performance of conventional spellcheckers. In this paper we demonstrate that S-capade is capable of correcting a significant portion of misspellings made by children where conventional correction tools fail.

Keywords: Spelling correction · Phonemic distance · Children's spelling

1 Introduction

Spelling errors are often considered one of two types: typographic or cognitive [22]. Typographic errors are the results of motor coordination slips; perhaps substituting a character for an adjacent one on the keyboard. Cognitive errors, on the other hand, stem from a misconception or lack of knowledge regarding the correct spelling of a word. One particular subset of these cognitive errors are known as phonetic errors where the writer produces a misspelling that, whilst not orthographically correct, captures the phonetic sequence of the target word.

These phonetic errors are particularly common in children's spelling, which has long been considered phonetic-based. In an examination of children's early spelling, Read [29] discussed the significant influence of speech sounds and

---

E. O'Neill and R. Young—Both the authors have equal contribution to this paper.

© Springer Nature Switzerland AG 2020
L. Espinosa-Anke et al. (Eds.): SLSP 2020, LNAI 12379, pp. 85–96, 2020.
https://doi.org/10.1007/978-3-030-59430-5_7

the relationships between them. Thus, whilst some misspellings might appear "bizarre" and deviate heavily from the target word, they tend to reflect the phonetic judgments of the child. Additionally, it is currently common in the classroom for children to be taught reading and writing using phonics: an approach which focuses on the relationships between letters and sounds [33]. As such, children are encouraged to use a 'sounding out' method when spelling unfamiliar words - an approach that is relied on heavily by low achieving spellers [7].

Despite the prevalence of phonetic-type errors, conventional spelling correction tools are not fully capable of correcting these types of misspellings and as such exhibit poorer performance on children's spelling. In this paper we present a correction method based on phonemic similarity that is capable of correcting phonetic misspellings of English made by children that deviate heavily from the target word. Kukich [22] grouped work on spelling correction into distinct tasks; detection of errors, isolated error correction, and context dependent error correction. This work focuses on isolated error correction, generating a list of real-word candidate corrections based on the phonetic properties of the misspelling. Similar to Hodge and Austin [17], our goal is to maximise recall through candidate generation as we envision this method as a component of an overall model that will handle candidate selection as a context-dependent task.

2   Related Work

Early spelling correction algorithms typically use character edit distances between misspellings and real-word corrections, relying on the finding that the majority of misspellings differ by a single edit operation (insertion, deletion, substitution, or transposition) [8]. These methods are suited to typographic misspellings. However, phonetic misspellings often deviate more substantially from the real-word target [22]. Improved performance was seen with the use of noisy-channel models which allow for multiple edit operations [4]. In particular, Brill and Moore [3] demonstrated significant performance improvements to the noisy channel model by calculating the probabilities of string-to-string edits and combining these when comparing a misspelling to real-word candidate corrections.

The incorporation of phonetic information into these methods proves advantageous to the correction of cognitive misspellings. Veronis [36] used a weighted edit-distance algorithm where the costs of edit operations were based on the phonetic similarity between graphemes. It is also common to convert words from their orthographic form to one which captures their phonetic features. For example, Soundex, described by Kukich [22] and patented by Russel and Ordell [30], maps words to a fixed length alpha-numeric code based on its characters. Numeric values are assigned to groups of letters that are phonetically similar. Thus words which are pronounced similarly will have the same encoding (e.g. 'sure' and 'shore' both have encoding S600). Edit-distance algorithms can be applied to these encodings to find real-word candidate corrections that are phonetically similar to a misspelling. However, Soundex has been criticised as being too general given its limited permutations [17,23]. Thus, phonetic transformation rules, determined by linguistic knowledge of the target language, are often used before encoding [17,28]. Alternatively, phonemic forms can be used directly by transforming a misspelling to its corresponding phoneme sequence using letter-to-sound-rules [9,21,23,34]. Other approaches to spelling correction include tackling the problem as one of Machine Translation [2,31] or as a synthesis/recognition task [32].

The method described in this paper combines elements from a number of these approaches. Misspellings are converted to their corresponding phonemic sequences using a machine learned grapheme-to-phoneme tool [5] instead of explicit letter-to-sound rules. Weighted edit distances are calculated between misspellings and real-word candidate corrections using a phoneme-to-phoneme distance matrix based on both the acoustic and distributional properties of the phonemes. Section 3 describes this method in detail, whilst Sect. 4 details the experimental setup for comparing this method with other spelling correction tools on various datasets. The results of this are presented in Sect. 5 where we demonstrate that S-capade is capable of correcting a significant proportion of children's misspellings beyond those corrected by other tools.

3   S-Capade Method

When a child uses a 'sounding out' approach to spelling they are approximating the sounds they perceive in the target word with letters they believe represent those sounds. As such, deviations from the correct spelling occur both as a result of incorrect phonemes being perceived, e.g. phoneme /V/[1] being perceived as /F/ resulting in the misspelling 'gif' (give), and of incorrect letters being chosen, e.g. representing the /AY/ phoneme with an 'i' in the misspelling 'ciber' (cyber). The majority of misspellings resulting from the latter case are handled by converting the graphemic misspelling to its phonemic form. In these instances the phonemic form typically matches that of the correct spelling. However, misspellings of the former variety map to phoneme sequences that are similar to that of the correct spelling but not necessarily identical. In these cases we require some measure of similarity at a phoneme level so that, for example, we can predict that 'gif' is more likely to be 'give' than 'gig' due to the /F/ phoneme being more similar to /V/ than /G/.

In this work, similarity is modelled using two features which have been shown to influence a native speaker's perception of phonemic similarity; namely the acoustic and distributional properties of the phonemes. Phonemic similarity is considered to be a function of confusability [13] - two phonemes can be thought of as similar if one is often mistakenly identified as the other. Previous work by Kane and Carson-Berndsen [19] investigated phoneme confusability using an under-specified recognition system. A target phoneme was removed during training so that at test time the system was forced to select an alternative phoneme - one which was acoustically similar to the target. The frequency with which one phoneme was identified as another was used as a measure of their acoustic similarity. The potential influence of a phoneme's distributional properties on

---

[1] Throughout this paper we use the ARPAbet notation when referring to phonemes.

perceived similarity was demonstrated in previous work by O'Neill and Carson-Berndsen [27]. Here, phonemes that often occurred in the same environment (having the same preceding and following phonemes) were shown to be perceived as more similar. A word2vec model, trained on the Brown Corpus [11], was applied at the phonemic level and used to generate phoneme embeddings. The distances between these embeddings, or vector representations, represented the distributional similarity between the corresponding phonemes. Both the acoustic and distributional properties were combined to form a phoneme-to-phoneme distance matrix where smaller distance values represented more similar phonemes. Significantly the distance matrix is not symmetric i.e. the distance between a target phoneme X being perceived as Y is not necessarily the same as the target phoneme Y being perceived as X. For example, it is likely that the /NG/, as in 'walking', will be pronounced as /N/; resulting in the misspelling 'walkin'. However it is much less likely that the /N/ phoneme, as in 'happen', will be pronounced as /NG/; resulting in the misspelling 'happeng'. The distance matrix employed in this work is able to make this distinction.

Candidate corrections are the possible real-word targets of a misspelling. Both the real-word candidate correction and the misspelling were first converted to their corresponding phonemic forms; the former using the CMU Pronouncing Dictionary [38] and the latter with a grapheme-to-phoneme tool trained on this dictionary [5]. To determine the degree of similarity between the two phoneme sequences, a distance score was calculated between the misspelling and real-word candidate using a weighted edit distance algorithm akin to that of Wagner and Fischer [37]. The cost for performing a substitution operation was defined as the distance between the two phonemes per the distance matrix. Deletion and insertion operations were treated as substitutions of a phoneme with the empty string and vice versa. Distance values for these operations were chosen heuristically based on existing literature regarding which phonemes typically undergo insertion (epenthsesis) and deletion (ellision) in speech [6, 10, 15, 18, 42]. A comparison of the character-level edit-distance and S-capades' phoneme-level weighted edit-distance used in this paper is given in Table 1. The misspelling 'sichweshan' and its real-word target 'situation' have a high character edit-distance. As such, non-phonetic spelling correction approaches are unable to correct this error. However, their phonetic similarity results in a very small edit distance using S-capade, thus making it more easily correctable.

Table 1. Character-level edit-distance vs S-capade's phonemic edit-distance

	Character-level	S-capade
Misspelling	s i c h w e s h e n	S IH CH W EH SH AH N
Real-Word Target	s i t u a t i o n	S IH CH UW EY SH AH N
Edit-Distance	7	1.1

4   Experimental Setup

In this section we describe the experimental setup designed to test the ability of S-capade to correct particularly deviant errors. As stated previously, the S-capade method is envisioned as a component of a larger system. It is not intended for the correction of typos but rather is specifically aimed at misspellings which lie beyond the scope of conventional spelling correction tools. As such, S-capade is not expected to outperform other tools but instead to uniquely target a greater proportion of errors on datasets likely to contain these particularly deviant errors i.e. those consisting of misspellings made by children.

4.1   Datasets

The baseline spelling correction methods, see Sect. 4.2, and the phonemic distance method discussed in Sect. 3 were evaluated and compared using a collection of five different misspelling datasets. Four of these datasets are publicly available, and were obtained in a pre-processed format from the Birkbeck University of London [25]. The fifth was acquired through a collaboration with an Irish Educational company, Zeeko [43]. Details of all datasets may be seen in Table 2. For each dataset, only misspellings where the target correction is one word are included. A single word target correction would be the misspelling 'hapen' corrected to 'happen'. An example of a target correction which is two words would be the misspelling 'alot' corrected to 'a lot'.

Table 2. Misspelling datasets

Dataset	Misspellings	Misspellings used	Target words	Publicly available
Birkbeck	36,133	33,887	6,068	Yes
Holbrook	1,791	1,562	1,177	Yes
Wikipedia	2,455	2,230	1,909	Yes
Aspell	531	515	437	Yes
Zeeko	232	232	163	No

- **Birkbeck** - native-speaker errors (British or American) [25]. Majority of errors from schoolchildren, university students or adult literacy students [24].
- **Holbrook** - extracts of writings from British secondary school students in their penultimate year of school [25].
- **Wikipedia** - common misspellings made by editors (British or American) on Wikipedia [25]. A common misspelling is one that occurs at least once a year on the site [39].
- **Aspell** - GNU spell checker dataset (British forms). Comprised of common misspellings [1].

- **Zeeko** - comprised of spelling mistakes from Irish primary school students [43]. The age range of respondents is 8–14 years old.

Across these five datasets there is a broad spectrum of literacy demographics; namely primary school students, secondary school students, university students, and Wikipedia article editors. We hypothesised that due to children's first efforts in spelling being based on a 'sounding out' approach, as discussed in Sect. 1, S-capade will perform better on datasets containing children's phonetic spelling attempts, which tend to have larger character edit distances. For example, in the Holbrook dataset 53% of misspellings have a character edit distance of 1, 31% have a character edit distance of 2 and 16% have an edit distance greater than 2. Conversely, in the Wikipedia dataset 69% of misspellings have an edit distance of 1, 28% of 2 and only 3% have an edit distance greater than 2. In the Zeeko dataset 91% of the misspellings are of two character edit distance or less.

4.2   Conventional Spelling Correction Comparison Tools

Three different conventional spelling correction tools are used for comparison in this paper - PySpellChecker, SymSpell and Aspell. All three tools are based on a character edit distance limit of 2, use British English dictionaries and generate a suggested spelling correction and a list of candidate corrections. S-capade is limited to a distance of two insertions and deletions of phonemes in a misspelling sequence for edit candidate generation (adapted from SymSpellPy [14,40]) and lookup. Any target words in the datasets that were not present in the tools' default dictionaries were manually added to ensure fairness of results.

- **PySpellChecker** - word permutations were created via insertions, deletions, replacements and transpositions [26] which were then compared to known words in a frequency dictionary [12].
- **SymSpell** - generates word permutations for comparison via the misspelling and valid words in the dictionary using deletes only [14]. Selection based on the smallest edit distance and highest frequency word [16,41].
- **Aspell** - performed word comparisons in a given dictionary and uses phonetic comparisons with other words [20]. This was done via table driven phonetic code allowing 'sounds like' word comparison and suggestions. This makes it the most relevant tool to compare to this paper's S-capade method.

4.3   Metrics

In Sect. 5, we compare the accuracy and recall of S-capade across the five datasets against the three conventional spelling correction tools, Pyspell, Symspell, and Aspell. For each misspelling, real-word candidates are ranked in order of distance and subsequently frequency. We define accuracy as whether or not the closest candidate matches the real-word target and recall as whether the real-word target is found in the top 10 closest candidates. Word correction overlap graphs, based on accuracy, are presented for each of the datasets comparing

S-capade with the Aspell spelling corrector. In these graphs, the common corrections between each method and the misspelling corrections made only by one or other method are shown. Aspell was chosen as the comparison for S-capade given its use of the 'sounds like' word correction approach, see Sect. 4.2.

5   Results and Discussion

The Birkbeck dataset results are presented in Table 3. With respect to accuracy, S-capade is comparable to PySpell and SymSpell, and outperforms both in terms of recall. Aspell outperforms S-capade in accuracy and recall. Of the 17,029 misspellings corrected between both methods, ~48% were word misspelling corrections common to both, ~32% were corrections made only by Aspell, and ~20% were corrections made only by S-capade. The coverage of misspelling corrections for the dataset between the two methods can be seen in Fig. 1.

Table 3. Birkbeck correction scores

Method	Accuracy	Recall
PySpell	35.3%	42.6%
SymSpell	34.74%	43.04%
Aspell	39.89%	66.03%
S-capade	34.43%	51.49%

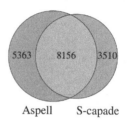

Aspell   S-capade

Fig. 1. Birkbeck: Aspell vs S-capade

Table 4 displays the results for the Holbrook dataset. Compared to the Birkbeck dataset results, the overall scores are similar. The most interesting result from this dataset can be seen in Fig. 2, which compares the misspelling correction coverage of the two methods for the Holbrook dataset. Of the 626 misspellings corrected between both methods, ~35.3% were word misspelling corrections common to both, ~32.3% were corrections made only by Aspell, and ~32.4% were corrections made only by S-capade. It can be seen that S-capade has a slightly greater correction coverage of misspellings when compared with Aspell. The Holbrook dataset is more likely to be comprised of phonetic spelling mistakes given

Table 4. Holbrook correction scores

Method	Accuracy	Recall
PySpell	29.32%	42.06%
SymSpell	27.46%	42.51%
Aspell	27.08%	67.93%
S-capade	27.14%	52.82%

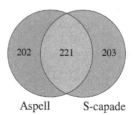

Aspell   S-capade

Fig. 2. Holbrook: Aspell vs S-capade

its demographic, discussed in Sect. 4.1, and as such shows how our approach corrects misspelling errors different to those corrected by Aspell.

Of the five datasets under analysis, S-capade performed the worst on the Wikipedia dataset, relative to the other spelling correction methods. This is visible in Table 5, where it obtained the lowest score for accuracy and recall. Compared with the overlap scores for the other datsets in Figs. 1, 2, 4, and 5, S-capade also had the smallest proportion of misspelling corrections. Of the 1,984 misspellings corrected between both methods, ~61% were word misspelling corrections common to both, ~29% were corrections made only by Aspell, and ~10% were corrections only made by S-capade. As discussed in Sect. 4.1, the Wikipedia dataset is made up of Wikipedia editors' common spelling mistakes. These are typically typographic misspellings, and as expected our phonetic approach does not produce competitive results for this dataset (Fig. 3).

Table 5. Wikipedia correction scores

Method	Accuracy	Recall
PySpell	78.39%	88.48%
SymSpell	80.99%	92.11%
Aspell	79.96%	97.04%
S-capade	63.14%	77.80%

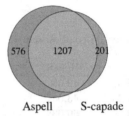

Aspell   S-capade

Fig. 3. Wikipedia: Aspell vs S-capade

The scores for the Aspell dataset can be seen in Table 6, where S-capade had similar performance to PySpell and SymSpell. Of the 351 misspellings corrected between both methods, ~50% were word misspelling corrections common to both, ~32% were corrections made only by Aspell, and ~18% were corrections made only by S-capade, as may be seen in Fig. 4. The Aspell dataset focuses on particularly bad spelling attempts; those which deviate from the real-word target by multiple edit operations. However, these are not necessarily phonetic misspellings and, as such, S-capade performs satisfactorily on this dataset.

Table 6. Aspell correction scores

Method	Accuracy	Recall
PySpell	49.32%	62.33%
SymSpell	53.20%	67.18%
Aspell	55.73%	85.6%
S-capade	46.41%	65.24%

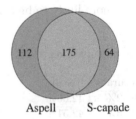

Aspell   S-capade

Fig. 4. Aspell: Aspell vs S-capade

Table 7. Zeeko correction scores

Method	Accuracy	Recall
PySpell	56.90%	72.41%
SymSpell	54.74%	70.69%
Aspell	54.74%	86.64%
S-capade	49.57%	76.29%

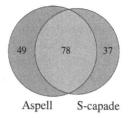

Aspell   S-capade

Fig. 5. Zeeko: Aspell vs S-capade

The scores for the Zeeko dataset may be seen in Table 7. After Holbrook, the Zeeko dataset resulted in the second best performance for S-capade with respect to recall relative to the comparison methods. Figure 5 shows that, of the 164 misspellings corrected by Aspell and S-capade, ∼47.5% were common corrections, ∼30% were corrections only made by Aspell, and ∼22.5% were corrections only made by S-capade. As discussed in Sect. 4.1, 91% of the Zeeko dataset misspellings are of 2 character edit distance or less. We believe this shows that despite the misspellings edit distance falling within the boundary of conventional tools, phonetic spelling errors require a different correction approach.

The CMU pronouncing dictionary was used by the S-capade method for phoneme-sequence-to-word lookups when correcting word misspellings. Figure 6 displays the breakdown in corrections made by S-capade, showing the split between either exact match lookup in the CMU dictionary using a phoneme sequence, in which case the edit distance is equal to zero, or using S-capade to calculate the phonemic distance between the misspelling and the real-word target. It can be seen that for four out of the five datasets, S-capade's distance method accounted for over 50% of the real-word candidate corrections made.

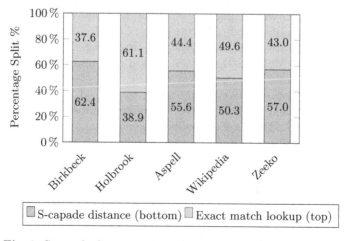

Fig. 6. S-capade distance calculation vs Exact dictionary match

The approach taken by S-capade resulted in interesting word corrections of phonetically spelt words with large character edit distances that conventional spelling correction tools were unable to correct. Table 8 shows some selected misspellings from the datasets that S-capade corrected, and the traditional character edit distance versus the phonemic edit distance generated by our approach.

Table 8. S-capade interesting word corrections

Target	Misspelling	Character distance	S-capade distance
Necessarily	Nessecarryally	8	1.62
Philosophy	Folocify	7	0.54
Situation	Sichweshen	7	1.10
Ecstasy	Extersee	6	0.46
Sufficient	Servishant	6	0.93
Procedure	Prosiegeur	5	0.59
Whistled	Wisheld	4	1.14
Council	Cousall	3	1.00
Actually	Achuly	3	1.28

6 Conclusions

In this paper, we have presented a phonemic-distance based approach to spelling correction that is capable of handling phonetic misspellings which conventional tools are unable to correct. The creativeness of children's spelling attempts has been shown to produce phonetic misspellings that heavily deviate from the real-word target. As such we see poorer performance of conventional spelling correction tools on datasets specifically consisting of children's spelling errors. The method described in this paper is shown to correct a significant portion of misspellings within these datasets that one of the top performing English spellcheckers, Aspell, cannot.

The phonemic-distance based approach is envisioned as a component in a fully context-dependent spelling correction system. Future work will look to incorporate this method into a spellchecker capable of handling both typographic and phonetic misspellings and of choosing the correct real-word target from a list of candidates based on the context of the misspelling. Further plans for improvement include investigating the effects of accent on the phonetic misspellings produced and the potential benefits of an accent-specific system on spelling correction accuracy.

Acknowledgements. This work was supported with the financial support of the Science Foundation Ireland grant 13/RC/2094 to Lero - the SFI Research Centre for Software (www.lero.ie). The ADAPT Centre for Digital Content Technology (www.adaptcentre.ie) is funded under the SFI Research Centres Programme (Grant 13/RC/2106). The authors would like to thank the team at Zeeko (https://zeeko.ie/) for supporting their research.

References

1. Atkinson, K.: Aspell spell checker test data (2002). http://aspell.net/test/cur-all/batch0.tab. Accessed 19 May 2020
2. Aw, A., Zhang, M., Xiao, J., Su, J.: A phrase-based statistical model for SMS text normalization. In: COLING/ACL, pp. 33–40 (2006)
3. Brill, E., Moore, R.C.: An improved error model for noisy channel spelling correction. In: ACL, pp. 286–293 (2000)
4. Church, K.W., Gale, W.A.: Probability scoring for spelling correction. Stat. Comput. **1**(2), 93–103 (1991)
5. CMUSphinx: Grapheme-to-phoneme tool based on sequence-to-sequence learning (2016). https://github.com/cmusphinx/g2p-seq2seq
6. Collins, B., Mees, I.M.: Practical Phonetics and Phonology: A Resource Book for Students. Routledge, London (2013)
7. Daffern, T., Critten, S.: Student and teacher perspectives on spelling. Aust. J. Lang. Literacy **42**(1), 40–57 (2019)
8. Damerau, F.J.: A technique for computer detection and correction of spelling errors. Commun. ACM **7**(3), 171–176 (1964)
9. Fisher, W.M.: A statistical text-to-phone function using ngrams and rules. ICASSP. **2**, 649–652 (1999)
10. Fourakis, M., Port, R.: Stop epenthesis in English. J. Phonetics **14**(2), 197–221 (1986)
11. Francis, W.N., Kucera, H.: Brown corpus manual (1979)
12. FrequencyWords: Frequency word list generator (2020). https://github.com/hermitdave/FrequencyWords. Accessed 21 May 2020
13. Gallagher, G., Graff, P.: The role of similarity in phonology. Lingua **2**(122), 107–111 (2012)
14. Garbe, W.: Symspell (2020). https://github.com/wolfgarbe/symspell. Accessed 21 May 2020
15. Gimson, A.C., Ramsaran, S.: An Introduction to the Pronunciation of English, vol. 4. Edward Arnold London, London (1970)
16. Google: Google books Ngram viewer (2012). http://storage.googleapis.com/books/ngrams/books/datasetsv2.html. Accessed 21 May 2020
17. Hodge, V.J., Austin, J.: An evaluation of phonetic spell checkers (2001)
18. Itô, J.: A prosodic theory of epenthesis. Nat. Lang. Linguist. Theory **7**(2), 217–259 (1989)
19. Kane, M., Carson-Berndsen, J.: Enhancing data-driven phone confusions using restricted recognition. In: INTERSPEECH, pp. 3693–3697 (2016)
20. Kevin Atkinson, G.A.: How aspell works (2004). http://aspell.net/0.50-doc/man-html/8_How.html. Accessed 21 May 2020
21. Khoury, R.: Microtext normalization using probably-phonetically-similar word discovery. In: WiMob, pp. 384–391 (2015)
22. Kukich, K.: Techniques for automatically correcting words in text. ACM Comput. Surv. (CSUR) **24**(4), 377–439 (1992)

23. de Mendonça Almeida, G.A., Avanço, L., Duran, M.S., Fonseca, E.R., Nunes, M.d.G.V., Aluísio, S.M.: Evaluating phonetic spellers for user-generated content in Brazilian Portuguese. In: International Conference on Computational Processing of the Portuguese Language, pp. 361–373 (2016)
24. Mitton, R.: Birkbeck spelling error corpus (1980). https://ota.bodleian.ox.ac.uk/repository/xmlui/handle/20.500.12024/0643. Accessed 19 May 2020
25. Mitton, R.: Corpora of misspellings for download (2007). https://www.dcs.bbk.ac.uk/~ROGER/corpora.html. Accessed 19 May 2020
26. Norvig, P.: Pyspellchecker (2020). https://pypi.org/project/pyspellchecker/. Accessed 21 May 2020
27. O'Neill, E., Carson-Berndsen, J.: The effect of phoneme distribution on perceptual similarity in English. In: INTERSPEECH, pp. 1941–1945 (2019)
28. Philips, L.: The double metaphone search algorithm. C/C++ users J. **18**(6), 38–43 (2000)
29. Read, C.: Children's Creative Spelling. Routledge, London (2018)
30. Russell, R., Odell, M.: Soundex. US patent 1,261,167 (1918)
31. Silfverberg, M., Kauppinen, P., Lindén, K.: Data-driven spelling correction using weighted finite-state methods. In: SIGFSM Workshop on Statistical NLP and Weighted Automata, pp. 51–59 (2016)
32. Stüker, S., Fay, J., Berkling, K.: Towards context-dependent phonetic spelling error correction in children's freely composed text for diagnostic and pedagogical purposes. In: INTERSPEECH (2011)
33. Torgerson, C., Brooks, G., Hall, J.: A Systematic Review of the Research Literature on the Use of Phonics in the Teaching of Reading and Spelling. DfES Publications, Nottingham (2006)
34. Toutanova, K., Moore, R.C.: Pronunciation modeling for improved spelling correction. In: Proceedings of the 40th Annual Meeting on Association for Computational Linguistics, pp. 144–151 (2002)
35. University College Dublin: S-capade github repository (2020). https://github.com/ucd-csl/Scapade. Accessed 15 Jul 2020
36. Veronis, J.: Computerized correction of phonographic errors. Comput. Humanit. **22**(1), 43–56 (1988)
37. Wagner, R.A., Fischer, M.J.: The string-to-string correction problem. JACM **21**(1), 168–173 (1974)
38. Weide, R.L.: The CMU pronouncing dictionary (1998). http://www.speech.cs.cmu.edu/cgi-bin/cmudict
39. Wikipedia: Wikipedia:lists of common misspellings (2020). https://en.wikipedia.org/wiki/Wikipedia:Lists_of_common_misspellings. Accessed 19 May 2020
40. Wolf Garbe, S.: Symspellpy (2020). https://github.com/mammothb/symspellpy. Accessed 21 May 2020
41. Wordlist, A.: Scowl (spell checker oriented word lists) (2019). http://wordlist.aspell.net. Accessed 21 May 2020
42. Yip, M.: English vowel epenthesis. Nat. Lang. Linguist. Theory **5**, 463–484 (1987). https://doi.org/10.1007/BF00138986
43. Zeeko: Free text survey responses (2020). https://zeeko.ie. Accessed 19 May 2020

Exploring Parameter Sharing Techniques for Cross-Lingual and Cross-Task Supervision

Matúš Pikuliak[(✉)] and Marián Šimko

Faculty of Informatics and Information Technologies, Slovak University of Technology in Bratislava, Ilkovicova 2, Bratislava, Slovakia
{matus.pikuliak,marian.simko}@stuba.sk

Abstract. Many languages still lack the annotated training data needed for supervised learning. This issue is often addressed by using auxiliary supervision and the so called transfer learning. In this work we focus on the problem of combining two types of auxiliary supervision – cross-lingual and cross-task. Previous work has shown promising results for this combination. Here, we aim to explore various advanced parameter sharing techniques to improve the results. We propose three distinct techniques with various properties and evaluate their performance on four Indo-European languages and four distinct NLP tasks (dependency parsing, language modeling, named entity recognition and part-of-speech tagging). We conclude that the proposed techniques significantly improve the performance for zero-shot learning.

Keywords: Transfer learning · Cross-lingual learning · Parameter sharing

1 Introduction

Machine learning, and more specifically deep learning, has become a dominant natural language processing research paradigm in recent years. This paradigm depends on the existence of annotated datasets to train the models. Creating such annotated datasets is notoriously expensive and, as a result, they usually exist only for a few particularly well researched languages. Other languages are often missing even the most basic datasets and as such they can not utilize the recent advancements in NLP.

Transfer learning is one of the proposed remedies for this problem. It is essentially a research direction that aims to reuse the existing annotated data for different models [26]. Two important paradigms for transfer learning in NLP are (1) *cross-lingual learning*, when we reuse the data from other languages, and (2) *cross-task learning*, when we reuse the data annotated for different tasks.

Recently, the idea of combining both cross-lingual and cross-task supervision gained some traction in the NLP community [11,19]. We have previously shown

© Springer Nature Switzerland AG 2020
L. Espinosa-Anke et al. (Eds.): SLSP 2020, LNAI 12379, pp. 97–108, 2020.
https://doi.org/10.1007/978-3-030-59430-5_8

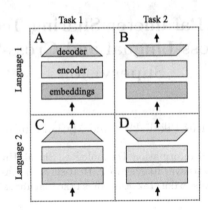

Fig. 1. Each of the four models in this 2 × 2 grid solves a specific task-language combination. If **A** is the target model, **B** provides cross-task supervision and **C** provides cross-lingual supervision. **D** is the coupling model between **B** and **C**. Color coded is the parameter sharing strategy – layers with the same color have identical parameters. Adapted from [23].

that the models that share neither a task nor a language with the target model can still be useful, if they couple the other models, as depicted in Fig. 1. These models are called the *coupling models* [23].

In this work, we follow our previous efforts by proposing three advanced parameter sharing techniques. Parameter sharing is the technique that is used for transferring knowledge between different models [4]. E.g. a model trained for Spanish POS tagging might share some parameters with a model trained for Czech dependency parsing. By sharing their parameters they are able to communicate with each other and learn from each other. Our advanced techniques improve their ability to share their parameters. The core idea of all the techniques is that we give the models information about what task they solve and in what language. They can incorporate this information into their learning process. The techniques differ in how exactly is this information used.

Our main contribution in this work is therefore a proposal of specialized parameter sharing techniques. We evaluate their performance in an experimental setup with four Indo-European languages (Czech, English, German, Spanish) and four NLP tasks (dependency parsing, language modeling, named entity recognition and part-of-speech tagging). The techniques we propose were able to significantly improve the results over the baselines shown in previous work. We also demonstrate that they work well with various text representation techniques. We release all the code and data[1].

In Section 2 we discuss related work about cross-lingual and cross-task supervision, or their combination. In Sect. 3 we describe the baseline parameter

---

[1] https://github.com/matus-pikuliak/crosslingual-parameter-sharing.

sharing model and our three proposed advanced techniques that improve it. In Sect. 4 we experimentally evaluate the proposed techniques and finally Sect. 5 concludes this paper.

2 Related Work

Cross-lingual learning is a transfer learning approach based on using annotated data from other languages. It was successfully used for various NLP tasks, such as machine translation [13], dependency parsing [8], sentiment analysis [25] and many others. There are several distinct approaches to cross-lingual learning. Annotation projection based approaches project the existing labels from the source languages to the target language to create distantly supervised data [12]. Model transfer approaches are based on the idea of creating language universal representations for the samples. Then a model trained on source language data can be directly used on target language data as well. Delexicalized text samples [21] or multilingual distributed representations [16] among others can be used as these representations. Finally, parameter sharing techniques are based on the idea of models with different languages sharing some of their parameters, i.e. some of their layers have identical behavior.

Cross-task learning is a learning approach when data annotated for different tasks are used as the auxiliary source of supervision. The most common types of cross-task supervision is to use pre-trained word embeddings [22] or language model encoders [6] to initialize the models or to get reasonable word representations. Parameter sharing based techniques were also used to improve results for many tasks, e.g. dependency parsing was improved via POS tagging [27] or emotion detection was improved via sentiment analysis [1].

Combination of cross-lingual and cross-task supervision is a topic that has received some attention in previous years. First, [19] combined these two paradigms using parameter sharing. They successfully improved results for low-resource NER. [23] added the coupling models, i.e. models that that do not provide direct cross-lingual or cross-task supervision, instead they fill the full grid of models. Recently, XTREME dataset [11] was proposed as a benchamrk for transfer learning that contains datasets for multiple tasks and multiple langauges.

3 Parameter Sharing Techniques

In this section we first describe the model grid that is used to combine cross-lingual and cross-task supervision. This grid is identical to the grid used in [23]. Then we propose our own techniques to improve the transfer of knowledge between different models within this grid.

3.1 Baseline

Our baseline is a grid of models as depicted in Fig. 1. Each model in the grid has a specific task and language assigned. E.g., one model can be used to solve Spanish POS tagging, while the other might be used to solve Czech dependency parsing. The models share some of their parameters, i.e. when the model has its parameters updated, it instantaneously updates the parameters in other models as well.

In this work we use zero-shot learning. One model is selected to be the zero-shot target model. This model is not trained directly with its data, instead it only uses the shared parameters trained in all the other models. The other models provide three types of supervision. Models that share the task, but solve it in different languages provide cross-lingual supervision. Models that solve other task in the same language provide cross-task supervision. Finally, models that share neither a task nor a language with the target model are called the coupling models. They regularize the other two types of models [23].

One training epoch consists of fixed number of training steps. One of the auxiliary models is randomly selected each training step and a training batch is run through it. The parameters updated through a stochastic gradient descent based training algorithm are then propagated to all the other models.

Model Architecture. The models themselves have a standard NLP architecture. First, there is a word embedding layer. Each word has an embedding assigned and the text is thus transformed into a sequence of embedding vectors $e_1, e_2, ..., e_N$, where N is the length of the sentence. By default, we assume that we have multilingual word representations, i.e. representations where words from different languages are in the shared semantic vector space [16]. These embeddings are then processed with an encoder – a bi-directional LSTM layer [9]. This layer creates a contextualized word representation c for each word: $c_1, c_2, ..., c_N = enc(e_1, e_2, ..., e_N)$. These contextualized representations model the words in the particular context of the input sentence.

Finally, task-specific decoders make prediction based on these contextualized word representations: $y = dec(c_1, c_2, ..., c_N)$. The modality of the output y depends on the task, e.g. for POS tagging it is a sequence of tags, while for dependency parsing it is a parse tree. The loss function value is calculated based on this prediction compared to the desired output.

Decoders. We consider four tasks in our work: dependency parsing, language modeling, named entity recognition and part-of-speech tagging. As mentioned previously, these tasks have different output modalities, so for each task we have a specialized task-specific decoder. NER and POS tagging are both sequence tagging tasks so for both of them we use a decoding based on *conditional random fields* algorithm [18]. Dependency parsing is done with a graph-based parser [20]. This parser calculates the score for each possible head-dependent relation between two words and a parse tree is then constructed based on these scores. Language modeling is done in the leave-one-out variant, i.e. we predict the word based on all the other words in the sentence. The details of how do the decoders look like and how exactly is the loss function defined are described in [23].

Parameter Sharing Strategies. We use different parameter sharing strategies for different layers. The word embeddings are language-specific, i.e. each language has its own embedding matrix. The embeddings are not trainable, thus no transfer learning happens within this layer. On the other hand, encoder is shared between all the models, i.e. each time one model updates its parameters, all the other models get them too. Decoders can not be shared across different tasks, since they have different architectures. They are therefore shared only cross-lingually, i.e. all the models solving the same task in different languages have the same decoder parameters. This parameter sharing scheme is also color-coded in Fig. 1.

3.2   Advanced Techniques

The model grid described so far was previously shown to effectively combine cross-lingual and cross-task supervision. In this work we propose three advanced parameter sharing techniques designed to improve the transfer learning capabilities of the models within this grid. All of them are based on adjusting the models so that they can work with the information about what particular language or task do they solve. They do not require any additional data, though they might increase the time and/or memory complexity of the model and can thus lead to longer training and inference times and higher memory requirements.

Private Encoders. The LSTM encoder we described above is global, i.e. it is shared between all the models in the grid. Here we propose to use private encoders, i.e. encoders that are visible only to some models instead. In addition to the globally shared encoder, we propose two additional types: *(1) Language-specific encoders*, which are shared between all the models with the same language, and *(2) Task-specific encoders*, which are shared between all the models that solve the same task. We can then use different combinations of these three encoders for each model. Each encoder processes the word embeddings and returns the sequence of contextualized embeddings. The final contextualized word representation for the X-th word $\mathbf{c}_X$ is then a concatenation of the particular representations for this word from individual encoders, i.e. for a model solving task T in language L we concatenate $\mathbf{c}_X^G$ from the global encoder, $\mathbf{c}_X^T$ from the task-specific encoder and $\mathbf{c}_X^L$ from the language-specific encoder into one final representation $\mathbf{c}_X$.

The main idea of this technique is that the private encoders should have the capability to develop language or task-specific strategies. The globally shared encoder learns about what is common for all the languages and tasks, while the private encoders learn what is specific. Note, that the private encoders increase the time and memory requirements significantly. Several encoders are virtually running in parallel.

Language and Task Embeddings. The second technique is based on using task and language-specific embeddings. Each task and/or language has a specific trainable embedding assigned. This embedding is appended to each word embedding before being processed by the encoder. E.g., for a model solving task T in language L we would change the word embedding representation for a word so that $e_X^* = e_X; e_T; e_L$, where e^* and e are the new and the old word embeddings. e_T and e_L are the task and language embeddings. Semicolon represents the concatenation of vectors.

This approach has a similar rationalization as the private encoders. The specific embeddings give the model the information about what task it solves and in what language. The encoder can then change its behavior based on this input, i.e. it can develop specific strategies. With private encoders we forced the model to develop these strategies by creating private model parts. Here we instead let it create the strategies internally within one shared encoder. This might give the model the ability to decide for itself, how strong should the signal from task and/or language be when the input is processed.

Compared to private encoders, this approach is less computationally expensive, since it does not add any additional operations. It merely increases the input size of the LSTM layer. Similarly, it has only minimal memory requirements, since it only adds the task and/or language embedding matrices. The number of tasks and/or languages is small (4 for both in our case). In contrast, private encoders introduce whole layers worth of parameters.

Adversarial Training. The third and final parameter sharing technique we propose is based on the idea of adversarial training. Adversarial training is used to create domain-invariant representations within the model [7] and it has even been used for cross-lingual learning before [14]. The main idea is to force the model to create language-*universal* representations within the model. I.e., the contextualized word representations should come from the same distribution in all the languages.

We implement the adversarial training with the so called *gradient reversal layer* (GRL) [7]. We extend each model with a classifier that classifies the language of contextualized representations **c**. This classifier predicts what was the original language of the word. The loss function of this classifier is then added to the overall loss of the model. The classifier itself is implemented as a multilayer perceptron with cross-entropy loss function.

This would normally lead to more language-specific representations, since the model would push the word representations from different languages apart, so that they can be distinguished more easily. That is why the GRL layer is used. This layer works as an identity function during the forward pass, but during the backward pass of the back-propagation it reverses the values of the gradient. This layer is used right after the contextualized word representations, so the language classifier has the opposite effect on them – the word representations from different languages become indistinguishable.

The target model encoder should create contextualized representations that are similar to representations that the decoder has seen before, i.e. that come from the same distribution. Our hypothesis is, that this might lead to better decoder performance, since it does not have to deal with the domain shift when it is applied to the target language data. Note that having language-universal representations is completely different from what the other two techniques aim to achieve. In contrast, they create language-specific strategies.

4   Experiments

4.1   Evaluation Setup

The overall evaluation setup is identical to [23] to ensure the comparability of our work. Here we briefly summarize how the evaluation is done.

As for datasets, we use the *Universal Dependencies* datasets for both part-of-speech tagging and dependency parsing. The dataset has universal tagsets for both tasks. Language modeling is done with corpora extracted from *Wikipedia*. NER has a combination of several dataset: *Groningen Meaning Bank* [3] for English, *GermEval 2014* [2] for German, *CoNLL 2002* [24] for Spanish and *Czech Named Entity Corpus* [17] for Czech. The tagging schemata were unified by pre-processing to conform to the standard IOB schema. We use MUSE multilingual word embeddings [5] as our default word representation.

We use the full 4×4 grid of models in all our experiments. Each time one model is designed to be the target model, while the other models provide auxiliary supervision. The performance of the target model is evaluated during the training. We use accuracy for POS tagging, labeled attachment score (LAS) for dependency parsing and chunk-based F1 score for NER as evaluation measure. We also aggregate all these scores into the so called average error reduction score (AER), which measures how much error was reduced compared to the selected baseline across all three tasks. Language modeling is used only as an auxiliary task, i.e. its performance is not evaluated.

4.2   Techniques Performance

Table 1 shows the performance of the proposed techniques. First, we show two baselines. A zero-shot target model trained purely with cross-lingual supervision. In this case we do not use the full grid, but merely one row of the grid. This is the standard multilingual learning setup, when we have annotated data present in multiple languages. We also use this as baseline when we calculate AER score for this table. The second, stronger baseline is when we use the full grid of auxiliary models, i.e. models providing cross-ligual supervision, models providing cross-task supervision and even the coupling models. The techniques we propose are designed for grids like these and are built on top of them. Therefore it is the

Table 1. Performance for transfer learning with various advanced techniques. We show whether the technique was applied along the task or language axis of the model grid. For private parameters we also show results when we do not use the globally shared encoder.

	DP	NER	POS	AER
Cross-lingual (AER baseline)	38.75	49.30	69.05	0.00
Full grid	46.25	56.62	84.09	32.40
Private parameters				
Task	53.19	55.35	**86.40**	38.70
Language	50.70	56.32	78.09	28.17
Task & Language without Global	57.10	56.38	85.14	42.14
Task & Language	57.87	**57.55**	85.95	**44.89**
Embeddings				
Task	57.79	56.58	84.84	42.51
Language	50.56	56.60	85.32	37.21
Task & Language	58.45	57.54	84.88	44.08
Adversarial training				
Language	**59.03**	57.26	84.79	44.13

best to compare the scores with these full grids to see how they changed after the techniques were applied.

When applicable, we compare how do individual techniques perform when they are applied along different axes of the grid, i.e. when they are applied for the tasks or for the languages. Adversarial training can be applied only along the language axis. Private encoders can be also applied without the globally shared encoder.

First, we can see that all the tasks were improved by all the techniques. However, dependency parsing has achieved the biggest improvement going from 46 LAS to almost 60. For both private encoders and embeddings, using the technique only along the task axis performs better than using it along the language axis. Similarly, in both cases the combination of the two yields the best performance. The resulting performance of these two approaches are very similar, even thought the private encoders add much more capacity to the model. We conclude that in this limited setup with 16 models the encoder can generalize well enough with the task and language embeddings.

In contrast, adversarial learning can be applied only along the language axis, but it still achieves competitive performance (and the best performance for dependency parsing). This is interesting, since for the two other techniques the task axis proved to be more important.

Compare the contextualized word representations created by the encoder with various techniques depicted in Fig. 2. We can see that the adversarial training creates language independent representations as expected, i.e. the representations from different languages can not be distinguished. On the other

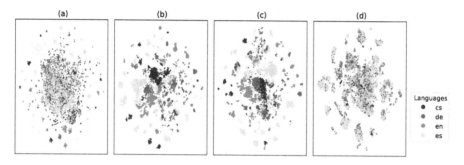

Fig. 2. TSNE visualization of word representations. (a) shows the MUSE embeddings before they go into the encoder, (b–d) show contextualized word embeddings from the encoder trained with Czech POS target model – (b) private encoders, (c) embeddings and (d) adversarial training.

hand, the other two techniques learn to create more language-specific representations. This is interesting, because all these techniques achieve similar performance improvement despite the fact, that they use seemingly incompatible approaches to representation learning within the model.

4.3 Text Representations

Besides using MUSE multilingual word embeddings we also experimented with two additional word representation techniques. First, we used MUSE embeddings, but we rotated the vector space for each language by shuffling the dimensions. This decoupled the connection between languages, but kept the relations between the words within individual languages. Second, we used a character-level LSTM to create word representations. Each word is processed character by character by the same LSTM layer to create a word representation. In this case, no pre-trained parameters were used to initialize the models.

The results from this experiment are shown in Table 2. AER is still calculated compared to the cross-lingual baseline trained with MUSE embeddings. Using full grid consistently outperforms cross-lingual supervision only. This shows that combining cross-lingual and cross-task supervision (with coupling models included) is viable approach even with these text representation approaches. The decoders are able to deal with languages they have not seen before even without the help of multilingual word embeddings.

We also show how the proposed techniques deal with these representations. Private encoders perform the best for rotated MUSE embeddings. It is possible that our approach to decouple the language spaces by shuffling the dimensions was too easy to reconstruct and the private encoders were able to rotate them back. Private encoders also work quite well with character-level representations. However, they were bested by adversarial training there. Adversarial training has especially good results for NER. We assume that the model was able to learn language universal features of named entities, such as capitalization or similar names (e.g. *America* in English and *Amerika* in Czech).

Table 2. Performance with various text representation techniques.

	DP	NER	POS	AER
MUSE				
Cross-lingual (AER baseline)	38.75	49.30	69.05	0.00
Full Grid	46.25	56.62	84.09	32.40
Rotated MUSE				
Cross-lingual	2.55	0.77	13.78	−174.87
Full grid	29.59	21.11	63.90	−57.02
+Private encoders	**48.63**	**36.95**	**77.15**	**−2.42**
+Embeddings	44.05	20.76	63.20	−45.16
+Adversarial training	47.97	27.05	66.73	−27.54
Character-level LSTM				
Cross-lingual	15.07	32.00	41.62	−89.29
Full grid	40.44	38.74	70.75	−21.02
+Private encoders	53.04	37.48	**80.27**	5.43
+Embeddings	48.50	37.04	73.66	−11.23
+Adversarial training	**53.61**	**44.95**	75.86	**8.75**

5 Conclusion

We believe that combining cross-lingual and cross-task supervision is an important research topic. Combination of various types of auxiliary supervision can lead to development of more universal NLP models that are able to tackle many tasks in many languages. All these can influence each other and learn from each other. Techniques like we proposed can lead to further development of these universal models.

We proposed three distinct techniques to improve the performance of transfer learning when cross-lingual and cross-task supervision are combined. These three techniques are the main contribution of our work. All of them proved to be effective under different circumstances. The increase in performance is significant, especially for dependency parsing. Compared to the two other tasks, dependency parsing is the hardest task that can not be solved on lexical level easily. Instead it requires a deep understanding of how syntax in different languages work. That is perhaps why it was able to utilize the proposed advanced parameter sharing techniques.

In the future we plan to experiment with pre-trained language models as encoders. These models achieved interesting results in cross-lingual learning [15]. The combination with cross-task supervision was not yet researched for them. Their huge size will probably require to rethink the parameter sharing techniques we use, e.g. private encoders might be too expensive to train. Instead, we can reuse some of the fine-tuning techniques that were developed for large monolingual language models, e.g. the so called *adapters* [10].

Acknowledgments. This work was partially supported by the Scientific Grant Agency of the Slovak Republic, grants No. VG 1/0725/19 and VG 1/0667/18 and by the Slovak Research and Development Agency under the contracts No. APVV-15-0508, APVV-17-0267 and APVV SK-IL-RD-18-0004.

References

1. Akhtar, M.S., Chauhan, D., Ghosal, D., Poria, S., Ekbal, A., Bhattacharyya, P.: Multi-task learning for multi-modal emotion recognition and sentiment analysis. In: Proceedings of the 2019 Conference of NAACL, Minneapolis, Minnesota, pp. 370–379. ACL (2019)
2. Benikova, D., Biemann, C., Reznicek, M.: Nosta-d named entity annotation for German: guidelines and dataset. In: Proceedings of the Ninth International Conference on Language Resources and Evaluation, LREC 2014, 26–31 May 2014, Reykjavik, Iceland, pp. 2524–2531. ELRA (2014)
3. Bos, J., Basile, V., Evang, K., Venhuizen, N.J., Bjerva, J.: The Groningen meaning bank. In: Ide, N., Pustejovsky, J. (eds.) Handbook of Linguistic Annotation, pp. 463–496. Springer, Dordrecht (2017). https://doi.org/10.1007/978-94-024-0881-2_18
4. Caruana, R.: Multitask learning: a knowledge-based source of inductive bias. In: Machine Learning, Proceedings of the Tenth International Conference, 27–29 June 1993, University of Massachusetts, Amherst, MA, USA, pp. 41–48 (1993)
5. Conneau, A., Lample, G., Ranzato, M., Denoyer, L., Jégou, H.: Word translation without parallel data. In: 6th International Conference on Learning Representations. Vancouver, Canada (2018)
6. Devlin, J., Chang, M.W., Lee, K., Toutanova, K.: BERT: pre-training of deep bidirectional transformers for language understanding. In: Proceedings of the 2019 Conference of NAACL, Minneapolis, Minnesota, pp. 4171–4186. ACL (2019)
7. Ganin, Y., Lempitsky, V.S.: Unsupervised domain adaptation by backpropagation. In: Proceedings of the 32nd ICML 2015, Lille, France, 6–11 July 2015. JMLR Workshop and Conference Proceedings, vol. 37, pp. 1180–1189. JMLR.org (2015)
8. Guo, J., Che, W., Yarowsky, D., Wang, H., Liu, T.: Cross-lingual dependency parsing based on distributed representations. In: Proceedings of the 53rd Annual Meeting of the ACL and the 7th IJCNLP, Beijing, China, pp. 1234–1244. ACL (2015)
9. Hochreiter, S., Schmidhuber, J.: Long short-term memory. Neural Comput. **9**(8), 1735–1780 (1997)
10. Houlsby, N., et al.: Parameter-efficient transfer learning for NLP. In: Chaudhuri, K., Salakhutdinov, R. (eds.) Proceedings of the 36th International Conference on Machine Learning, ICML 2019, 9–15 June 2019, Long Beach, California, USA. Proceedings of Machine Learning Research, vol. 97, pp. 2790–2799. PMLR (2019). http://proceedings.mlr.press/v97/houlsby19a.html
11. Hu, J., Ruder, S., Siddhant, A., Neubig, G., Firat, O., Johnson, M.: XTREME: a massively multilingual multi-task benchmark for evaluating cross-lingual generalization. CoRR abs/2003.11080 (2020)
12. Hwa, R., Resnik, P., Weinberg, A., Kolak, O.: Evaluating translational correspondence using annotation projection. In: Proceedings of the 40th Annual Meeting of the ACL, Philadelphia, USA, pp. 392–399. ACL (2002)
13. Johnson, M., et al.: Google's multilingual neural machine translation system: enabling zero-shot translation. Trans. ACL **5**, 339–351 (2017)

14. Joty, S., Nakov, P., Màrquez, L., Jaradat, I.: Cross-language learning with adversarial neural networks. In: Proceedings of the 21st CoNLL, Vancouver, Canada, pp. 226–237. ACL (2017)
15. Karthikeyan, K., Wang, Z., Mayhew, S., Roth, D.: Cross-lingual ability of multilingual BERT: an empirical study. In: 8th International Conference on Learning Representations, ICLR 2020, Addis Ababa, Ethiopia, 26–30 April 2020. OpenReview.net (2020)
16. Klementiev, A., Titov, I., Bhattarai, B.: Inducing crosslingual distributed representations of words. In: Proceedings of COLING 2012, pp. 1459–1474. The COLING 2012 Organizing Committee, Mumbai, India (2012)
17. Kravalova, J., Zabokrtsky, Z.: Czech named entity corpus and SVM-based recognizer. In: Proceedings of the 2009 Named Entities Workshop: Shared Task on Transliteration (NEWS 2009), pp. 194–201. ACL (2009)
18. Lafferty, J.D., McCallum, A., Pereira, F.C.N.: Conditional random fields: probabilistic models for segmenting and labeling sequence data. In: Proceedings of the 18th ICML, Williams College, Williamstown, USA, pp. 282–289. Morgan Kaufmann (2001)
19. Lin, Y., Yang, S., Stoyanov, V., Ji, H.: A multi-lingual multi-task architecture for low-resource sequence labeling. In: Proceedings of the 56th Annual Meeting of the ACL, Melbourne, Australia, pp. 799–809. ACL (2018)
20. McDonald, R., Pereira, F., Ribarov, K., Hajič, J.: Non-projective dependency parsing using spanning tree algorithms. In: Proceedings of HLT-EMNLP, Vancouver, British Columbia, Canada, pp. 523–530. ACL (2005)
21. McDonald, R., Petrov, S., Hall, K.: Multi-source transfer of delexicalized dependency parsers. In: Proceedings of the 2011 EMNLP, Edinburgh, Scotland, UK, pp. 62–72. ACL (2011)
22. Mikolov, T., Sutskever, I., Chen, K., Corrado, G.S., Dean, J.: Distributed representations of words and phrases and their compositionality. In: 27th NIPS Proceedings, 5–8 December 2013, Lake Tahoe, Nevada, United States, pp. 3111–3119 (2013)
23. Pikuliak, M., Šimko, M.: Combining cross-lingual and cross-task supervision for zero-shot learning. In: Sojka, P., Kopeček, I., Pala, K., Horák, A. (eds.) TSD 2020. LNCS (LNAI), vol. 12284, pp. 162–170. Springer, Cham (2020). https://doi.org/10.1007/978-3-030-58323-1_17
24. Sang, E.F.T.K.: Introduction to the conll-2002 shared task: language-independent named entity recognition. CoRR cs.CL/0209010 (2002)
25. Wan, X.: Co-training for cross-lingual sentiment classification. In: Proceedings of the Joint Conference of the 47th Annual Meeting of the ACL and the 4th International Joint Conference on Natural Language Processing of the AFNLP, Suntec, Singapore, pp. 235–243. ACL (2009)
26. Wang, D., Zheng, T.F.: Transfer learning for speech and language processing. In: Asia-Pacific Signal and Information Processing Association Annual Summit and Conference, APSIPA 2015, Hong Kong, 16–19 December 2015, pp. 1225–1237 (2015)
27. Zapotoczny, M., Rychlikowski, P., Chorowski, J.: On multilingual training of neural dependency parsers. In: Ekštein, K., Matoušek, V. (eds.) TSD 2017. LNCS (LNAI), vol. 10415, pp. 326–334. Springer, Cham (2017). https://doi.org/10.1007/978-3-319-64206-2_37

A Discourse-Informed Approach for Cost-Effective Extractive Summarization

Marta Vicente[(✉)] and Elena Lloret

Department of Software and Computing Systems, University of Alicante,
Alicante, Spain
{mvicente,elloret}@dlsi.ua.es

Abstract. This paper presents an empirical study that harnesses the benefits of Positional Language Models (PLMs) as key of an effective methodology for understanding the gist of a discursive text via extractive summarization. We introduce an unsupervised, adaptive, and cost-efficient approach that integrates semantic information in the process. Texts are linguistically analyzed, and then semantic information, specifically synsets and named entities, are integrated into the PLM, enabling the understanding of text, in line with its discursive structure. The proposed unsupervised approach is tested for different summarization tasks within standard benchmarks. The results obtained are very competitive with respect to the state of the art, thus proving the effectiveness of this approach, which requires neither training data nor high-performance computing resources.

Keywords: Text summarization · Positional Language Models · Statistical methods

1 Introduction

In today's society, information overload hampers efficient and effective data processing and management. Efforts to deal with such situation have revealed how summarization techniques become valuable assets, able to provide different resources for facilitating information understanding through the accomplishment of their main goal, not other than to condense data without losing meaning [20].

In recent years, Deep Learning (DL) approaches have been widely adopted and, not only in summarization, but in most of the Natural Language Processing (NLP) tasks, have become the state of the art[1]. However, DL still poses two major limitations: 1) the huge amount of training data needed to create robust models; and 2) the costly amount of computational resources necessary to develop these models [26].

---

[1] NLP-progress is a repository to track the progress in NLP, that includes the datasets and the current state of the art for the most common NLP tasks. (nlpprogress.com, last accessed in July 2020).

© Springer Nature Switzerland AG 2020
L. Espinosa-Anke et al. (Eds.): SLSP 2020, LNAI 12379, pp. 109–121, 2020.
https://doi.org/10.1007/978-3-030-59430-5_9

This paper refocuses attention on statistical methods as opposed to machine learning-based methods, and presents a Discourse-Informed approach for Cost-effective Extractive Summarization (DICES). We have selected as statistical grounding a specific type of language model known as Positional Language Model (PLM) which provides an unsupervised method that does not require human annotation or intervention to get good results. We shape it to incorporate semantic information gathered from the document, instead of merely using words, while considering the placement of the relevant information within the document.

Our motivation here is twofold: first, at a technical level, to overcome the limitations of the *bag of words* approaches and propose a way to understand and process the text not as a simple set of words but as a succession of messages, whose full meaning is accessible beyond the sentence level at the discourse dimension; secondly, at a societal level, our approach represents a more digitally inclusive tool for public and private sector organizations that have tighter budgets for accessing Information and Communication Technologies.

In a fast changing world, any method that is flexible and adaptive is arguably highly desirable, since it can be easily used in different contexts and with different data, without compromising performance. Our approach is feasible with less resources than would be necessary for deep or machine learning approaches.

The main contributions of this work can be summarized as:

- A proposal of a discourse-informed statistical model, which incorporates semantics to gain a better understanding of the source that foster the improvement of the resulting summary.
- A design of an unsupervised, lightweight and simple yet effective framework that could be easily adapted to different tasks and languages.
- A collection of experiments which have been conducted on different summarization tasks (multi-document and headline/very short summarization) over a standard benchmark (DUC2004), with no heavy load of computational resources, to empirically verify the effectiveness of our approach. Evaluation results are encouraging and demonstrate that DICES is competitive with state-of-the-art approaches.

The remainder of this paper is structured as follows. In Sect. 2, we introduce some previous relevant work on summarization. The definition of our approach is explained in Sect. 3, where we detail the statistical foundations along with the different stages to obtain a proper summary. Section 4 describes the tasks and dataset, together with the experimental setup and the evaluation procedure. The results and their analysis are covered in Sect. 5. We conclude with Sect. 6, where we provide a recap and mention plans for future work.

2   Related Work

For brevity, in this section we focus specifically on representative summarization methods within the extractive context, as well as those that underline the importance of discourse. We also introduce some works where PLMs have proven to be useful in different areas of NLP.

Most of the research presented in recent years includes neural approaches. For these systems, summarization becomes a task were the selection of sentences is undertaken as a classification problem. Encoder-decoder architectures are common [4,19] and so is reinforcement learning [3,32], although research into new combinations of neural components grows fast and constantly. However, these approaches still need huge amounts of training data, which is not always available, such in the cases of very specific domains or tasks. In this sense, DICES can deal with whichever amount of available data, because its effectiveness does not depend on such factor.

Although a large part of existing research deals with the text at a sentence level and relies on occurrence frequency, a few attempts have been made to incorporate discourse and semantics in the field. Structured attention to induce trees was the proposal of [15], while relying in Rhetorical Structural Theory [18] is the case for [16]. These systems have a strong and expensive linguistic component that needs performing dependency parsing or rhetorical analysis to get the relation between the units of the document. Our approach, DICES, represents the semantics and structure of the components from a statistical perspective, which imply shallow features and resources.

A different sort of approaches segments the document in other meaning units, as [6], whose segmentation is aspect or topic based. In contrast, DICES granularity permits wider possibilities also allowing to include this type of feature within DICES processing through the tuning of a seed, which will be introduced in Sect. 3.

Regarding the use of PLMs, such approach has proven to be useful and cost-effective in different areas of NLP, such as information retrieval in the clinical domain [1], automatic story generation [29] or information discovery in social networks [33]. Additionally, they were applied in the context of CL-SciSumm 2017 Shared Task, in order to identify fragments of text from scientific papers cited or paraphrased in posterior publications [9]. Although this task was closely related to summarization, the use of PLM for this task was not as effective as the results obtained by other statistical methods, such as TF-IDF. However, due to the inherent nature of PLMs, we strongly believe that they can have a positive impact for summarization—when it comes to determine where the important information is—that is worthy to test. As far as we know, there are no other previous attempts to solely use PLMs for summarizing purposes.

3   DICES Approach

DICES is based on the idea that a deeper understanding of the document will lead to better results in terms of summarization. From our perspective, this understanding comes from the semantics of the discourse, which is considered as a structured collection of coherent sentences that share concepts and topics. The positional information is fundamental and we introduce it in our proposal inspired by the work in Information Retrieval developed by [17].

In this section, we first describe the statistical foundations of our proposal as the way to provide a representation of the document on such terms. Next, we explain how this representation is used to obtain the required summary.

3.1   Positional Language Models Fundamentals

Taking into account all the positions i within document D, PLMs provides a mechanism to calculate the relevance of each element w that belongs to the document's vocabulary V in every position of D, based on the element's distance to other occurrences of the same element throughout D.

The closer the elements appear to the position being evaluated, the higher the score obtained, with the whole text considered as context, and not only the scope of a single sentence.

In this manner, one PLM is computed for each and every position of the document:

$$P(w \mid i) = \frac{\sum_{j=1}^{|D|} c(w,j) \times f(i,j)}{\sum_{w' \in V} \sum_{j=1}^{|D|} c(w',j) \times f(i,j)} \tag{1}$$

where $c(w,j)$ indicates that term w exists in position j, $|D|$ refers to D's length and $f(i,j)$ to the propagation function rating the distance between i and j.

3.2   PLM for Summarization

Having explained the model foundations, and thus the PLM module, a more detailed procedure needs to be designed to adapt the model to the task of summarization. We can define 3 phases necessary for the achievement of our objective, as well as several parameters that will shape some of them.

First, the **definition of the vocabulary** is performed in order to identify which type of terms best suits the task's objective. At this stage, we obtain a representation of the text that involves both the vocabulary and the position of its elements. Next, we **select a seed**, i.e., a set of words that can be relevant to the text and whose constitution depends on the corpus of origin itself, from whose documents we extract the vocabulary. Finally, the processing of the PLM against the seed vocabulary allows us to establish scores for the text elements, which will be transformed into a **ranking of sentences** from which the highest scored ones will be selected to produce the final summary, up to a specific length.

3.3   The Vocabulary Definition

First, it is necessary to define which type of elements will constitute the vocabulary for the PLM. A straightforward approach, such as selecting the plain words as they appear in the text, would involve a sparsity problem that can be overcome by looking for more integrative terms. A further step by which to increase abstraction and thus, reduce such sparsity, implies using lemmas instead. However, looking for a deeper and more comprehensive approach, we could explore more meaningful constructs, and thus consider forms as sets of synonyms or deeper semantic, syntactic structures.

For the current configuration, we opted for a type of entity that incorporates the sense of the terms from a shared meaning point of view. In this manner, the vocabulary is composed of the synsets corresponding to nouns, verbs and adjectives.

Besides, the named entities that appear along the text are incorporated into the vocabulary. This decision aligns with our semantic goal, which in this case was to capture the meanings, and therefore, the semantic information they convey. Freeling [22] is an open-source tool which provides several layers of linguistic analysis, and we use it to obtain the vocabulary information, both the synsets from WordNet [10] and the named entities.

3.4 Seed Selection

In DICES summarization process, the next step involves the selection of a seed. This seed must be constituted by elements that permit the detection of the relevant segments of the discourse. The seed processing can begin with a sentence or with a set of terms, which need to be analyzed with the same tools as the source text to obtain the same type of elements. A second vocabulary V_s is then built from them.

3.5 Sentence Ranking and Selection

Let V denote the source vocabulary, with elements $\{w_1, .., w_{jVj}\}$, and V_s the vocabulary extracted from the seed, a filter vector F is generated with as many positions as elements have the original vocabulary V. If the element w_j from V belongs to V_s, then $F[j] = 1$; $F[j] = 0$, otherwise. Now it is possible to obtain a Score Vector (SC) providing a unique value for every position i within the document, whose computation involves the PLMs previously calculated, and the elements of the seed:

$$SC[i] = \sum_{w \in V} P(w \mid i) \times F \qquad (2)$$

SC becomes a detector of important areas, with maximum values when the accumulation of relevant elements given by PLMs is higher.

From the SC, we are able to obtain the positions of interest—those with higher scores—within the document and retrieve as candidates the sentences to which these positions belong.

Considering such information, a sentence score S_{score} is computed for each of them:

$$S_{\text{score}} = \sum_{k \in S} SC[k] \qquad (3)$$

where S refers to the sentence to be scored and k indicates the positions within the document for that sentence.

Generally, when a summary is created, a parameter is set that determines the length of the summary. Therefore, to get the optimal set of sentences, we sequentially select the highest scoring ones, until the required length is fulfilled.

4 Experiments and Evaluation

In order to evaluate DICES, several experiments were conducted on different task over a standard benchmark. In this Section we introduce them, together with some implementation details, and explain how the resultant summaries were automatically evaluated to get our comparable results.

4.1 Tasks and Dataset

Depending on the source of the summary, we can speak about single-document summarization (SDS), if the source of the summary is only one document, or multi-document summarization (MDS), when the source is a collection of texts. Moreover, it is possible to distinguish between indicative summaries, that provide the aboutness of the original piece of text, and an informative summary, that includes more facts and could be read instead of the original source [20].

Taking into account such distinctions, one of the objectives when proposing DICES was to demonstrate that it could be effectively adapted to deliver different types of summaries under multiple scenarios. In this section, we will describe the dataset and tasks that allowed us to do so. They were selected for their renown to enable a quality comparison with previous systems.

The Dataset. Some of the most popular datasets used to address such tasks proceed from the Document Understanding Conferences (DUC). Among them, we chose DUC2004 because, not only they include tasks aimed at SDS and MDS, but the required summaries were as well quite different, which allowed us to enrich the evaluation of our system's adaptability. On the one side, the SDS task aimed at generating a very short summary (headline), with a length limit of 65 bytes. In this case we were not producing an informative summary, but an indicative one.

On the other side, the required length for the MDS task should be 665 bytes at most, producing an informative summary in this case. The same news articles in English provided for the SDS task were grouped in 50 clusters now, for each of which a summary should be produced.

4.2 Experimental Setup

Several implementation details regarding the propagation function, the definition of the seed and the strategy to perform summarization over a multi-document source were adjusted in order to apply DICES to the dataset and tasks.

The Propagation Function. The first decision regards to the definition of the propagation function introduced in Sect. 3.1, and represented as *f(i,j)* in Eq. 1. It was also necessary to define its *sigma* parameter, which is responsible for the spread of the kernel curve, representing the semantic scope of a term. Following the work of [29], we set the σ parameter to 25 and a Gaussian kernel was selected as propagation function, in this manner:

$$f(i,j) = e^{\frac{-(i-j)^2}{2\sigma}} \tag{4}$$

where i and j represent the position for which the PLM is calculated and the position in which the second occurrence is found, respectively.

Definition of the Seed. The function of the seed in the process of summarization is to act as a discriminating factor that allows the detection of areas of importance and, ultimately, significant sentences in the document so as to discard information that can be dismissed.

In the present work, to select a good seed we rely on the assumption that, due to the type of textual genre to which they belong, the documents of the DUC2004 dataset follow the standardized *inverted pyramid structure* [23], according to which the most important or interesting information is included in the first sentence—namely, the *Lead Sentence*. The remainder of the text develops, completes and provides fundamental details regarding that first statement. By selecting this initial assertion as seed, DICES can exploit the potential that PLMs provide in relation to the position of salient elements, leveraging the essential information contained in the *Lead Sentence*.

Therefore, the extraction of the seed is a straightforward operation for the documents processed for the SDS task, whereas one further step is needed in the MDS task. In this case, the first sentences of each document belonging to the same cluster are recovered and concatenated to create the collective seed required. Once the seed segment is chosen, it is processed with linguistic tools, and then synsets and named entities are extracted to finally obtain the seed vocabulary V_s.

MDS Documents Preparation. Just as particular processing is required in relation to the seed of the MDS task, the input of the summation process for a multi-document source also needs prior treatment. Hence, in order to get the summary of a set of documents belonging to the same cluster, the strategy consists of concatenating the bodies, providing such aggregates as single input for the PLM module.

4.3 The Evaluation

The evaluation of the summaries was conducted considering their ground truth and their relation in terms of n-gram overlap using ROUGE tool[13]. Each of the system summaries was evaluated against four models, released by DUC2004 for each document and cluster, in both SDS and MDS tasks.

ROUGE is a popular recall-oriented metric typically used to evaluate quality in summarization, circumstance that allowed us to compare DICES with state-of-the-art systems, based on different n-gram sizes.

We have also included two term-frequency (*Tf*) baselines: *Tf-Idf* [24] and *Tf-Isf* [21]. The former one, *Tf-Idf*, takes into account the whole corpus and computes for each term of the corpus vocabulary its *inverse document frequency* (*idf*), considering the number of documents on which the term appears. The *inverse sentence frequency* (*isf*), on the other hand, is computed for every term within a unique document, independent of the rest of the corpus, and implies counting the number of sentences in which the term appears. The sentences for the calculation of the *isf* are equivalent to the documents for computing the *idf*.

5   Results and Discussion

In this section, we present our results on each of the tests and compare our model with several state-of-the-art approaches. Regarding the measures presented, we found that all the systems were reporting for evaluation ROUGE unigram (R1) and bigram (R2) overlapping, and sometimes ROUGE longest subsequence overlap (RL). Similarly occurs with F-score and recall. In order to get the clearest idea of our system's performance, we have included all the significant cases.

5.1   Very Short Summarization on DUC2004

Generation of headlines or very short summaries, with a strong limitation on size, has emerged as a powerful trend in recent years. One of the earliest related tasks was announced in DUC2004. Results for this task are reported in Table 1, recall (left) and F-score (right).

Table 1. ROUGE scores for different systems on the single-document DUC2004 task, modality very short summaries

DUC2004-SD	R (%)				F-score(%)		
System	R1	R2	RL	System	R1	R2	RL
Tf-Idf	20.16	5.60	17.72	Tf-Idf	18.79	5.20	16.52
Tf-Isf	20.18	5.61	17.74	Tf-Isf	18.80	5.21	16.54
Lead	22.25	–	–	Pointer-Gen	31.43	6.03	10.01
BestDuc04	25.65	–	–	LexRank	**34.44**	7.11	11.19
Li_18	29.33	10.24	25.24				
Tak_19	32.85	11.78	28.52				
DICES04-SD	**46.88**	**14.94**	**38.31**	DICES04-SD	23.98	**7.43**	**19.06**

We compare DICES performance with the *Lead* baseline provided by the organizers and the best system of the challenge. Our approach comfortably outperforms standard baselines, including the *Tf-Idf* and *Tf-Isf* approximations, but also outperforms state-of-the-art neural approaches *Li_18* [12] and *Tak_19* [28] with a simple yet effective solution in terms of recall. Additionally, we compare DICES F-Score with *Pointer-Gen* [25]—an encoder-decoder abstractive approach—and *LexRank* [5], a different type of method, graph-based, that uses the PageRank algorithm, showing our system improvement over both of them in the longest n-gram overlapping ROUGE metrics.

5.2   Multi Document Summarization on DUC2004

Table 2 presents ROUGE scores on the DUC2004 MDS task. DICES is compared with several strong models, either in terms of recall (left) or F-score (right).

Regarding recall, we compare and outperform the Lead baseline and the best system, but also later approaches as *TakOku* [27] or *Wang* [31]. It is worth noting that for *MDS Chali* [2] and *Submodular* [14], DICES beats them in recall, but not in F-score, where our results are slightly worse. We also report F-scores from *Pointer-Gen* and *LexRank*, and contrast our system to the basic baselines provided by the term frequency approaches, *Tf-Idf* and *Tf-Isf*, which are considerably improved by DICES.

Table 2. ROUGE scores for different systems on the multi-document DUC2004 task

DUC2004-MD	R (%)			F-score (%)	
System	R1	R2	System	R1	R2
Tf-Isf	32.39	6.05			
Lead	32.42	6.40	Pointer-Gen	31.43	6.03
Tf-Idf	32.56	6.01	Tf-Isf	32.16	6.02
BestDUC04	38.28	**9.21**	Tf-Idf	32.25	5.97
TakOku	39.35	–	LexRank	34.44	7.11
Wang	39.07	–	BestDuc	37.94	–
Submodular	39.35	–	Submodular	38.39	–
MDS-Chali	39.53	–	MDS-Chali	**39.83**	–
DICES04-MD	**40.99**	8.52	DICES04-MD	36.88	**7.66**

5.3   Overall Discussion

One of the objectives we pursued when we decided to design and test DICES, considering that we do so at a time when neural systems are on the rise, was to demonstrate that it was viable to achieve competitive results in scenarios with less data, computational resources and time. The results show that, even with less data and processing, most of the outcomes are remarkable.

Regarding the DL approaches that appear in the comparison, the size of the data could explain precisely the difference in the results, since it is this size which can determine the data usage for the testing stage when there are not enough examples for the proper training of the model.

With reference to non neural models, it is possible that DICES' consideration of the semantic level of the discourse causes this difference in results. However, although PLM works with semantic chains of elements, we do not perform coreference resolution. Some preliminary experiments were carried out in this regard, but results from the tools employed (Freeling and an AllenNLP [7] model, based in [11]) were not as satisfactory as expected. The identification of the coreferential elements was inaccurate, thus introducing noise into our approach and noticeably increasing the execution time. Furthermore, the results show the good performance of the system, even without using any similarity measure or method to avoid redundancy.

An analysis of the resulting summaries made it possible to detect a series of common errors originated in the linguistic preprocessing stage. For instance, we detected that punctuation (quotation mostly), either correct or incorrect, affects the behavior of language analyzers. Also, the inadequate performance of lexical disambiguation for the accurate identification of concepts/synsets may increase or reduce vocabulary size thus compromising the final results.

In spite of all this, DICES shows outstanding results and a remarkable capacity to adapt. Its good performance has been demonstrated in the different summarization tests. It could in fact be adapted to more restricted tasks, such as those oriented by queries, topics or users preferences by using them as seeds within the process. DICES methodology is also language-independent. Although we only evaluated the approach for English, it could be easily adapted to other languages, presuming the existence of a linguistic analyzer for the target language.

6   Conclusion and Future Work

This paper proposes DICES, an extractive model which enables the gist of a news item to be understood. A simple yet powerful method that not only detects and locates the parts of the document containing the relevant information, but also recovers the corresponding sentences to create different types of summaries.

DICES adopts a PLM as its core, a statistical model that has proven to be effective in other NLP disciplines. This model was designed to overcome the limitation of the *bag of words* approach, for which information on term frequency prevails over that information related to the structure of the text, or the succession of the elements that constitute it. The PLM jointly embodies positional and semantic information to perform an improvement on the generation of summaries.

Furthermore, DICES shows a remarkable characteristic compared to the set of systems that today exploit the possibilities of deep learning. As our system does not use machine learning, there is no need for large amounts of training data, neither excessive computational or temporal resources. Besides, its adaptation to different domains is considerably straightforward.

Hence, we can speak of a lightweight, efficient, unsupervised and extremely adaptable tool, which with small variations to the algorithm—based on off-the-shelf and available linguistic analysis tools (e.g., Freeling, StanfordNLP, Wordnet)—is readily adaptable to different languages.

This paper presents results that indicate the successful evaluation of DICES in single and multiple document summarization tasks for the news domain over the DUC2004 dataset, although we have already extended its assessment over different datasets (DUC2002 and CNN-DM [8]) with optimistic outcomes in [30].

DICES offers plenty of possibilities for future work. Not only testing the approach with different languages, but also adapting it to different domains and types of summaries. Making the seed comply with certain requirements (users profiles, topics) opens a line in guided summarization. Besides, we plan to use DICES in abstractive scenarios as well as for different language generation tasks.

Acknowledgments. This research work has been funded by the Spanish Government through the projects: "Modelang: Modeling the behavior of digital entities by Human Language Technologies" (RTI2018-094653-B-C22) and "INTEGER Intelligent Text Generation" (RTI2018-094649-B-I00), also by Generalitat Valenciana through "SIIA: Tecnologías del lenguaje humano para una sociedad inclusiva, igualitaria, y accesible" (PROMETEU/2018/089). This paper is also based upon work from COST Action CA18231 "Multi3Generation: Multi-task, Multilingual, Multi-modal Language Generation".

References

1. Boudin, F., Nie, J.Y., Dawes, M.: Positional language models for clinical information retrieval. In: 2010 Proceedings of EMNLP, pp. 108–115 (2010)
2. Chali, Y., Uddin, M.: Multi-document summarization based on atomic semantic events and their temporal relationships. In: Ferro, N., et al. (eds.) ECIR 2016. LNCS, vol. 9626, pp. 366–377. Springer, Cham (2016). https://doi.org/10.1007/978-3-319-30671-1_27
3. Chen, Y.C., Bansal, M.: Fast abstractive summarization with reinforce-selected sentence rewriting. In: Proceedings of the ACL, vol. 1, pp. 675–686 (2018)
4. Cheng, J., Lapata, M.: Neural summarization by extracting sentences and words. In: 54th Annual Meeting of the ACL - Long Papers 1, pp. 484–494, March 2016
5. Erkan, G., Radev, D.R.: LexRank: graph-based lexical centrality as salience in text summarization. J. Artif. Intell. Res. **22**, 457–479 (2004)
6. Frermann, L., Klementiev, A.: Inducing document structure for aspect-based summarization. In: Proceedings of the ACL, vol. 1, pp. 6263–6273 (2019)
7. Gardner, M., et al.: AllenNLP: a deep semantic natural language processing platform. arXiv preprint arXiv:1803.07640 (2018)
8. Hermann, K.M., et al.: Teaching machines to read and comprehend. In: Advances in Neural Information Processing Systems, pp. 1693–1701 (2015)

9. Karimi, S., Moraes, L.F., Das, A., Verma, R.M.: University of Houston@ CL-SCiSumm 2017: positional language models, structural correspondence learning and textual entailment. In: BIRNDL@ SIGIR (2), pp. 73–85 (2017)

10. Kilgarriff, A., Fellbaum, C.: WordNet: an electronic lexical database. Language **76**(3), 706 (2000)

11. Lee, K., He, L., Lewis, M., Zettlemoyer, L.S.: End-to-end neural coreference resolution. In: Proceedings of EMNLP (2017)

12. Li, H., Zhu, J., Zhang, J., Zong, C.: Ensure the correctness of the summary: incorporate entailment knowledge into abstractive sentence summarization. In: Proceedings of COLING, pp. 1430–1441 (2018)

13. Lin, C.Y.: ROUGE: a package for automatic evaluation of summaries. In: Text Summarization Branches Out, pp. 74–81. ACL (2004)

14. Lin, H., Bilmes, J.: Multi-document summarization via budgeted maximization of submodular functions. In: Proceedings of the NAACL, pp. 912–920 (2010)

15. Liu, Y., Titov, I., Lapata, M.: Single document summarization as tree induction. In: Proceedings of the NAACL, vol. 1, pp. 1745–1755 (2019)

16. Liu, Z., Chen, N.: Exploiting discourse-level segmentation for extractive summarization. In: Proceedings of the 2nd Workshop on New Frontiers in Summarization, pp. 116–121. ACL (2019)

17. Lv, Y., Zhai, C.: Positional language models for information retrieval. In: Proceedings of the 32nd International ACM SIGIR, pp. 299–306. ACM (2009)

18. Mann, W.C., Thompson, S.A.: Rhetorical structure theory: description and construction of text structures. In: Kempen, G. (ed.) Natural Language Generation. NATO ASI Series (Series E: Applied Sciences), vol. 135, pp. 85–95. Springer, Dordrecht (1987). https://doi.org/10.1007/978-94-009-3645-4_7

19. Nallapati, R., Zhou, B., dos Santos, C., Gulcehre, Ç., Xiang, B.: Abstractive text summarization using sequence-to-sequence RNNs and beyond. In: Proceedings of the SIGNLL Conference, pp. 280–290. ACL (2016)

20. Nenkova, A., McKeown, K.: Automatic summarization. Found. Trends® Inf. Retrieval **5**(2), 103–233 (2011)

21. Neto, J.L., Santos, A.D., Kaestner, C.A., Freitas, A.A.: Document clustering and text summarization. In: Proceedings of the International Conference on Practical Applications of Knowledge Discovery and Data Mining, pp. 41–55 (2000)

22. Padró, L., Stanilovsky, E.: FreeLing 3.0: Towards wider multilinguality. In: Proceedings of the LREC, pp. 2473–2479. ELRA (2012)

23. Pottker, H.: News and its communicative quality: the inverted pyramid–when and why did it appear? J. Stud. **4**(4), 501–511 (2003)

24. Salton, G., Buckley, C.: Term-weighting approaches in automatic text retrieval. Inf. Process. Manag. **24**(5), 513–523 (1988)

25. See, A., Liu, P.J., Manning, C.D.: Get to the point: summarization with pointer-generator networks. In: Proceedings of the ACL, vol. 1, pp. 1073–1083 (2017)

26. Strubell, E., Ganesh, A., McCallum, A.: Energy and policy considerations for deep learning in NLP. In: Proceedings of the ACL, pp. 3645–3650 (2019)

27. Takamura, H., Okumura, M.: Text summarization model based on maximum coverage problem and its variant. In: Proceedings of the EACL, pp. 781–789 (2009)

28. Takase, S., Okazaki, N.: Positional encoding to control output sequence length. In: Proceedings of NAACL, vol. 1, pp. 3999–4004. ACL (2019)

29. Vicente, M., Barros, C., Lloret, E.: Statistical language modelling for automatic story generation. J. Intell. Fuzzy Syst. **34**(5), 3069–3079 (2018)

30. Vicente, M., Lloret, E.: Relevant content selection through positional language models: an exploratory analysis. Procesamiento del Lenguaje Natural **65**, 75–82 (2020)
31. Wang, D., Zhu, S., Li, T., Gong, Y.: Multi-document summarization using sentence-based topic models. In: Proceedings of the ACL, pp. 297–300. ACL (2009)
32. Wu, Y., Hu, B.: Learning to extract coherent summary via deep reinforcement learning. In: Proceedings of the AAAI, pp. 5602–5609 (2018)
33. Yan, R., Li, X., Liu, M., Hu, X.: Tackling sparsity, the achilles heel of social networks: language model smoothing via social regularization. In: Proceedings of the ACL, vol. 2, pp. 623–629 (2015)

Towards eXplainable AI in Text Features Engineering for Concept Recognition

Andreas Waldis⬤, Luca Mazzola(✉)⬤, and Alexander Denzler

School of Information Technology, Lucerne University of Applied Sciences and Arts,
Rotkreuz, Switzerland
{andreas.waldis,luca.mazzola,alexander.denzler}@hslu.ch

Abstract. The rapid and pervasive development of methods from Artificial Intelligence (**AI**) affects our everyday life. Its application improves the users' experience of many daily tasks. Despite the enhancements provided, such approaches have a substantial limitation in the shortfall of people's trust connected with their lack of explainability. In natural language understanding (**NLU**) and processing (**NLP**), a fundamental objective is to support human interactions using sense-making of the language for communication. Such methods try to comprehend and reproduce the self-evident processes of human communication. This applies either in receiving speech signals or in extracting relevant information from a text. Furthermore, the pervasiveness of **AI** methods in the workplace and on the free time demands a sustainable and verified support of users' trust, as a natural condition for their acceptance. The objective of this work is to introduce a framework for the calculation and selection of understandable text features. Such features can increase the confidence placed into adopted **NLP** solutions. The following work outlines the **Text Feature Framework** and its text features, based on statistical information coming from a general text corpus. The showcase experiment uses those features to verify them on the concept recognition task. The results shows their capability to explain a model and its predictions. The resulting concept recognition models are competitive with other methods existing in the literature. It has the definitive advantage of being able to externalize the supporting evidence for a choice of concept identification.

Keywords: Natural language processing · Information retrieval · Explainable artificial intelligence · Concept recognition · Feature engineering · Feature selection

1 Introduction

These days, **AI** is ubiquitous in our life. It is part of almost any technology that supports us, be it in private or in our job. Depending on the situation, those technologies suggest a restaurant for dinner, guides us through the traffic jam, corrects our writing, or suggest maintenance of an industrial machine.

L. Espinosa-Anke et al. (Eds.): SLSP 2020, LNAI 12379, pp. 122–133, 2020.
https://doi.org/10.1007/978-3-030-59430-5_10

Like in all fields of **AI**, **NLP** and **NLU** experienced rapid development of new approaches. Those methods often follow a similar structure: (1) transforming a text input into a numeric representation, (2) apply a task-specific algorithm, and (3) back-transform the results in a human-understandable format. Over the past years, reinventions made remarkable progress in the transformation of text into a computer-usable representation. Mikolov et al. showed with Word2Vec [14] a first example of representing a word in a high dimensional space (word embeddings), followed by Glove - introduced by Jeffrey Pattington et al. [16]. A few years later, Peters et al. [17] and Devlin et al. [5] introduced the principle of contextual word embeddings. While the previously invented word embeddings produce the same vector for one word, these contextual word embeddings differ based on the context. Many methods used these variations of word embeddings with a big success - thanks to their expressive power. However, at the same time, their high dimensional and abstract space makes it hard to understand the behavior of generated models or the influence of a single dimension. This interpretability is a crucial aspect to trust technology. According to a study of PricewaterhouseCoopers consultancy firm (available online), a majority of the US business leaders (72%) believe in the capabilities of **AI**. Simultaneously, 67% of them see the risk connected with the lack of trust. Adadi et al. shows in [1] four ways of how explainable artificial intelligence (**XAI**) can increase this trust by (1) justify decisions (2), control decisions, (3) improve decisions, and (4) explore decisions.

With this work, we aim to increase the trust of **NLP** or **NLU** algorithms by showing a way of calculating, selecting, and applying understandable text features. Subsequently of this section, we briefly explore the state of the art of related methods (Sect. 2) before we introduce the **Text Feature Framework** in Sect. 3. This framework consists of the pipeline to calculate features to describe a text sample of varying length and its context. Since these calculations following a mathematical formulation, a certain feature value is comprehensible and covers a characteristic of a sample. We demonstrate, with a showcase experiment (Sect. 4), how to use the framework to build interpretable models that distinguish between concepts and non-concepts with these features. In Sect. 5, we evaluate the resulting models concerning internal measures, as the concept identification capacity, and qualitative ones. The latter one consists, in particular, of evaluating the resulting models on simultability, decomposability, and post-hoc interpretability. Such explanations are crucial for this showcase since the judgment of reasonable concepts changes from person to person and is affected by latent aspects. Thus, the explicitation of a model and its decisions is essential to increase the models' trust. Eventually, Sect. 6 draws the conclusions on our framework and its potential for **NLP** and **NLU** approaches, and closes with our thoughts about further research we would like to pursue.

2   Related Work

The following section gives an overview of the related work and essential topics such as automated concept recognition, text features, feature selection, and model interpretability.

AUTOMATED CONCEPT RECOGNITION is the task of recognizing concepts within a given text. Concepts can be seen as n-grams with a higher amount of information than any other random picked n-gram (non-concept) [15] - for example *Republic of Ecuador* vs. *on either side of.* There are semantic approaches like considering word connections [8], a combination of statistic and linguistic methods [15], or convolutions neural networks (**CNN**) [22]. We see in the latter one promising performance results, but also a lack of interpretability of the resulting predictions.

MODEL INTERPRETATION has three main objectives according to Lipton [13]. The explanation of an entire model (simulatability), of single components (decomposability), and its predictions (post-hoc interpretability). Wei et al. showed a way to explain a model by treating it as a black box and derive the feature importance with its predictions [23]. An example of decomposability is the work of Friedman et al. [7]. Their approach measures the change of the model output by adjusting the value of a single feature. This adjustment allows approximating the dependence of predictions on a single feature. The work of Ribeiro et al. [18] is an example of post-hoc interpretability. They showed a method to explain how the prediction is made with regards to every single feature and the corresponding value.

TEXT FEATURES captures numeric properties of a piece of text. Christopher et al. list a variety of frequency based features like the term frequency (tf), or inverse document frequency (idf) [4]. There are other less known ones like the residual inverse document frequency [2] ($ridf$), or the maximum spread distance [11] (msd). A second feature group consists of probabilistic based feature like pointwise mutual information [4] (pmi), likelihood ratio (lr), odds ratio (or) [20], t-score and z-score [6] (t,z), chi-score [3] (chi).

FEATURE SELECTION helps to understand the data, reduces the training time, and increase the predictive power by combating the curse of dimensionality [9]. The selection process ranks the features according to internal or external measurements. Internal ones calculate the importance of every feature with regards to the target variable y. This calculation depends on the kind of y: point-biserial correlation for the dichotomous case [21], one-way ANOVA test for a categorical one, and the Pearson correlation in the case of a numeric variable. External measurements train, for example, a tree-based model to predict y [19]. After the training, the internal feature importance can be used for ranking the features.

3   Text Feature Framework

With the proposed framework, we aim to provide a way of calculating and selecting a wide range of understandable text features. Figure 1 shows an overview

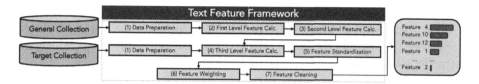

Fig. 1. Overview of the framework

of this process. The idea is to use statistical information (step 1–3), extracted from an extensive general collection (as Wikipedia), to derive a broad set of traceable text features (step 4–7). As all calculation steps following fixed mathematical formulations, the text features are comprehensible - a crucial property for interpretability. The resulting set of features can be used, for example, in a classification task like concept recognition as input. The following section shows the feature structure and introduces the seven steps of pre-processing, feature calculation right down to feature selection.

FEATURE STRUCTURE: The different text features describes the different characteristics of a text sample. In this work, we consider a sample as an n-gram (up to seven words) and its surrounding words. Every of the almost 160 text features belongs to one out of three feature categories and one feature group. The category indicates the type of feature: (1) either frequency-based like the term frequency, (2) probabilistic-based e.q. the conditional probability, or (3) similarity-based - for example, the cosine or euclidean similarity. At the same time, the feature group defines what part of a sample to consider. The n-gram- (N) and the surrounding features (S) characterize the n-gram of the sample itself and the word before and after it. While the transition-features (T) describes the word pairs on the beginning and end of the n-gram. Either the word on the left (w_{-1}) and the first word (w_1) or the word on the right (w_{n+1}) and the last word (w_n) of the n-gram.

DATA PREPARATION: The first step of the pipeline takes care of pre-processing the raw text collections (*General Collection* and *Target Collection*). This step lowers the text, replace special characters, split it into tokens, stems them, and create samples according to the previously seen structure.

FIRST LEVEL FEATURE CALCULATION: The next step uses the preprocessed text from of the *General Collection* to extract stem occurrences, co-occurrences, and spreadings. This includes the calculation of the following four matrices:

- The term frequency matrix $TF_{m \times n}$ captures the frequencies of all the m stems within the n documents of the collection.
- The prior-matrix $PR_{m \times m}$ and posterior-matrix $PO_{m \times m}$ capture the co-occurrences of every stem m with every other one. While the first one captures the occurrence of a stem s_i before another stem s_j, the latter one records the occurrence of s_i after s_j.

– The fourth matrix $NSD_{m \times n}$ contains the normalized spreading distance of all m stems in all n documents. This distance represents the number of stems between the first and the last occurrence of a stem in a document - normalized by the total number of stems in a document.

SECOND LEVEL FEATURE CALCULATION: This step uses the four resulting matrices of the previous step for further pre-calculations. This includes the following calculations:

– The mean μ and standard deviation (std. dev.) σ for all m stems of the matrices TF, PR, PO, and NSD.
– The document frequency df of each stem as the number of documents that contains it within all documents of the collection.
– The inverse document frequency idf, and the residual inverse document frequency $ridf$ for all m stems. The latter one is difference of the idf value and $log(\frac{1}{(1-e^{\mu_s})})$ where μ_s is the mean tf of a stem s for one document.
– The calculation of the $TFIDF_{m \times n}$, and $TFRIDF_{m \times n}$ matrix uses the precalculated TF, idf, and $ridf$ for all stems m and documents n.
– We measure the cosine or euclidean similarity of two stems on the base of the three matrices $TFIDF$, $TFRIDF$, and PR. Since they are high dimensional sparse matrices, they suffer from the curse of dimensionality. To overcome this drawback, we use the Truncated SVD algorithm [10] to reduce the dimension to 200 ($TFIDF_{200}$, $TFRIDF_{200}$, and PR_{200}).

THIRD LEVEL FEATURE CALCULATION: This final calculation step takes care of the feature calculation for the preprocessed samples of the *Target Collection*. For example cos_{tfidf}, one of the transition-features, measures the cosine similarity of two stems - either (s_{-1}, s_1) or (s_n, s_{n+1}) - with their vector representation coming from the matrix $TFIDF_{200}$. To get a fixed number of features for a sample of varying length, we assume that the single values of each stem follows a Gaussian distribution. This allows us to calculate the statistic of those values - as the mean μ and std. dev. σ. This calculation follows three possibilities:

– Each stem s has one specific value such as the inverse document frequency (idf). Based on these values, we calculate the mean (e.g. idf_μ) and std. dev. (e.q. idf_σ).
– A stem s is represented as a statistic - like the term frequency. In this case we have a mean tf_μ and std. dev. tf_σ for every s (one row of the matrix TF). We use those two lists of values to calculate the compound statistic as the mean and the std. dev. of the tf_μ values ($tf_{\mu_\sigma}, tf_{\mu_\mu}$) and the mean and the std. dev. of the tf_σ values ($tf_{\sigma_\sigma}, tf_{\sigma_\mu}$).
– A feature describes a pair of stems s_1, s_2 - as the pointwise mutual information (pmi). To get a fixed representation, we calculate the feature for every stem pair first and the statistic of these values second. We consider either every stem pair based on the sequence ($pmi_{seq_\mu}, pmi_{seq_\sigma}$) of appearance $(s_1, s_2), (s_2, s_3), ..., (s_{n-1}, s_n)$ or any possible combination ($pmi_{all_\mu}, pmi_{all_\sigma}$) of pairs $(s_1, s_2), (s_1, s_3), ..., (s_{n-1}, s_n)$.

FEATURE STANDARDIZATION, WEIGHTING, CLEANING: The last part of the pipeline cleans up the features and selects the most important ones. In the first step, the z-normalization scales the features to a mean of zero and std. dev. of one by subtracting the mean and dividing by the std. dev. Afterward, internal or external measurements weight influence of a feature to the target variable y. The last step cleans this weighted list of features by removing features with a high correlation of higher-ranked features (Pearson correlation of 0.9 or higher).

4   Design of Experiment

This section shows the experimental usage of the proposed feature framework for concept recognition. This application consists of the calculation and ranking of the different features, their usage, and an evaluation. All of this step use four different datasets: (1) 5.5 million English Wikipedia articles, (2) a set of 150'000 news articles from various networks (available on Kaggle-9, (3) the DUC dataset (available on nist), and (4) the Hulth dataset [12].

FEATURE CALCULATION: The calculation of the features follows to seven steps of the framework - as in Fig. 1. The first phase use the pre-processed 5.5 million Wikipedia articles as *General Collection* to extract statistical information (see step one), and make pre-calculations (as in step two). Then, the second phase calculates all the features, according to step three, for six million samples of the *Target Collection*. This samples are coming from the news dataset with 150'000 articles to extract six million samples - following the structure in Fig. 1. The third phase weights and sorts the single features by measure the influence of every feature to the target label on the six million samples. The labels indicate if the n-gram of a sample is a concept or not, according to the list of Wikipedia titles. We use different ways to measure the influence of the features:

- The point-biserial correlation of the target label and a feature for all bi-gram samples (***total_2***), tri-gram samples (***total_3***), tetra-gram samples (***total_4***), or the full set of samples (***total_n***).
- The mean of the point-biserial correlation (*mean*) for all groups of samples clustered by their n-gram length.
- The mean and maximum feature importance from 20 cross-validation runs of a Decision Tree (***dec_tree_max***, ***dec_tree_mean***) and Random Forest (***rand_forest_max***, ***rand_forest_mean***).

The last step of this third phase cleans the nine sorted lists of feature importance by removing redundant ones. A pair of features is to be said as redundant when their Pearson correlation exceeds a defined threshold - in this case 0.9 (90%).

TRAINING: The training process trains in total 2'304 different concept recognition models, by permuting the following hyperparameters:

- FEATURE WEIGHTS, the 64 list of sorted features.
- NUMBER OF FEATURE, 10, 20 or 30 top features based on the sorted list of feature weights.

- NUMBER OF SAMPLES, one, two or three million out of the six millions samples from the news dataset.
- MODEL TYPE, either Multinominal Naive Bayes (**NB**), Logistic Regression (**LR**), Decision Tree (**DT**), or Random Forest (**RF**).

The training of each model divides the samples into a training (80%) and validation set (20%), first. Second, it runs a 20-fold cross-validation on the training set and trains the final model on the full training set.

EVALUATION: The evaluation of the trained models focuses on stability, performance, and interpretability of the concept recognition. We use the precision, recall, f1-score, and mean concept length as performance metrics. The mean concept length is defined as the average number of words within the recognized concepts. The three parts of the evaluation look as follows:

- The first part measures the validation performance of every model, and the stability - as the mean and std. dev. of the precision based on 20 cross-validation runs. The validation performance is calculated as the f1-score of the final model on the validation set.
- Second, the evaluation measures the average performance of all the models on four datasets - the full Hulth and DUC dataset, 1'000 unseen news articles, and 1'000 randomly selected Wikipedia articles. Using four different kinds of datasets ensures that the resulting models do not overfit with regards to the kind of documents of the training corpus.
- The final part focus on interpreting a model and its predictions - according to the three objectives of XAI [13]. Those interpretations measure the impact of the single features (simultability), the dependence of the prediction on their different values (decomposability), and the exploration of a single prediction with regards to the different feature values (post-hoc interpretability).

5 Results

The following section shows the result of the stability, performance, and interpretability evaluation.

STABILITY: We use the stability to measure the generalizability as the std. dev. of the precision and the f1-score. Thus, a lower std. dev. value indicates a higher stability. We observe an average std. dev. precision and f1-score of 2.4%, 51% for all models, along with a negative Pearson correlation of -0.533 with the validated f1-score. In detail, we see that the tree based models (**DC** and **RF**) have higher scores (0.59%, 70% and 0.68%, 68%) than **LR** (4.6%, 34.6%) and **NB** (3.8%, 29%). In terms of time complexity, Naive Bayes models are trained the fastest (mean of 5 s), compared to Logistic Regression and Decision Tree models with 223 s, and the Random Forest with 972 s. Furthermore, models using the **dec_tree_mean** feature set has the highest scores (0.35%, 76%) compared to the others with a stability score of 1.4% to 3.3 % and f1-score of 71% to 42%.

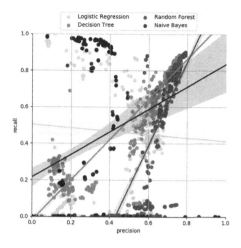

Fig. 2. Scatter plot of precision and recall of all models

PERFORMANCE: The second step of the evaluation measures the performance of all models on the four different datasets. Figure 2 shows the average precision and recall of every model for the four datasets. Decision Tree models have an almost linear relationship between precision and recall. The Random Forest models strengthen the precision, and the other twos favor, in general, a larger recall score. Besides, we observe, on average, an std. dev. of 0.03 of the precision, and 0.02 of the recall within the four test sets, A closer look reveals more detailed results with regards to the f1-score and mean concept length. The tree base models (**DT** and **RF**) have a f1-score of 0.53, 0.49 and mean concept length of 1.83, and 1.46. Additional **LR** and **NB** models have mean length of 1.86 and a f1-score of 0.35, and 0.21. The tree base feature measurements have an f1-score between 0.53 to 0.56 and a mean length of 1.19 to 1.44. In contrast, the internal measurements have a mean f1-score of 0.33 to 0.41 and mean length between 1.74 to 1.84. Overall we measure a Pearson correlation between the f1-score and the mean concept length of -0.61. Table 2 shows the comparison of models trained with the proposed text features and the **CNN** models. This comparison includes the precision, recall, and f1-score of the model with the highest, the lowest, and the median score. The table contains the complete feature set (precision *pr*, recall *re*, f1-score *f1*, mean length *avg*) of the single selected models. Overall the models trained with the text features have higher precision and f1-score than the **CNN** models while the **CNN** models achieve a lot better recall scores.

INTERPRETABILITY: The usage of our proposed understandable text features can help to understand the ongoing decision processes of a model and reveals new insights into the data. We show, following, how to fulfill the three objectives formulated by Lipton [13], using the four model types trained with top ten features, according to the **total_ n** ranking, and three million samples:

Table 1. On the **LEFT**, comparison of feature impact for the four model types, and on the **RIGHT** the local analysis of classifying *Western Hemisphere* as a concept

Feature	Importance	RF	DT	LG	NB	RF 78.5%	DT 100%	LG 41.1%	NB 99%
pmi_{all_μ}	0.45	5	4	4	8	0.056	0.1349	0.0678	0.042
pmi_{seq_μ}	0.45	8	7	5	9	0.056	0.1349	0.0678	0.042
nsd_{σ_μ}	0.27	2	3	1	1	0.0089	0.033	-0.057	-0.0167
$tfridf_{\sigma_\sigma}$	0.26	7	6	6	3	-0.03	-0.028	-0.036	-0.0178
z_{all_μ}	0.22	9	9	10	7	0.0013	0.0054	0.0014	0.011
idf_μ	0.20	1	2	8	5	0.018	0.056	0.0073	0.012
chi_{seq_μ}	0.17	10	10	9	10	-0.015	0.0015	0.0099	-0.005
pri_{σ_μ}	0.16	3	1	3	2	-0.0176	-0.0384	-0.0537	-0.0089
pri_{σ_σ}	0.14	6	8	2	4	-0.0249	-0.0388	0.078	-0.0079
$apmi_{all_\mu}$	0.13	4	5	7	6	-0.065	-0.16	-0.078	-0.0027

Table 2. Comparison of the concept recognition performance with the previous approach (**CNN**)

Metric		Text features				CNN			
		pr	re	f1	avg	pr	re	f1	avg
Precision	Median	**0.60**	0.61	0.60	1.11	**0.28**	0.99	0.45	1.46
	Min	**0.10**	0.16	0.12	3.38	**0.24**	0.99	0.39	1.60
	Max	**0.80**	0.92	0.86	1.1	**0.33**	0.94	0.48	1.28
Recall	median	0.70	**0.71**	0.70	1.22	0.26	**0.98**	0.41	1.49
	Min	0.32	**0.10**	0.15	2.15	0.32	**0.94**	0.47	1.46
	Max	0.13	**0.99**	0.22	2.61	0.26	**0.99**	0.40	1.33
f1	Median	0.59	0.54	**0.57**	1.13	0.29	0.99	**0.44**	1.46
	Min	0.11	0.10	**0.11**	3.4	0.24	0.99	**0.38**	1.6
	Max	0.81	0.912	**0.86**	1.1	0.32	0.94	**0.48**	1.28

- SIMULTABILITY, Table 1 shows the importance of the ten features along with a rank approximation of them for the different models. This approximation uses ten-thousand samples to approximate the influence of the features proposed by Wei et al. [23]. One can see that the feature nsd_{σ_μ} (the mean of the standard deviations of the normalized maximum spreading distance of every stem of the n-gram) has a potentially high impact. In contrast, the chi_{seq_μ} feature (the mean *chi* value of the word pairs in an n-gram) is less important for all models. Furthermore, the feature idf_μ (mean *idf* value of the stems within an n-gram) seems to be more important for tree-based models and less for Naive Bayes or Logistic Regression.
- DECOMPOSABILITY, Fig. 3 shows the partial dependence curve [7] of the feature idf_μ for the different features. In contrast to the previously shown importance, this method shows how the different feature values affect the prediction. It reveals that for tree-based models (**DT**, **RF**), changing the idf_μ increases the probability of observing a concept ($p(Concept)$). While for the other two

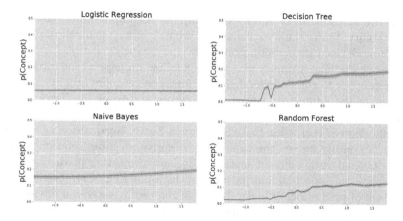

Fig. 3. Comparison of the partial dependence curve of the feature idf_μ of the *N-Gram* for all the types of model

models, this feature has a marginal impact. With this information and the knowledge that a high *idf* value is a sign for rarity, we can hypothesize that the tree-based models favour classifying samples as concepts containing stems, that are rare in general.

- POST-HOC INTERPRETABILITY, the way of analyzing a single prediction (as in "Model Interpretation" in Sect. 2) allows exploring the impact of single feature values to a prediction. Table 1 shows that the models **DT**, **RF**, and **NB** classify the n-gram *Western Hemisphere* correctly as concept with varying certainty from 78.5% to 100%. Furthermore, we can see the influence of the features on the prediction - a positive value increases the certainty, and a negative score decreases it. Thus, the tight misclassification (41.1%) of the **LG** model origins in the values of the features nsd_{σ_μ}, $apmi_{all_\mu}$, or pri_{σ_μ}. Furthermore, these interpretations confirm the positive influence of the *idf* feature on the tree-based models.

6   Conclusions

The results of the showcase experiment reveal that our proposed feature framework helps to build understandable models to recognize concepts. We noted high concept recognition performance and high stability. Besides, we see that the most promising models are trained using a Decision Tree and features weighted by the tree-based approach. These models have high f1-scores and need less time to train compared to Random Forest models - with slightly lower scores. Additionally, those models gain better f1-score and precision than the **CNN** approach.

Generally, our presented framework produces understandable and meaningful text features. They can encode a sample with a dynamic number of words within fixed dimensions. This structure enables us to take into account the surrounding context. Furthermore, we showed with the experiment that these features help to fulfill three objectives of **XAI** - simultability, decomposability, and post-hoc interpretability. Using these explanations, we can justify, control, improve, and explore a model and its decision processes.

With our findings in mind, we see three follow up aspects for further work. First, we propose to run an extended experiment to get more insights about how generalizable the expressive power and interpretability of the **Text Feature Framework** are. Such an extension could involve the usage of the text features for classification or regression tasks like Named Entity Recognition or Sentiment Analysis. Secondly, we see the capability to derive an interpretation for other models - trained with different features. By back-projecting predictions to our feature space, we expect to find patterns in the input to give an understandable explanation of predictions. Finally, based on the result, we see an advantageous effect on considering the context (neighbor words) of a sample. Instead of doing this explicit, we propose to explore the opportunities of models that encode the context implicit by construction - like Recurrent Neural Networks or Transformer Networks.

References

1. Adadi, A., Berrada, M.: Peeking inside the black-box: a survey on explainable artificial intelligence (XAI). IEEE Access **6**, 52138–52160 (2018)
2. Armstrong, S., Church, K.W., Isabelle, P., Manzi, S., Tzoukermann, E., Yarowsky, D.: Natural Language Processing Using Very Large Corpora. TLTB, vol. 11. Springer, Dordrecht (2013). https://doi.org/10.1007/978-94-017-2390-9
3. Bortz, J., Döring, N.: Forschungsmethoden und Evaluation für Human-und Sozialwissenschaftler: Limitierte Sonderausgabe. Springer, Heidelberg (2007). https://doi.org/10.1007/978-3-540-33306-7
4. Christopher, D.M., Prabhakar, R., Hinrich, S.: Introduction to Information Retrieval. Cambridge University Press, Cambridge (2008)
5. Devlin, J., Chang, M.W., Lee, K., Toutanova, K.: BERT: pre-training of deep bidirectional transformers for language understanding. arXiv preprint arXiv:1810.04805 (2018)
6. Evert, S.: The statistics of word cooccurrences: word pairs and collocations. Ph.D. thesis, IMS, University of Stuttgar (2005)
7. Friedman, J., Hastie, T., Tibshirani, R.: The Elements of Statistical Learning. SSS, vol. 1. Springer, New York (2001). https://doi.org/10.1007/978-0-387-21606-5
8. Gelfand, B., Wulfekuler, M., Punch, W.: Automated concept extraction from plain text. In: AAAI 1998 Workshop on Text Categorization, pp. 13–17 (1998)
9. Guyon, I., Elisseeff, A.: An introduction to variable and feature selection. J. Mach. Learn. Res. **3**, 1157–1182 (2003)
10. Halko, N., Martinsson, P.G., Tropp, J.A.: Finding structure with randomness: probabilistic algorithms for constructing approximate matrix decompositions. SIAM Rev. **53**(2), 217–288 (2011)
11. Hofmann, K., Tsagkias, M., Meij, E., de Rijke, M.: A comparative study of features for keyphrase extraction in scientific literature. In: Proceedings of the 18th ACM Conference on Information And Knowledge Management, Hong Kong, China (2009)

12. Hulth, A.: Improved automatic keyword extraction given more linguistic knowledge. In: Proceedings of the 2003 Conference on Empirical Methods in Natural Language Processing, pp. 216–223. Association for Computational Linguistics (2003)
13. Lipton, Z.C.: The mythos of model interpretability. Queue **16**(3), 31–57 (2018)
14. Mikolov, T., Sutskever, I., Chen, K., Corrado, G.S., Dean, J.: Distributed representations of words and phrases and their compositionality. In: Advances in Neural Information Processing Systems, pp. 3111–3119 (2013)
15. Parameswaran, A., Garcia-Molina, H., Rajaraman, A.: Towards the web of concepts: extracting concepts from large datasets. Proc. VLDB Endow. **3**(1–2), 566–577 (2010)
16. Pennington, J., Socher, R., Manning, C.D.: GloVe: global vectors for word representation. In: Proceedings of the 2014 Conference on Empirical Methods in Natural Language Processing (EMNLP), pp. 1532–1543 (2014)
17. Peters, M., et al.: Deep contextualized word representations. In: Proceedings of the 2018 Conference of the North American Chapter of the Association for Computational Linguistics: Human Language Technologies, Volume 1 (Long Papers), pp. 2227–2237. Association for Computational Linguistics, New Orleans, June 2018
18. Ribeiro, M.T., Singh, S., Guestrin, C.: Why should I trust you?: explaining the predictions of any classifier. In: Proceedings of the 22nd ACM SIGKDD International Conference on Knowledge Discovery and Data Mining, pp. 1135–1144. ACM (2016)
19. Sugumaran, V., Muralidharan, V., Ramachandran, K.: Feature selection using decision tree and classification through proximal support vector machine for fault diagnostics of roller bearing. Mech. Syst. Signal Process. **21**(2), 930–942 (2007)
20. Szumilas, M.: Explaining odds ratios. J. Can. Acad. Child Adolesc. Psychiatry **19**(3), 227 (2010)
21. Tate, R.F.: Correlation between a discrete and a continuous variable. Point-biserial correlation. Ann. Math. Stat. **25**(3), 603–607 (1954)
22. Waldis, A., Mazzola, L., Kaufmann, M.: Concept extraction with convolutional neural networks. In: Proceedings of the 7th International Conference on Data Science, Technology and Applications (DATA 2018), vol. 1, pp. 118–129 (2018). https://doi.org/10.5220/0006901201180129
23. Wei, P., Lu, Z., Song, J.: Variable importance analysis: a comprehensive review. Reliab. Eng. Syst. Saf. **142**, 399–432 (2015)

Speech Processing

A Comparison of Metric Learning Loss Functions for End-To-End Speaker Verification

Juan M. Coria$^{(\boxtimes)}$ⓘ, Hervé Bredinⓘ, Sahar Ghannayⓘ, and Sophie Rossetⓘ

Université Paris-Saclay, CNRS, LIMSI, 91400 Orsay, France
{coria,bredin,ghannay,rosset}@limsi.fr

Abstract. Despite the growing popularity of metric learning approaches, very little work has attempted to perform a fair comparison of these techniques for speaker verification. We try to fill this gap and compare several metric learning loss functions in a systematic manner on the VoxCeleb dataset. The first family of loss functions is derived from the cross entropy loss (usually used for supervised classification) and includes the congenerous cosine loss, the additive angular margin loss, and the center loss. The second family of loss functions focuses on the similarity between training samples and includes the contrastive loss and the triplet loss. We show that the additive angular margin loss function outperforms all other loss functions in the study, while learning more robust representations. Based on a combination of SincNet trainable features and the x-vector architecture, the network used in this paper brings us a step closer to a truly end-to-end speaker verification system, when combined with the additive angular margin loss, while still being competitive with the x-vector baseline. In the spirit of reproducible research, we also release open source Python code for reproducing our results, and share pretrained PyTorch models on `torch.hub` that can be used either directly or after fine-tuning.

Keywords: Speaker identification and verification · Additive angular margin loss · Contrastive loss · Loss function · Metric learning · Triplet loss

1 Introduction

Given an utterance x and a claimed identity a, speaker verification aims at deciding whether to accept or reject the identity claim. It is a supervised binary classification task usually addressed by comparing the test utterance x to the enrollment utterance x_a pronounced by the speaker a whose identity is claimed. Speaker identification is the task of determining which speaker (from a predefined

This work was supported by the French National Research Agency (ANR) via the funding of the PLUMCOT project (ANR-16-CE92-0025) and was granted access to the HPC resources of IDRIS under the allocation 2019-AD011011182 made by GENCI.

L. Espinosa-Anke et al. (Eds.): SLSP 2020, LNAI 12379, pp. 137–148, 2020.
https://doi.org/10.1007/978-3-030-59430-5_11

set of speakers $a \in S$) has uttered the sequence x. It is a supervised multiclass classification task addressed by looking for the enrollment utterance x_a the most similar to the test utterance x. After a preliminary speech segmentation step, speaker diarization aims at grouping speech turns according to the identity of the speaker.

Whether we address speaker verification (this paper), speaker identification, or speaker diarization, the objective is to find a pair (f, d) of representation function f and comparison function d with the following ideal property. Given an utterance x_a pronounced by a given speaker, any utterance x_p pronounced by the same speaker should be closer to x_a than any speech sequence x_n uttered by a different one:

$$d(f(x_a), f(x_p)) < d(f(x_a), f(x_n)) \tag{1}$$

State-of-the-art for speaker verification (like the *x-vector* approach [25]) follows this principle. Their representation function $f(x) = n(h(x))$ is the composition of a handcrafted feature extraction step h (e.g. filter banks or MFCCs) and a neural network n trained for closed-set speaker recognition on a large collection of utterances from a large number of speakers. Its comparison function d is the composition of a trained Linear Discriminant Analysis (LDA) transform l, trained Probabilistic LDA (PLDA) scoring p [10], and adaptive s-norm score normalization s [13]:

$$d(f(x), f(x')) = s(p(l(f(x)), l(f(x')))) \tag{2}$$

Metric learning techniques aim at simplifying the comparison function d to the most simple distance function (e.g. euclidean or cosine distance), delegating all the complexity to the representation function f (usually a trained neural network) that should ensure intra-class compactness and inter-class separability. Figure 1 depicts these concepts graphically in two dimensions. Given training utterances $\{x_i\}$, the neural network f produces representations $\{f(x_i)\} \in \mathbb{R}^m$ such that the angular distance θ between two utterances is small if they were pronounced by the same speaker (compactness) and large otherwise (separability).

A number of loss functions have been proposed to train such representation functions. While these approaches were mostly introduced for computer vision [8] and facial recognition in particular [4,12,23,28], they have been rapidly adopted in other domains, like speaker verification [1,3], language identification [6] and even sentence embedding in natural language processing [22].

Speaker verification suffers from many of the same issues as face recognition, since utterances from a single speaker might differ in noise, phonetic content, mood, etc. This is why we consider intra-class compactness and inter-class separability highly desirable properties for speaker embeddings as well. Recent work in speaker verification [5] has even shown that a simple cosine distance scoring with a metric learning loss can perform equally or better than a PLDA scoring on the same architecture.

Our main contribution is the systematic comparison of six metric learning loss functions for speaker verification, according to several criteria including performance, training time, and robustness. These losses can be loosely separated

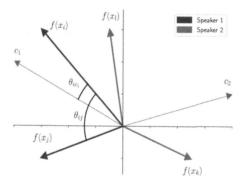

Fig. 1. Metric learning approaches aim at making representations of utterances of the same speaker close to each other, while separating utterances of different speakers as much as possible. In this example, the angular distance θ_{ij} between $f(x_i)$ and $f(x_j)$ should be small because utterances x_i and x_j were both pronounced by speaker #1, while the distance between $f(x_l)$ and $f(x_i)$ should be large because x_l is from speaker #2. Some metric learning functions internally rely on centers c_k that are trained jointly with the representation function f and can be seen as a canonical representation of each speaker

into two families (contrast-based and classification-based) and include the regular cross entropy loss, the additive angular margin loss [4], the center loss [28], the congenerous cosine loss [12], the contrastive loss [8] and the triplet loss [23]. In particular, we show (like others did before us for face recognition [26]) that the additive angular margin loss is better with respect to all considered criteria. More generally, margin-based loss functions (additive angular margin, contrastive, and to a lesser extent triplet loss) lead to representations that can be compared directly without heavy back end computations. Moreover, we show empirically that score normalization provides no significant improvement to our best models.

On the back end of the original x-vector approach, each one of LDA transform l, PLDA scoring p and adaptive s-norm score normalization s needs its own (ideally disjoint) set of training data, making the approach quite complex and data-hungry. This is our main motivation behind the use of a metric learning approach. Some existing end-to-end architectures in the literature avoid PLDA as well [11,27,29] but still rely on handcrafted features. Therefore, on the front end, we combine SincNet [20] trainable feature extraction with the x-vector network architecture to build a fully trained representation function f that processes the waveform directly and does not rely on handcrafted features: $f(x) = n(h(x))$ becomes $f(x) = n(x)$. SincNet features have proven to outperform handcrafted features for some tasks [18,21] and have been used in conjunction with an angular margin loss in [17] for speaker recognition on the simple TIMIT dataset. We believe our best models constitute a step towards a truly (front) end to (back) end neural speaker verification approach in this regard.

Finally, a more practical contribution is the joint release of the Python open-source code for training speaker embeddings with PyTorch and models pre-trained on VoxCeleb speaker verification, which we argue is much simpler than the (*de facto* standard) use of *Kaldi* [19] for this purpose.

2   Loss Functions

This section defines the loss functions considered in the study and divides them in two families: the ones relying on classification with cross entropy loss, and the ones that rely on similarity between examples.

2.1   Classification-Based Losses

The first family of loss functions is derived from the cross entropy loss $\mathcal{L}_{\mathrm{CE}}$, initially introduced for multi-class classification:

$$\mathcal{L}_{\mathrm{CE}} = -\frac{1}{N} \sum_{i=1}^{N} \log \left[\frac{\exp(\sigma_{iy_i})}{\sum_{k=1}^{K} \exp(\sigma_{ik})} \right] \tag{3}$$

where N is the number of training examples (here, audio chunks x_i), K the number of classes (here, speakers) in the training set, y_i the class of training sample x_i, and σ_i the output of a linear classification layer with weights $C \in \mathbb{R}^{m \times K}$ and bias $b \in \mathbb{R}^K$:

$$\sigma_i = f(x_i) \cdot C^T + b \tag{4}$$

To facilitate the comparison with other metric learning loss functions, Eq. 4 can be rewritten as follows:

$$\forall k \quad \sigma_{ik} = \|f(x_i)\| \cdot \|c_k\| \cdot \cos \theta_{ic_k} + b_k \tag{5}$$

where θ_{ic_k} is the angular distance between the representation $f(x_i)$ of training sample x_i, and c_k the kth row of matrix C. Because the bias b is jointly trained with the representation function f, the latter may learn to rely on the former to discriminate classes. A partial solution is to remove the bias:

$$\forall k \quad \sigma_{ik} = \|f(x_i)\| \cdot \|c_k\| \cdot \cos \theta_{ic_k} \tag{6}$$

where the kth row of matrix C can then be seen as a canonical representation of the kth speaker. Although removing the bias does improve performance slightly, this only partially solves the problem as the representation function f may still learn to encode speaker variability in their norm, which could in turn lead to a co-adaptation between representations and the classification layer. Hence, the congenerous cosine loss [12] goes one step further by forcing the model to only rely on the angular distance between $f(x_i)$ and c_k:

$$\forall k \quad \sigma_{ik} = \alpha \cdot \cos \theta_{ic_k} \tag{7}$$

where the hyper-parameter α scales the cosine, further penalizing errors and favoring correct predictions.

None of the above loss functions address intra-class compactness specifically. The additive angular margin loss [4] introduces a margin to penalize the angular distance between $f(x_i)$ and c_{y_i}:

$$\forall k \ \sigma_{ik} = \begin{cases} \alpha \cdot \cos(\theta_{ic_k} + m) & \text{if } y_i = k \\ \alpha \cdot \cos \theta_{ic_k} & \text{otherwise} \end{cases} \tag{8}$$

where m is the margin. This loss explicitly forces embeddings to be closer to their centers by artificially augmenting their distance by the margin.

The center loss [28] takes a different approach and adds a term to the cross entropy loss that penalizes the distance between training samples and a (jointly learned) representation $\gamma_k \in \mathbb{R}^m$ of their class k:

$$\mathcal{L} = \mathcal{L}_{\text{CE}} + \frac{\lambda}{2} \sum_{i=1}^{N} 1 - \cos \theta_{i\gamma_{y_i}}^2 \tag{9}$$

2.2   Contrast-Based Losses

While classification-based loss functions assume that the class of each training sample is known, this second family of loss functions relies solely on binary *same/different* annotations: given a pair of training samples (x_i, x_j), the pair is said to be positive when $y_i = y_j$ and negative otherwise.

The contrastive loss [8] aims at making representations of positive pairs $\mathcal{P}$ closer to each other, while pushing negative pairs $\mathcal{N}$ further away than a positive margin $m \in \mathbb{R}^+$:

$$\mathcal{L} = \sum_{(x_i,x_j)\in\mathcal{P}} (1 - \cos \theta_{ij})^2 + \sum_{(x_i,x_j)\in\mathcal{N}} \max(m - (1 - \cos \theta_{ij}), 0)^2 \tag{10}$$

where θ_{ij} is the angular distance between $f(x_i)$ and $f(x_j)$.

The triplet loss [23] is defined in a similar way, but instead of pairs, it relies on triplets $(x_a, x_p, x_n) \in \mathcal{T}$, such that $y_a = y_p$ and $y_a \neq y_n$:

$$\mathcal{L} = \sum_{(x_a,x_p,x_n)\in\mathcal{T}} \max(\cos \theta_{an} - \cos \theta_{ap} + m, 0) \tag{11}$$

and aims at making the representation of positive samples x_p closer to the anchor sample x_a than the representation of any other negative samples x_n by a positive margin $m \in \mathbb{R}^+$.

Because positive pairs $\mathcal{P}$, negative pairs $\mathcal{N}$ and triplets $\mathcal{T}$ need to be sampled from the training set, they bring an additional computational cost that may slow down the training process. Moreover, if tuples do not maximize the training signal (e.g. due to many positives and negatives already satisfying Eq. 1), convergence issues may appear [9,23]. These issues are usually addressed by selecting tuples carefully in a process known as *mining*, making the whole process even more costly without any guarantee of the training stability.

To circumvent these issues, we use a slightly modified implementation of the triplet loss in our experiment:

$$\mathcal{L}_T = \sum_{(x_a,x_p,x_n)\in\mathcal{T}} \text{sigmoid}(\alpha \cdot (\cos\theta_{an} - \cos\theta_{ap})) \tag{12}$$

where α plays the same role as in Eqs. 7 and 8. This idea was first introduced by [6], and can be interpreted as an approximation of the area under the ROC curve [15]. We hypothesized that the use of sigmoid may force all triplets to provide a normalized training signal, making large errors saturate to 1. Getting rid of the positive truncation also ensures that positive pairs keep getting closer and negatives pairs further apart, reducing the interest of keeping the positive margin.

While classification-based loss functions can only be used in a fully supervised setup, contrast-based loss functions that only rely on *same/different* labels can be used in self-supervised scenarios [18,21] (e.g. by only using pairs with a high estimated probability of being positive or negative).

3   Experiments

3.1   Experimental Protocol

Experiments are conducted using VoxCeleb datasets [3,16], containing utterances in English. The whole VoxCeleb 2 development set (5994 speakers) serves as our training set. The VoxCeleb 1 development set (1211 speakers) is split into two parts: 41 speakers (whose name starts with U, V, or W) serve as our development set (1000 trials per speaker), the remaining 1170 speakers are used as cohort for adaptive s-norm score normalization. Final evaluation is performed on the official VoxCeleb 1 test set.

Each loss function comes with its own set of hyper-parameters, further described in Sect. 3.3. Their optimal values are selected during a preliminary grid search experiment, training the model with each configuration for 20 hours and evaluating it on the development set in terms of equal error rate. The configuration leading to the best equal error rate is selected and used for further training the model for a total of 200 h. Once training is completed, the best epoch is selected as the one leading to the best equal error rate on the development set. Finally, we apply the corresponding model on VoxCeleb 1 official test set (40 speakers) and report the equal error rate and corresponding 95% confidence interval computed with the FEERCI package [7]. We also report the equal error rate after adaptive s-norm score normalization (whose cohort size is tuned on the development set).

3.2   End-to-End Architecture

As stated in the introduction, the network architecture used in this set of experiments combines SincNet trainable feature extraction [20] with the standard x-vector architecture [25] to build a fully end-to-end speaker verification system. Both SincNet and x-vector use the configuration proposed in the original papers (except for the SincConv layer of SincNet that uses a stride of 5 for efficiency).

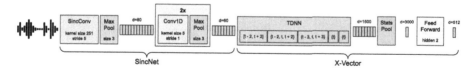

Fig. 2. The end-to-end architecture used throughout the paper combines SincNet trainable features with the standard TDNN x-vector architecture

As depicted in Fig. 2, the network takes the waveform as input and returns 512-dimensional speaker embeddings. In practice, we use a 3 s-long sliding window with a 100 ms step to extract a sequence of speaker embeddings that are then averaged to obtain just one speaker embedding per file. These average speaker embeddings are then simply compared with the cosine distance.

3.3   Implementation Details

All models were trained on GPU (NVIDIA Tesla V100) with Stochastic Gradient Descent using a fixed learning rate selected during the initial hyper-parameter grid search: we tried .001, .01, and .1. Mini-batches were built by stacking 3s audio chunks extracted randomly from the training set, making sure each speaker was equally represented. Following a successful technique from previous work [14], on-the-fly augmentation was used by dynamically adding random background noise from the MUSAN dataset [24] with a random signal-to-noise ratio between 10 dB and 20 dB.

For classification-based loss functions, the batch size was fixed to 128 (from 128 different speakers). For contrast-based loss functions that expect pairs (or triplets) of training samples, a fixed number of audio chunks from a fixed number of different speakers were stacked to build mini-batches, before forming all possible pairs (or triplets) out of it. Both numbers were added to the set of hyper-parameters for these loss functions: we tried 20 and 40 for the number of speakers per batch, 2 and 3 for the number of audio chunks per speaker. The best hyper-parameter configurations found during the initial grid search are summarized in Table 1.

4   Results

Performance – Fig. 3 summarizes the performance of the proposed end-to-end architecture when trained with each loss function. We report the equal error rate

Table 1. Optimal hyper-parameters. LR stands for "learning rate". Hyper-parameters marked with * were not tuned

Loss function	LR	Hyper-parameters
Cross entropy loss	10^{-1}	
Congenerous cosine loss	10^{-1}	$\alpha = 10$
Additive angular margin loss	10^{-2}	$\alpha = 10$ $m = 0.05$
Center loss	10^{-1}	$\lambda = 1$
Contrastive loss	10^{-1}	$m = 0.4$ 3 chunks $\times$ 20 speakers
Triplet loss	10^{-2}	$\alpha = 10^{*}$ 3 chunks $\times$ 40 speakers

on VoxCeleb 1 test set. The provided 95% confidence intervals show that additive angular margin loss significantly outperforms all other loss functions. When combined with adaptive s-norm score normalization, it even achieves competitive performance with respect to the x-vector baseline that relies on handcrafted features (and for which we could not compute confidence intervals without access to the system output).

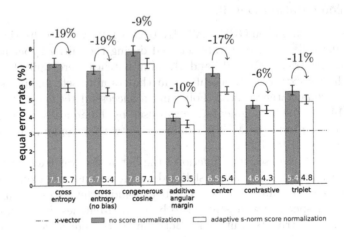

Fig. 3. Equal error rate on VoxCeleb 1 official test set, with or without adaptive s-norm score normalization. Relative improvement brought by score normalization is reported with curved arrows at the top. 95% confidence intervals are depicted as vertical error lines. Performance of x-vector baseline [25] is reported for reference

Robustness – A closer look at the relative improvement brought by the score normalization step shows that additive angular margin loss and contrastive loss are the only ones for which the difference is not statistically significant, which means that score normalization can be omitted in these models without significant performance loss. This also suggests that the use of a margin leads to representations that are both better (in terms of performance) and more robust to domain mismatch.

Training time – Despite training the models for 200 h each, some of them were still improving on the development set when the time limit was reached: the congenerous cosine loss and the contrast-based (contrastive and triplet) losses. A closer look at convergence time with respect to the amount of data seen by each model is presented in Table 2. We observe that the difference in training time is also correlated to the amount of audio chunks seen, which shows that in general this slower convergence is due to the need for more training examples rather than implementation differences. While the relative slowness of the contrastive loss and triplet loss can be explained by the fact that they both rely on on-the-fly tuple mining, we are still unsure as to why congenerous cosine is so slow.

Table 2. Convergence time for each model in terms of examples seen and training time. The contrastive loss, congenerous cosine loss and triplet loss need more training time and examples to converge

Loss function	Epochs	Audio chunks (in millions)	Time
Cross entropy loss	208	30	60 h
Center loss	240	35	70 h
Additive angular margin loss	560	81	160 h
Triplet loss	680	98	>200 h
Congenerous cosine loss	709	102	>200 h
Contrastive loss	846	122	>20 0h

5   Conclusion

Overall, additive angular margin loss is better than the other loss functions that were considered in this study both in terms of performance and robustness, and with a reasonable convergence time. The only drawback we identify is the fact that it can only be used in a fully supervised learning scenario (contrary to our second best model, the contrastive loss). Moreover, our two best models show no significant improvement after score normalization, achieving competitive performance with respect to the x-vector baseline even without the heavy front and back-end computations.

As stated in the introduction, a model pretrained on VoxCeleb 2 with additive angular margin loss is available on `torch.hub`. Comparing two utterances for speaker verification is achieved with a few lines of commented Python code:

```
1   # load pretrained model from torch.hub
2   import torch
3   model = torch.hub.load('pyannote/pyannote-audio', 'emb')
4
5   # extract embeddings for the whole files
6   emb1 = model({'audio': '/path/to/file1.wav'})
7   emb2 = model({'audio': '/path/to/file2.wav'})
8
9   # compute distance between embeddings
10  from scipy.spatial.distance import cdist
11  import numpy as np
12  distance = np.mean(cdist(emb1, emb2, metric='cosine'))
```

Reproducible Research

The companion Github repository[1] provides instructions to reproduce the main findings of this comparison. It is based on the `pyannote.audio` [2] toolkit that can be used to train (or fine-tune pretrained) models on a different dataset.

References

1. Bredin, H.: TristouNet: triplet loss for speaker turn embedding. In: 2017 IEEE International Conference on Acoustics, Speech and Signal Processing (ICASSP), pp. 5430–5434. IEEE (2017)
2. Bredin, H., et al.: pyannote.audio: neural building blocks for speaker diarization. In: 2020 IEEE International Conference on Acoustics, Speech and Signal Processing (ICASSP), pp. 7124–7128. IEEE (2020)
3. Chung, J.S., Nagrani, A., Zisserman, A.: VoxCeleb2: deep speaker recognition. In: Interspeech, pp. 1086–1090 (2018)
4. Deng, J., Guo, J., Zafeiriou, S.: ArcFace: additive angular margin loss for deep face recognition. In: 2019 IEEE Conference on Computer Vision and Pattern Recognition (CVPR), pp. 4685–4694 (2019)
5. Garcia-Romero, D., McCree, A., Snyder, D., Sell, G.: JHU-HLTCOE System for VoxSRC 2019 (2019). http://www.robots.ox.ac.uk/~vgg/data/voxceleb/data_workshop/JHU-HLTCOE_VoxSRC.pdf
6. Gelly, G., Gauvain, J.: Spoken language identification using LSTM-based angular proximity. In: Interspeech, pp. 2566–2570 (2017)
7. Haasnoot, E., Khodabakhsh, A., Zeinstra, C., Spreeuwers, L., Veldhuis, R.: FEERCI: a package for fast non-parametric confidence intervals for equal error rates in amortized O(m log n). In: Bromme, A., Uhl, A., Busch, C., Rathgeb, C., Dantcheva, A. (eds.) 2018 International Conference of the Biometrics Special Interest Group, BIOSIG 2018. IEEE (2018). https://doi.org/10.23919/BIOSIG.2018.8553607
8. Hadsell, R., Chopra, S., LeCun, Y.: Dimensionality reduction by learning an invariant mapping. In: 2006 IEEE Computer Society Conference on Computer Vision and Pattern Recognition (CVPR 2006), vol. 2, pp. 1735–1742. IEEE (2006)

---

[1] `github.com/juanmc2005/SpeakerEmbeddingLossComparison`.

9. Hermans, A., Beyer, L., Leibe, B.. In defense of the triplet loss for person re-identification. arXiv preprint arXiv:1703.07737 (2017)

10. Ioffe, S.: Probabilistic linear discriminant analysis. In: Leonardis, A., Bischof, H., Pinz, A. (eds.) ECCV 2006. LNCS, vol. 3954, pp. 531–542. Springer, Heidelberg (2006). https://doi.org/10.1007/11744085_41

11. Li, Y., Gao, F., Ou, Z., Sun, J.: Angular softmax loss for end-to-end speaker verification. In: 2018 11th International Symposium on Chinese Spoken Language Processing (ISCSLP), pp. 190–194. IEEE (2018)

12. Liu, Y., Li, H., Wang, X.: Rethinking feature discrimination and polymerization for large-scale recognition. arXiv preprint arXiv:1710.00870 (2017)

13. Matejka, P., et al.: Analysis of Score Normalization in Multilingual Speaker Recognition. In: Interspeech, pp. 1567–1571 (2017)

14. Mclaren, M., Castán, D., Nandwana, M.K., Ferrer, L., Yilmaz, E.: How to train your speaker embeddings extractor. In: Proceedings of the Odyssey 2018 the Speaker and Language Recognition Workshop, pp. 327–334 (2018)

15. Mingote, V., Miguel, A., Ortega, A., Lleida, E.: Optimization of the area under the ROC curve using neural network supervectors for text-dependent speaker verification. Comput. Speech Lang. **63**, 101078 (2020)

16. Nagrani, A., Chung, J.S., Zisserman, A.: VoxCeleb: a large-scale speaker identification dataset. In: Interspeech, pp. 2616–2620 (2017)

17. Nunes, J.A.C., Macêdo, D., Zanchettin, C.: Additive margin SincNet for speaker recognition. In: 2019 International Joint Conference on Neural Networks (IJCNN), pp. 1–5. IEEE (2019)

18. Pascual, S., Ravanelli, M., Serrà, J., Bonafonte, A., Bengio, Y.: Learning problem-agnostic speech representations from multiple self-supervised tasks. In: Interspeech, pp. 161–165 (2019)

19. Povey, D., et al.: The kaldi speech recognition toolkit. In: IEEE 2011 Workshop on Automatic Speech Recognition and Understanding. IEEE Signal Processing Society, December 2011, IEEE Catalog No.: CFP11SRW-USB

20. Ravanelli, M., Bengio, Y.: Speaker recognition from raw waveform with SincNet. In: 2018 IEEE Spoken Language Technology Workshop (SLT), pp. 1021–1028 (2018)

21. Ravanelli, M., et al.: Multi-task self-supervised learning for robust speech recognition. In: 2020 IEEE International Conference on Acoustics, Speech and Signal Processing (ICASSP), pp. 6989–6993. IEEE (2020)

22. Reimers, N., Gurevych, I.: Sentence-BERT: sentence embeddings using siamese BERT-networks. In: EMNLP/IJCNLP (2019)

23. Schroff, F., Kalenichenko, D., Philbin, J.: FaceNet: a unified embedding for face recognition and clustering. In: IEEE Conference on Computer Vision and Pattern Recognition (CVPR), pp. 815–823 (2015)

24. Snyder, D., Chen, G., Povey, D.: MUSAN: a music, speech, and noise corpus. arXiv preprint arXiv:1510.08484 (2015)

25. Snyder, D., Garcia-Romero, D., Sell, G., Povey, D., Khudanpur, S.: X-Vectors: robust DNN embeddings for speaker recognition. In: 2018 IEEE International Conference on Acoustics, Speech and Signal Processing (ICASSP), pp. 5329–5333 (2018)

26. Srivastava, Y., Murali, V., Dubey, S.R.: A performance comparison of loss functions for deep face recognition. arXiv preprint arXiv:1901.05903 (2019)

27. Wan, L., Wang, Q., Papir, A., Moreno, I.L.: Generalized end-to-end loss for speaker verification. In: 2018 IEEE International Conference on Acoustics, Speech and Signal Processing (ICASSP), pp. 4879–4883. IEEE (2018)

28. Wen, Y., Zhang, K., Li, Z., Qiao, Y.: A discriminative feature learning approach for deep face recognition. In: Leibe, B., Matas, J., Sebe, N., Welling, M. (eds.) ECCV 2016. LNCS, vol. 9911, pp. 499–515. Springer, Cham (2016). https://doi.org/10.1007/978-3-319-46478-7_31
29. Zhang, C., Koishida, K.: End-to-end text-independent speaker verification with triplet loss on short utterances. In: Interspeech, pp. 1487–1491 (2017). https://doi.org/10.21437/Interspeech.2017-1608

ANN-MLP Classifier of Native and Nonnative Speakers Using Speech Rhythm Cues

Ghania Droua-Hamdani[✉]

Centre for Scientific and Technical Research on Arabic Language Development (CRSTDLA),
Algiers, Algeria
gh.droua@post.com

Abstract. In this paper, speech rhythm metrics were used in classification of native vs. nonnative speakers. The speech corpus exploited is a part of West Point corpus. Nonnative speakers (14) are English participants who read the same set of Arabic text then their Arabic counterpart (15). Seven rhythm metrics from all vowels and consonants were calculated from 145 sentences using two rhythm models: Interval Measures (IM) and Compensation/Control Index (CCI). Rhythm data were use as input vector of ANN-MLP classifier. The classifier was trained and tested using different configurations of the input vectors. The best accuracy of the engine achieved (80.7%) when we used all speech rhythm input vectors.

Keywords: Rhythm metrics · Modern Standard Arabic · MLP-NN classifier · Native speakers · Nonnative speakers

1 Introduction

Speech prosody of native or non-native speakers is one of the main features contributing to the perception of a foreign accent [1]. Prosody deals with those elements of speech that are not individual phonetic units such as vowels and consonants but are properties of larger segments of speech like utterances. These contribute to linguistic functions such as intonation, stress, and rhythm. This paper is part of a larger project studying the speech prosody of Modern Standard Arabic and its impact on evaluation of the automatic speakers' recognizers. Among the prosodic features that can distinguish between speakers' accent, rhythm is one of the most robust and well-studied parameters. Over the last decades, speech rhythm has been the focus of a great deal of research in particular in language comparison, language acquisition, recognition of emotion, spoken language and speech accent identification [1–5].

The current research deals with speech rhythm data that were extracted from recordings of native (L1) and nonnative (L2) speakers. Texts used for the purpose is a Modern Standard Arabic (MSA). The speech material is taken from West Point corpus [6]. ANN classifier system was built to recognize both (Arabic vs. English) speakers. The ANN input vectors were performed with speech rhythm values. Many varieties of Artificial Neural Networks (ANNs) have appeared over the years, with widely varying properties. Indeed, they have been successfully applied to several speech recognition tasks as

© Springer Nature Switzerland AG 2020
L. Espinosa-Anke et al. (Eds.): SLSP 2020, LNAI 12379, pp. 149–156, 2020.
https://doi.org/10.1007/978-3-030-59430-5_12

in speech language identification and speech regional accent identification [7–11]. The kind used in the study is a Multilayer Perceptron (MLP)-ANN.

Modern Standard Arabic (MSA) is the official Arabic language in 22 countries. MSA phonetic system is composed of 28 consonants (C) and six vowels (three short vowels (v) vs. three long vowels (V). Three properties characterize MSA phonetic alphabet: pharyngeal consonants, emphatic consonants and gemination (consonant doubling).

The organization of the paper is as follows: Sect. 2 gives some notions on speech rhythm models. Section 3 presents the methodology followed in the study. Section 4 carries out results of different rhythm experiments and classifier accuracies. Section 5 concludes this work.

2 Speech Rhythm Metrics

Based on the auditory impression that speech events components reoccur periodically in the speech stream, languages can be categorized according to whether they are stress-timed languages (Arabic, English, etc.); syllable-timed (French, Spanish, etc.) and mora-timed (Japanese, etc.) [12]. To quantify variation in speech rhythm, researchers implemented many algorithms basing on phonemes' duration (consonant and vowels). While [13] developed a set of features called Interval Measures (IM) that were normalized later by [14]. White et al. [15] advocated for Pairwise Variability Indices (PVI). Bertinetto et al. [16] proposed the Compensation and Control Index (CCI) focusing on syllable complexity. Speech is perceived as a sequence of events in time, rhythm is used to refer to the way these events are distributed in time. The IM approach involves computing of three separate measures from the segmentation of speech signals into vocalic (V) and consonantal (C) units. These measures are: ΔV, ΔC and %V.

- ΔV: standard deviation of vocalic intervals
- ΔC: standard deviation of consonantal intervals
- %V: percentage of utterance duration composed of vocalic intervals

The time-normalized metric measures (VarcoV/C) were used when it was observed that the consonantal interval measure is inversely proportional to speech rate.

PVI model is based on the temporal succession of the vocalic and consonantal intervals. The model suggests that the rPVI should be used for the consonantal intervals, while the nPVI (normalized Pairwise Variability Index) should be used for the vocalic intervals.

The formulas to compute nPVI and rPVI are respectively:

$$nPVI = 100 \times \frac{\left(\sum_{k=1}^{m-1} \left| \frac{(d_k - d_{k+1})}{(d_k + d_{k+1})/2} \right| \right)}{(m-1)}$$

$$rPVI = \frac{\left(\sum_{k=1}^{m-1} |d_k - d_{k+1}| \right)}{(m-1)}$$

where m is the number of intervals, and d is the duration of the kth interval.

CCI algorithm states that controlling languages are supposed to show low levels of compensation at intra and inter-syllabic in comparison to compensating languages. Therefore, the CCI reveals level of compression (lengthening or shortening) acceptable in a language according to the context.

$$cci = \frac{100}{(m-1)} \sum_{k-1}^{m-1} \left| \frac{d_k}{n_k} - \frac{d_{k+1}}{n_{k+1}} \right|$$

where m is the number of intervals, d for duration, and n for number of segments within the relevant interval.

3 Method

3.1 Speakers

Speech material used for the study was taken from the West Point corpus, which was collected and processed by the Department of Foreign Languages at the United States Military Academy at West Point and the Center for Technology-Enhanced Language Learning (CTELL) [6]. West Point speech files were recorded from native and non-native Arabic speakers. The corpus consists of collections of four main MSA scripts. The corpus consists of 8,516 speech files. Each speech file represents one person reading one prompt from one of four prompt scripts. The files were recorded as 16-bit PCM raw audio files, with a sampling rate of 22.05 kHz, at normal speech rate. Native speakers (75) have read 7270 speech files and non-native speakers (35) produced 1246 speech files. Recordings of 29 speakers reading five same sentences from script 1 were used for the purpose. In total, 145 recordings were used in the analysis. Table 1 shows the number and gender of speakers in the sample.

Table 1. Distribution of native and non-native speakers in Modern Standard Arabic (MSA) corpus

. Native speakers (L1)		Non-native speakers (L2)	
Male	Female	Male	Female
5	10	6	8
Total	15	14	

3.2 Measurement

Speech materials, speaking style and segmentation procedures can affect rhythm metric scores considerably. These differences yield wide variability in rhythm metric results across languages and studies. To reduce this variability, the author did the segmentation and the annotation of all speech material manually. Therefore, a set of 145 recordings of L1 (Arabic) and L2 (English) speakers were segmented into vowel (V) and consonant (C) intervals and then we extracted durations of all the units.

3.3 MLP-NN Classifier

A Multilayer Perceptron (MLP) is a class of Artificial Neural Network. MLP design consists of at least three layers of nodes: an input layer, a hidden layer and an output layer. Each of the layers is composed by interconnected sets of neurons. MLPs are fully connected; therefore, each node in one layer connects with a certain weight to every node of the next layer. Input layer of this network has N units for an N dimensional input vector. For training, MLP utilizes a supervised learning gradient called back-propagation. During the training phase, the weights are optimized in order to minimize the error function. Sigmoid function is one of commonly used activation function. Under experimental conditions, the problem of finding an appropriate architecture for the network (weight, number of layers and neurons, etc.) means that the MLP-NN engine must be trained several times.

The block-diagram of the ANN-MLP of a proposed approach is illustrated in Fig. 1.

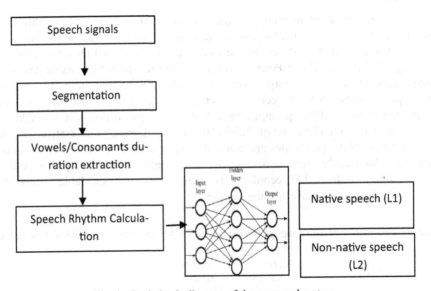

Fig. 1. Basic bock-diagram of the proposed system

4   Results

Seven rhythm metrics were computed from durations of vowels and consonants extracted from speech material of L1 and L2 speakers using both algorithms mentioned before -Interval Measures (%V, ΔV, and ΔC), two time-normalized indices (VarcoV, VarcoC), and Compensation and Control Index (CCI-C, CCI-V). Table 2 reports the average values of each of the seven rhythm metrics applied to the whole extracted data.

Speech rhythm values computed in first step were used to form the MLP input data. The engine was built using one hidden layer. Feature vector was split into three data

Table 2. Average Modern Standard Arabic (MSA) rhythm metrics (ms) for L1/L2 speakers.

Metrics	L1 speakers	L2 speakers
%V	42.41	40.12
ΔV	49.42	45.58
ΔC	53.29	43.90
VarcoV	65.14	58.64
VarcoC	50.87	49.79
CCIV	135.56	132.44
CCIC	130.97	85.46

sets: training, validation and testing data set. The speech rhythm MLP classifier was based on a back-propagation algorithm, a hyperbolic tangent and the logistic sigmoid function. The nodes in this network were all sigmoid activated. The node weights were adjusted based on corrections that minimize the error in the entire output. The training set was used to teach the network. The feed-forward algorithm assigned random weight value from input layer towards the output layer. The back-propagation algorithm went through the network iteratively, updated the weight in each layer backwards from the output layer towards the input layer then. The size of the MLP is 20 neurons.

To determine the best speech rhythm measure that allowed the MLP system to classify speakers according to their mother language English/Arabic speakers, we learned and tested the engine many times using several type of input vectors. The first configuration included each kind of speech rhythm scores separately i.e. we learned and tested seven different type of input values related to vowel vs. consonant durations - %V, ΔV, ΔC, VarcoV, VarcoC, CCI-V and CCI-C- respectively. The aim of this experiment is to assess the response of the engine when vowels or consonants rhythm scores were used individually as in put vectors. Thus, the study intended to determine the best kind of speech data that can categorize both set of native vs. nonnative speakers. Table 3 shows the outcomes of matrices of confusion for each input vector.

Table 3. Classifier's accuracies for independent input vector

Metrics	%V	ΔV	ΔC	VarcoV	VarcoC	CCIV	CCIC
Accuracy.(%)	62.8	60	63.4	56.6	60.7	57.9	62.1

Using each kind of input vectors individually, two upshots are point out from Table 1: the first result concerns the classification rates, which are globally unsatisfactory for both vocalic and consonantal rhythm measures. The second result underlined is that we had the best ratios when we have used consonant rhythm values as input vectors (63.4%, 60.7% 62.1%) in comparison with the utilization of vocalic input values). This conclusion is true for all rhythm models used. The deviation between ratios (vocalic and consonantal input vectors) is $\approx 4\%$.

The second suggestion related to input's vector configuration of the MLP consists on selecting all speech rhythm scores computed from each algorithm separately. The rhythm data comprised then both vocalic and consonantal durations. The aim of the is to assess the response of the MLP when we use different rhythm models. Thus, we composed three main input vectors: interval measures (IM), time-normalized measures (VarcoX) and Compensation and Control Indices (CCI) which included these speech rhythm values (%V, ΔV and ΔC), (VarcoV and VarcoC) and (CCI-V and CCI-C) respectively. The MLP classifier was trained and tested for each kind of vector. Table 4 gives the results of matrices of confusion for different combinations input vectors.

Table 4. Classifier's accuracies for combined Models

Vectors	IM	VarcoX	CCI	IM, VarcoX, CCI
Accuracy (%)	70.3	60.7	71.7	**80.7**

The outcomes put forward that the accuracies of the recognizer increased significantly in comparison with the accuracies given by Table 3. Depending on the type of data, which means that according to the speech rhythm model used, the MLP ratios vary. The best rate was achieved when we utilized CCI values combination (71.7%). The last investigation consisted on the employment of a mixture of all rhythm data computed by all algorithms (IM, VarcoX and CCI). As it can be seen, from Table 4, an important improvement of the accuracy of the recognizer is observed. The MLP ratio reached 80.7%. This result can be considered as a satisfactory rate that allowed the system to recognize two different classes. Thus, when an association of the whole of the data is operated as an input vector, the engine globally succeeded to categorize native and nonnative speakers i.e. Arabic speakers from English ones when the language used is Arabic.

5 Conclusion

In this paper, we have used speech rhythm metrics in classification of Arabic native vs. nonnative speakers. The speech corpus exploited is a part of West Point corpus. Nonnative speakers are English participants who read the same set of Arabic text than their Arabic counterpart. For the study, we used 145 recording produced by 29 participants (15 L1/14 L2). We computed seven rhythm metrics from all vowels and consonants of the speech material. Rhythm data were calculated using two models: Interval Measures (IM) and Compensation/Control Index (CCI). To proceed to the classification of speakers, we built a MLP-ANN engine, which expected to distinguish two classes of speakers basing on speech rhythm cues. The MLP classifier was trained and tested using different configurations according to the input vectors, which were dependent on kinds of computed segments and models used. When the vowels/consonants data were entered individually, the response of the system is insufficient. However, the recognizer gives better results when consonant vectors were assessed whatever the model used. The deviation noticed between ratios is about 4%. This suggests that the system is sensitive to difference in consonant durations between native and non-native speakers. The second configuration consisted on training and testing the MLP using together vowels and consonants rhythm values for each model. The accuracies of the recognizer increased significantly in comparison with the accuracies given in the first experiment. The improvement is about $\approx$ 10%. The best accuracy of the MLP was reached (80.7%) when we used a combination of all speech rhythm values that were computed using all models. This result can be considered as a satisfactory rate that allowed the system to recognize two different classes of speakers when speech rhythm metrics are used as input data. Thus, the classifier succeeded globally to categorize native (Arabic) and nonnative (English) speakers when the language used is Arabic.

References

1. Vázquez, L.Q., Romero, J.: The improvement of Spanish/Catalan EFL students' prosody by means of explicit rhythm instruction. ISAPh 2018 International Symposium on Applied Phonetics. Aizuwakamatsu, Japan (2018)
2. Anh-Thư, T., Nguyễn, T.: L2 English rhythm by Vietnamese speakers: a rhythm metric study. Linguist. J. **12**(1), 22–44 (2018)
3. Droua-Hamdani, G., Selouani, S.A., Boudraa, M., Cichocki, W.: Algerian Arabic rhythm classification. In: Proceedings of the third ISCA Tutorial and Research Workshop Experimental Linguistics, ExLing 2010, August 2010, Greece, pp. 37–41. ISCA International Speech Communication Association (2010)
4. Droua-Hamdani, G., Boudraa, M.: Rhythm metrics in MSA spoken language of six Algerian regions. In: 15th International Conference on Intelligent Systems Design and Applications (IEEE-ISDA 2015), 14–16 December, Marrakech, Morocco (2015)
5. Gholipour, A., Sedaaghi, M.H., Shamsi, M.: The contribution of prosody to the identification of Persian regional accents. In: 2012 IEEE Symposium on Industrial Electronics and Applications, Bandung, 2012, pp. 346–350 (2012). https://doi.org/10.1109/isiea.2012.649 6658
6. Linguistic data consortium LDC. http://www.ldc.upenn.edu
7. Zhu, Q., Stolcke, A., Chen, B.Y., Morgan, N.: Using MLP features in SRI's conversational speech recognition system. In: Interspeech 2005 – Eurospeech, 4–8 September, Lisbon, Portugal (2005)
8. Park, J., Diehl, F., Gales, M.J.F., Tomalin, M., Woodland, P.C.: Training and adapting MLP features for Arabic speech recognition. In: 2009 IEEE International Conference on Acoustics, Speech and Signal Processing, Taipei, pp. 4461–4464 (2009). https://doi.org/10.1109/icassp. 2009.4960620
9. Shuju, S., Yanlu, X., Xiaoli, F., Jinsong, Z.: Automatic detection of rhythmic patterns in native and L2 speech: Chinese, Japanese, and Japanese L2 Chinese. In: 10th International Symposium on Chinese Spoken Language Processing (ISCSLP), Tianjin, pp. 1–4 (2016). https://doi.org/10.1109/iscslp.2016.7918481
10. Bartz, C., Herold, T., Yang, H., Meinel, C.: Language identification using deep convolutional recurrent neural networks. In: Neural Information Processing, pp. 880–890. Springer International Publishing (2017)

11. Droua-Hamdani, G.: Classification of regional accent using speech rhythm metrics. In: International Conference on Speech and Computer, pp. 75–81 (2019)

12. Abercrombie, D.: Elements of General Phonetics. Edinburgh University Press, Edinburgh (1967)

13. Ramus, F., Nespor, M., Mehler, J.: Correlates of linguistic rhythm in the speech signal. Cognition **73**, 265–292 (1999)

14. Dellwo, V.: Rhythm and speech rate: a variation coefficient for deltaC. In: Peter Lang, F., Karnowski, P., Szigeti, I. (eds.) Language and Language Processing, Paper presented at the 38th Linguistic Colloquium, 231241 (2006)

15. Grabe, E., Low, E.L.: Durational variability in speech and the rhythm class hypothesis. Papers Lab. Phonol. **7**, 515–546 (2003)

16. Bertinetto, P.M., Bertini, C.: On modelling the rhythm of natural languages. In: Proceedings of the 4th International Conference on Speech Prosody, Campinas, pp. 427–430 (2008)

Deep Variational Metric Learning for Transfer of Expressivity in Multispeaker Text to Speech

Ajinkya Kulkarni[✉], Vincent Colotte, and Denis Jouvet

Université de Lorraine, CNRS, Inria, LORIA, 54000 Nancy, France
{ajinkya.kulkarni,vincent.colotte,denis.jouvet}@loria.fr

Abstract. In this paper, we propose to use the deep metric learning based multi-class N-pair loss, for text-to-speech (TTS) synthesis. We use the proposed loss function in a recurrent conditional variational autoencoder (RCVAE) for transferring expressivity in a French multispeaker TTS system. We extracted the speaker embeddings from the x-vector based speaker recognition model trained on speech data from many speakers to represent the speaker identity. We use mean of the latent variables to transfer expressivity for each emotion to generate expressive speech in the desired speaker's voice. In contrast to the commonly used loss functions such as triplet loss or contrastive loss, multi-class N-pair loss considers all the negative examples which make each class of emotion distinguished from one another. Furthermore, the presented approach assists in creating a robust representation of expressivity irrespective of speaker identities. Our proposed approach demonstrates the improved performance for transfer of expressivity in the target speaker's voice in a synthesized speech. To our knowledge, it is for the first time multi-class N-pair loss and x-vector based speaker embeddings are used in a TTS system.

Keywords: Text-to-speech · Variational autoencoder · Deep metric learning · Expressivity

1 Introduction

Text-to-speech synthesis is basically the artificial production of human speech from text. The traditional formulation of a text-to-speech (TTS) system often leaves the expressivity contained in a text. Expressive speech synthesis aims at generating synthesized speech by adding expressivity such as emotion, speaking style, etc reflecting the complex emotional states from a textual sentence. To make the artificially produced speech more realistic, a system should be able to impute certain linguistic factors such as intonation, rhythm, stress, etc usually termed as prosody. In this paper, we have presented generating synthesized emotional speech for multiple speakers. We have considered six different emotions as expressivity to transfer into a multispeaker TTS system.

© Springer Nature Switzerland AG 2020
L. Espinosa-Anke et al. (Eds.): SLSP 2020, LNAI 12379, pp. 157–168, 2020.
https://doi.org/10.1007/978-3-030-59430-5_13

Deep neural network based expressive speech synthesis has made comparatively progressive improvement in their performances in the recent times [6,9,11]. Several approaches have been proposed to transfer expressivity either by controlling the prosody parameters in latent space for speech synthesis or by transferring the expressivity using interpolation of conditional embeddings of speaker identity and prosody embedding [5,6]. The work done by [11], proposed expressivity transplantation as an extension to speaker adaptation using Latent Hidden Unit Contribution (LHUC) units. In [1,4], the variational autoencoder (VAE) framework has been adapted within the end-to-end TTS systems such as voiceLoop, and tacotron. They transform parameterized speech into latent representation and disentangle the latent speech attributes such as prosody, and speaker. But, these approaches are limited to single speaker text-to-speech system. A limited number of work has focused on integrating expressiveness into the multispeaker TTS system [5,6]. In [7], for synthesizing clean speech with controllable speaking style the authors have used a two level conditional generative model based on variational autoencoder. Most of the works uses 'global style token' or GST which is basically a style embedding to learn the expressiveness for multispeaker TTS system [8]. They created the style token embedding considering variation in prosody as well as speaking style except emotion.

Although, emotion is an essential feature in human-computer interface, not much work has done on synthesizing emotional speech using different types of emotion such as joy, anger, etc. It is difficult to effectively model synthetic emotional speech using different emotions. Besides, there is unavailability of emotional corpora featuring the different types of emotion. Moreover, it is time consuming annotating and collecting a huge dataset of emotional speech is not feasible. In this paper, we propose multi-class N-pair loss [15], a novel loss function to transfer different emotions into a multispeaker expressive TTS system for French. Deep metric learning has gained wide recognition in the computer vision and image classification domain [14]. They have used it mainly for training discriminative models. Whereas, we exploit the idea of using N-pair loss for generative model. The proposed loss function is used in a recurrent conditional variational autoencoder (RCVAE) to produce speech with multiple emotions. The multi class N-pair loss is learning objective function of deep metric learning. Our proposed approach of using N-pair loss assists in creating a robust representation of emotion in latent space irrespective of speaker identities.

Additionally, to enable multispeaker setting in TTS, we use speaker embeddings as an explicit condition in RCVAE framework. We derived the speaker embedding from speaker encoder pretrained with x-vectors. The x-vector maps the variable-length utterances to text independent fixed dimensional embeddings which are trained using a deep neural network that discriminates between speakers [16]. The speaker embeddings corresponds to the activations of the last hidden layer of speaker encoder network.

The rest of the paper is organized as follows: Sect. 2 presents the multispeaker expressive TTS approach which relies on RCVAE architecture and deep metric learning. In Sect. 2.1, we present the implementation of the acoustic model by

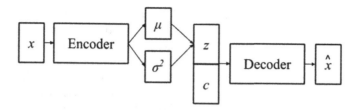

Fig. 1. RCVAE architecture used for training acoustic model. Here, x is a sequence of acoustic features to be reconstructed as $\hat{x}$, c is condition (textual features, speaker embedding) μ and σ are mean and variance parameters provided by the encoder network, and used to generate the latent variable z.

a RCVAE architecture trained using the multi-class N-pair loss metric learning. Sect. 2.2 discusses the speaker embeddings created for French speakers using a pre-trained speaker recognition model. Section 4.1 describes the pre-processing of speech and text data for the training of the multispeaker expressive TTS system. Section 4.2 describes the experimentation set up and Sect. 4 demonstrates the results obtained using the RCVAE model with and without using multi-class N-pair loss to show its impact on the transfer of expressivity. Section 5 presents the discussion on the obtained results and conclusion is presented in Sect. 6.

2   Multispeaker Expressive TTS

We build our TTS system using parametric speech synthesis approach, which is divided into duration model and acoustic model. In this section, we present the implementation of the acoustic model with multi-class N-pair loss in a RCVAE architecture as it is described in Sect. 2.1. We used an explicit duration model to predict the number of acoustic feature frames required to synthesize the speech for a given text. Hence, for predicting duration for each phoneme, we used a bidirectional long short term memory (BLSTM) based neural network as explained in [27]. Section 2.2 illustrates the implementation of speaker embedding as a adaptation technique from pre-trained speaker recognition.

2.1   Model Architecture

Variational autoencoders were introduced in 2013 by Kingma and Rezende independently [17,18]. The main components of a variational autoencoder are an encoder, a decoder, and the loss function used for training. For the RCVAE architecture, we implemented a BLSTM based encoder network. The input of the encoder is a sequence of acoustic features, x, along with condition c. Here, the condition c corresponds to textual features, duration information, and speaker embedding. The activation of hidden states of BLSTM layer is given to feedforward layers to estimate both mean vector and variance vector. The mean and variance are further used to describe the encoder's latent variable, z. Similarly, the decoder network consists of BLSTM layers. The usage of BLSTM based recurrency allows the model to extract long term context from acoustic features. The input of the decoder network are a latent variable z and the condition c. The decoder generates the sequence of predicted acoustic features $\hat{x}$, as shown in Fig. 1. During the inference, we sample z from the latent space distribution.

The loss function in VAE corresponds to the reconstruction loss plus a regularization term defined with the Kullback-Leibler (KL) divergence. The reconstruction loss represents the expectation over the reconstruction of acoustic features, $logP(x|z,c)$. The KL divergence measure indicates how close the learned distribution $Q(z|x,c)$ is to the true prior distribution $P(z|c)$. Recurrent network based VAE frameworks often leads to sudden drop in KL divergence [19]. To deal with this problem, we added variable weight, λ to KL divergence term as a KL annealing cost, as is is mentioned in Eq. 1. This assists to enhance the disentangled latent space representation with good interpretability of the latent variable.

$$
\begin{aligned}
Loss \;=\; & E_z[logP(x|z,c)] + \lambda KL[Q(z|x,c)\|P(z|c)] \\
& + log(1 + \sum_{i=1}^{N-1} exp(z^\top z_i^- - z^\top z^+))
\end{aligned} \tag{1}
$$

We use mean of latent variables as representation of emotion for expressivity transfer. Hence, the desired latent space should have well separated cluster's corresponding to the various emotions. This indicates better clustering of emotion may lead to improved performance of expressivity transfer in TTS system. Therefore, we proposed to use multi-class N-pair loss in variational inference as deep variational metric learning. Multi-class N-pair loss has shown superior performance compared to triplet loss or contrastive loss by considering one positive sample and $N-1$ negative samples for N classes [15]. This loss criteria increases the intercluster distance from $N-1$ negative samples and decreases the intracluster distance between positive samples and training examples. We employed mean of latent variables of emotion for mining the positive and the negative samples. In our case, positive samples refer to latent variables from the same emotion class and negative samples correspond to examples of different emotion classes. For N classes, z^+ is a positive sample, and $\{z_i^-\}_1^{N-1}$ samples from negative classes as stated in Eq. 1. This usage of multiple negative samples in training leads to faster convergence of the model creating a robust representation of emotion.

The RCVAE acoustic model's t-distributed stochastic neighbor embedding (t-SNE) plot shows the overlap of clusters of emotions, as illustrated in Fig. 2. We used the mean of latent variables of emotions to transfer the expressivity. If latent space has an unclustered representation of emotion, it may lead to poor transfer of expressivity. The t-SNE plot of the RCVAE N-pair acoustic model shows well-clustered emotion in latent space. The orange cluster in the t-SNE plot represents neutral speech. It is undesirable to synthesize expressive speech with modification in the target speaker's voice. This clustering of neutral speech for multiple speakers reflects the improvement in preserving the speaker's identity while transferring the expressivity. We build a RCVAE acoustic model without N-pair loss as a baseline system to evaluate the improvement in expressivity using deep metric learning.

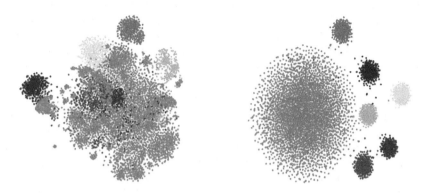

Fig. 2. t-SNE plot of latent representation of RCVAE acoustic model (left side) and RCVAE acoustic model with N-pair loss (right side). Each color represents the emotion. (Color figure online)

2.2   Speaker Embedding

The RCVAE encoder-decoder network is explicitly conditioned on the speaker embedding. We created speaker embeddings from pretrained speaker recognition model to capture the speaker's information. These embeddings should represent speaker characteristics irrespective of the textual content. For generating such embeddings, we develop a speaker encoder network from speaker recognition model trained on French speech synthesis corpora. Later, we use this speaker encoder to derive the speaker embedding.

To derive the speaker embeddings, we used x-vectors to train a feedforward neural network based speaker recognition model for discriminating between the speakers of our French speech synthesis corpora. The x-vector are deep neural network based embeddings trained on time-delay neural networks with a statistical pooling layer trained for the speaker recognition task [16]. We extracted x-vectors from the pretrained speaker recognition model trained on the vox-celeb corpus available in the Kaldi tool [20,21]. Finally, we obtained the speaker embeddings as an output of the last hidden layer of feedforward neural networks in the French speaker recognition model. The separation of speaker encoder and RCVAE framework results in lowering the complexity of network as well as requirement for multispeaker training data.

3   Experimentation

3.1   Data Preparation

We used 4 speech corpora, namely Lisa [12], a French female neutral corpus (approx. 3 h), Caroline [26], a French female expressive corpus (approx. 9 h), Siwis [23], a French female neutral corpus (approx. 3 h), and Tundra [24], a French male neutral corpus (approx. 2 h). Caroline's expressive speech corpus consists of several emotions, namely joy, surprise, fear, anger, sadness, and disgust (approx. 1hr for each emotion and 3 h for neutral). For each emotion, there are approximately 500 utterances for a total of 1 h duration. All the speech signals were used at a sampling rate of 16 kHz. Each speech corpus is divided into train, validation, and test sets in the ratio of 80%, 10%, 10% respectively.

We parameterized speech using the WORLD vocoder [22] with 187 acoustic features computed every 5 ms, namely 180 spectral features as Mel generalized cepstrum coefficients (mgc), 3 log fundamental frequencies (lf0), 3 band-aperiodicities (bap) and 1 value for voiced-unvoiced information (vuv). Based on the mean and standard deviation values, the acoustic features extracted from the WORLD vocoder were z-normalized. We used the front-end text processor from SOJA-TTS (developed internally in our team) for converting French text to linguistic features also known as context labels (dimension 180) which include pentaphone information.

3.2   Experimentation Setup

The RCVAE architecture consists of 2 BLSTM layers of 256 hidden units for both encoder network and decoder, The latent variable is of dimension 50. The training is done using a learning rate of 0.0001. The Adam optimizer initialized with default parameters, a batch size of 10 and a lambda factor of 0.001. The model was trained until the 100th epoch. To ensure better convergence of model parameters, the multi-class N-pair loss was activated only after the first 5 epochs. In the training phase, we used precomputed means of latent variables for each emotion from the previous epoch. These precomputed means are used in multi-class N-pair loss as positive and negative samples. For the baseline model, we trained the RCVAE acoustic model without multi-class N-pair loss with the same configuration as described above.

In the inference phase, we used the mean of latent variables computed for each emotion as a latent variable to synthesize each particular emotion. As mentioned before, we implemented a duration model explicitly for each speaker using a BLSTM network of 512 hidden units with the same configuration of batch size, learning rate, and optimizer as for the RCVAE architecture. For speaker embeddings, for all speech samples in corpora, we extracted 512-dimensional x-vector using the speaker recognition model trained on the voxceleb corpus [20]. Then, we implemented a 5 layer of feedforward neural network, and trained it to classify 4 French speakers (corresponding to our speech synthesis corpora) with (512-256-128-64-16) hidden units, using cross-entropy loss criteria, Adam optimizer, and

50 epochs of training. We extracted speaker embedding for each speech sample by taking the output of activations of the last hidden layer of dimension 16.

4   Results

We first computed Mel cepstrum distortion (MCD) on test data between reference acoustic features and those generated by acoustic models. The obtained results are presented in Table 1. One of the challenge we encountered was the fact that there is no reference emotional acoustic features available for Lisa, Tundra, and Siwis. Therefore, we evaluated the performance of transfer of expressivity using a subjective evaluation.

Table 1. Objective evaluation using MCD results

Model	MCD
RCVAE	5.795
RCVAE + N-pair	**5.472**

4.1   Evaluation of Multispeaker TTS

We carried out a Mean opinion score (MOS) [25] perception test for evaluating our multispeaker text-to-speech synthesis system. For the perception test, each listener had to score the synthesized speech stimuli from 1 to 5, where 1 is bad and 5 is excellent, considering intelligibility, naturalness, and quality of the speech stimuli. 12 French listeners participated in the perception test; each listener had to score 5 stimuli for each speaker-emotion pair randomly chosen from the test set. The results of the test are shown in Table 2 with an associated 95% confidence interval. The presented score for Caroline speaker in Table 2 represents the average score obtained for Caroline's neutral voice and all Caroline emotions (with associated confidence interval).

The scores for all others speakers have comparably similar results, in which Lisa speaker received the highest score for both the models trained with and without deep metric learning. Due to limited training data (1 h) for each emotion for Caroline's voice, performance of Caroline's speech synthesis for emotion is lower compared to Caroline's neutral speech synthesis. The results presented in Table 2 show that deep variational learning approach leads to better results compared to RCVAE acoustic model without N-pair loss. This is in line with the better separation between emotions in the latent space, as observed from the t-SNE plots in Fig. 2.

Table 2. MOS score for evaluation of multispeaker TTS system

MOS	Caroline neutral	Caroline emotion	Lisa neutral	Siwis neutral	Tundra neutral
RCVAE	2.7 ± 0.4	2.1 ± 0.2	2.8 ± 0.7	2.6 ± 0.8	2.7 ± 0.2
RCVAE + N-pair	**3.2 ± 0.4**	**2.6 ± 0.2**	**3.1 ± 0.6**	**3.0 ± 0.5**	**2.9 ± 0.4**

Table 3. Speaker similarity scores when transfer of expressivity

Speaker similarity	Lisa	Siwis	Tundra
RCVAE	2.3 ± 0.2	2.2 ± 0.1	2.7 ± 0.3
RCVAE + N-pair	**3.0 ± 0.1**	**2.7 ± 0.3**	**2.9 ± 0.2**

Table 4. Expressive similarity scores when transferring expressivity

Expressive similarity	Lisa	Siwis	Tundra
RCVAE	1.4 ± 0.4	1.5 ± 0.3	1.7 ± 0.5
RCVAE + N-pair	**1.9 ± 0.3**	**1.9 ± 0.4**	**2.0 ± 0.2**

4.2   Evaluation of Transfer of Expressivity

We used speaker similarity score and expressive similarity to evaluate the performance of the proposed architecture transferring expressivity onto other speaker voices. The linguistic contents of the speech stimuli and reference stimuli are not the same during the evaluation. In the speaker similarity perception test, we instructed listeners to provide a score about the similarity between the original speaker speech stimuli and synthesized expressive speech in a range of 1 (bad speaker similarity) to 5 (excellent speaker similarity). Likewise, we also directed listeners to score expressivity observed in the synthesized expressive speech stimuli on a scale of 1 (bad similarity) to 5 (excellent similarity) depending on the closeness of expressive characteristics in speech stimuli compared to original expressive speech stimuli. 12 French listeners participated in a perception test, each listener scored 3 sets of stimuli for each target speaker-emotion pair. The results of expressive similarity and speaker similarity are shown in Tables 3 and 4, with associated 95% confidence interval. Figures 3 and 4 display respectively speaker similarity and expressive similarity scores for each emotion and each speaker. Figures 3 and 4 show that similar results for all emotion are observed for the three speaker's voices, Siwis speaker got slightly lower score compared to other speakers.

The obtained results show that the addition of deep metric learning (multi-class N-pair loss) certainly improves the representation of expressivity, which leads to better transfer of expressivity. Furthermore, speaker similarity showed that while transferring expressive knowledge, addition of N-pair loss to architecture improve retainment of the speaker characteristics. Also results from Table 3

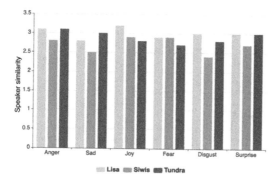

Fig. 3. Speaker similarity scores per emotion and speaker's voice, using RCVAE model trained with N-pair loss

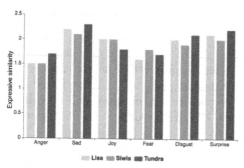

Fig. 4. Expressive similarity scores per emotion and speaker's voice, using the RCVAE model trained with N-pair loss

show that the system is able to equally transfer the expressivity not only from female (Caroline) to female (Lisa, Siwis) speakers but also from female (Caroline) to male (Tundra) speaker. Our proposed approach shows better performance for Lisa speaker than previous layer adaptation [12] approach for both speaker similarity and expressive similarity. From Figs. 3 and 4, Tundra speaker shows that sad and surprise are the emotions perceived as close to expressive characteristics with respect to the original reference speech provided in evaluation. While anger is the least perceive emotion for all speakers. In Fig. 3., we can observe that transferring anger emotion to target speakers received higher speaker similarity scores.

5   Discussion

We investigated the transfer of expressivity considering the emotional aspect of speech. The Caroline expressive speech corpus was recorded with several emotions irrespective of emotional information derived from the textual content. The available training expressive speech data is limited to 1hr per emotion. This

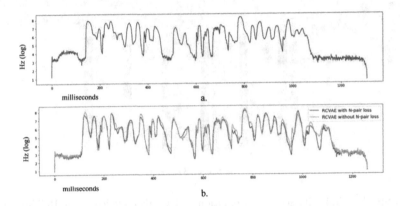

Fig. 5. lf0 trajectories for same utterance generated for a. neutral emotion for Lisa speaker, b. anger emotion for Lisa speaker synthesized using RCVAE without N-pair loss (blue) and using RCVAE with N-pair loss (orange). (Color figure online)

poses a challenge in training complex deep neural network frameworks for which large training data is usually expected. Due limited availability of training data for expressive speech corpus, we opt for parametric speech synthesis framework. The current state-of-art TTS frameworks focus mainly on transferring prosody or speaking style. These frameworks use precomputed means of emotions to perform the interpolation. In our approach, multiclass N-pair loss reduces the distance between latent variables belonging to the same emotion class. This creates a tightly bounded representation of expressivity. For instance, we can notice that trajectory of lf0 in Fig. 5.a is certainly modified after transferring anger emotion as shown in Fig. 5.b. The contour of lf0 for RCVAE acoustic model trained with N-pair loss (blue) has higher local differences (between high and low lf0 values) than the RCVAE acoustic model trained without N-pair loss (orange). This contributes to explain the better expressivity score obtained in contrast to the acoustic model without N-pair loss. We activated the N-pair loss objective after few training epochs to have a warm start for the network. Also, this ensures that reconstruction loss is converging in the right direction first. This avoids the overfitting of the clustering of latent variables. The variational metric learning provides benefits of variational inference along with a robust representation of emotion.

6   Conclusion

We presented variational autoencoder architecture trained with multi-class N-pair loss for transferring expressivity in a multispeaker text-to-speech synthesis for French. Multi-class N-pair loss function is used for the disentanglement of information in the latent space which is a deep metric learning objective. The deep variational metric learning enforce the better clustering of emotions in latent space representation.

In the presented work, speaker embeddings allow inheriting knowledge from the speaker recognition task in the TTS system. We trained speaker encoder network on speakers from our French speech synthesis corpora. The speaker representation learned in such a way ease the convergence of multispeaker TTS system. The perception tests conducted show that the proposed approach retains the target speaker voice while transferring the expressivity. This is the first approach that uses deep metric learning in a variational inference to improve the performance of latent space representation in transferring the expressivity. In the future, we would like to adopt a similar RCVAE based deep variational metric learning in an end-to-end TTS system.

Acknowledgements. Experiments presented in this paper were carried out using the Grid5000 testbed, supported by a scientific interest group hosted by Inria and including CNRS, RENATER and several Universities as well as other organizations. (see https:// www.grid5000.fr).

References

1. Wang, Y.: Tacotron: a fully end-to-end text-to-speech synthesis model. J. CoRR, arxiv.org, vol. abs/1703.10135 (2017)
2. Ping, W., et al.: Deep Voice 3: 2000-speaker neural text-to-speech, CoRR, arxiv.org, volume abs/1710.07654 (2017)
3. Sotelo, J., et al.: Char2Wav: end-to-end speech synthesis. In: ICLR (2017)
4. Taigman, Y., Wolf, L., Polyak, A., Nachmani, E.: VoiceLoop: voice fitting and synthesis via a phonological loop. In: ICLR (2017)
5. Zhang, Y.-J., Pan, S., He, L., Ling, Z.-H.: Learning latent representations for style control and transfer in end-to-end speech synthesis. In: ICASSP (2018)
6. Akuzawa, K., Yusuke, I., Yutaka, M.: Expressive speech synthesis via modeling expressions with variational autoencoder. In: Interspeech (2018)
7. Hsu, W.N., et al.: Hierarchical generative modeling for controllable speech synthesis. In: ICLR (2019)
8. Wang, Y., et al.: Style tokens: unsupervised style modeling, control and transfer in end-to-end speech synthesis. In: ICML (2018)
9. Skerry-Ryan, R.J., et al.: Towards end-to-end prosody transfer for expressive speech synthesis with tacotron. In: ICML (2018)
10. Lee, Y., Kim, T.: Robust and fine-grained prosody control of end-to-end speech synthesis. In: ICASSP (2019)
11. Parker, J., Stylianou, Y., Cipolla, R.: Adaptation of an expressive single speaker deep neural network speech synthesis system. In: ICASSP (2018)
12. Kulkarni, A., Colotte, V., Jouvet, D.: Layer adaptation for transfer of expressivity in speech synthesis. In: Language & Technology Conference (LTC) (2019)
13. Lin, X., Duan, Y., Dong, Q., Lu, J., Zhou, J.: Deep variational metric learning. In: Ferrari, V., Hebert, M., Sminchisescu, C., Weiss, Y. (eds.) ECCV 2018. LNCS, vol. 11219, pp. 714–729. Springer, Cham (2018). https://doi.org/10.1007/978-3-030-01267-0_42
14. Kaya, M., Bilge, H.Ş.: Deep metric learning: a survey. In: Symmetry, vol. 11 (2019). ISSN 2073–8994
15. Sohn, K.: Improved deep metric learning with multi-class N-pair loss objective. In: NIPS (2016)

16. Snyder, D., Garcia-Romero, D., Sell, G., Povey, D., Khudanpur, S.: X-Vectors: robust DNN embeddings for speaker recognition. In: ICASSP (2018)
17. Kingma, D.P., Max, W.: Auto-encoding variational bayes. CoRR, arxiv.org, abs/1312.6114 (2013)
18. Rezende, D.J., Mohamed, S., Wierstra, D.: Stochastic backpropagation and approximate inference in deep generative models. In: ICML (2014)
19. Bowman, S.R., Vilnis, L., Vinyals, O., Dai, A.M., Jozefowicz, R., Bengio, S.: Generating sentences from a continuous space. In: SIGNLL Conference on Computational Natural Language Learning (2016)
20. Chung, J.S., Nagrani, A., Zisserman, A.: VoxCeleb2: deep speaker recognition. In: Interspeech (2018)
21. Povey, D., et al.: The Kaldi speech recognition toolkit. In: ASRU Conference (2011)
22. Morise, M., Yokomori, F., Ozawa, K.: WORLD: a vocoder-based high-quality speech synthesis system for real-time applications. In: IEICE Transactions (2016)
23. Yamagishi, J., Honnet, P.E., Garner, P., Lazaridis, A.: The SIWIS French Speech Synthesis Database (2017)
24. Stan, A., et al.: TUNDRA: a multilingual corpus of found data for TTS research created with light supervision. In: Interspeech (2013)
25. Streijl, R.C., Winkler, S., Hands, D.S.: Mean opinion score (MOS) revisited: methods and applications, limitations and alternatives. Multimed. Syst. 22(2), 213–227 (2014). https://doi.org/10.1007/s00530-014-0446-1
26. Dahmani, S., Colotte, V., Girard, V., Ouni, S.: Conditional variational auto-encoder for text-driven expressive audiovisual speech synthesis. In: Interspeech (2019)
27. Wu, Z., Watts, O., King, S.: Merlin: an open source neural network speech synthesis system. In: ISCA Speech Synthesis Workshop (SSW9) (2016)

Generative Adversarial Network-Based Semi-supervised Learning for Pathological Speech Classification

Nam H. Trinh[✉] and Darragh O'Brien

ADAPT Centre, School of Computing, Dublin City University, Dublin, Ireland
nam.trinh@adaptcentre.ie, darragh.obrien@dcu.ie

Abstract. A challenge in applying machine learning algorithms to pathological speech classification is the labelled data shortage problem. Labelled data acquisition often requires significant human effort and time-consuming experimental design. Further, for medical applications, privacy and ethical issues must be addressed where patient data is collected. While labelled data are expensive and scarce, unlabelled data are typically inexpensive and plentiful. In this paper, we propose a semi-supervised learning approach that employs a generative adversarial network to incorporate both labelled and unlabelled data into training. We observe a promising accuracy gain with this approach compared to a baseline convolutional neural network trained only on labelled pathological speech data.

Keywords: Semi-supervised learning · Generative adversarial networks · Pathological speech classification

1 Introduction

Deep learning for healthcare applications has attracted significant research effort in recent years [14,24,26]. One such application is the use of neural networks for pathological speech classification. A challenge in this field is the scarcity of labelled training data [4,7,19,30]. Labelled medical data acquisition often requires significant human expertise and raises privacy and ethical concerns.

While labelled data availability is limited, unlabelled data are typically plentiful. Semi-supervised learning (SSL), incorporating both labelled and unlabelled data [33,34], presents a potential means of alleviating the labelled data shortage problem and thus improving overall classification performance in pathological speech classification when faced with a limited training dataset. Recently, Generative Adversarial Networks (GANs) (introduced in [9]) have been applied for SSL and have achieved considerable success with benchmark image datasets, e.g. MNIST, CIFAR-10, and SHVN.

Supported by the ADAPT Research Centre and funded by Science Foundation Ireland (SFI) under grant No. 17/RC/PHD/3488.

L. Espinosa-Anke et al. (Eds.): SLSP 2020, LNAI 12379, pp. 169–181, 2020.
https://doi.org/10.1007/978-3-030-59430-5_14

In this paper, we explore a GAN-based SSL approach for pathological speech classification that attempts to mitigate the data shortage problem. We evaluate our proposed approach by comparing its performance with that of a baseline CNN under the same training configuration. Our contributions are:

- An approach to applying GAN-based semi-supervised learning for pathological speech classification,
- An empirical experiment comparing the performance of the proposed approach with that of a baseline CNN using three popular pathological speech datasets.

The paper is organized as follows: we summarize some related work in Sect. 2. In Sect. 3, we present the proposed GAN-based SSL approach for pathological speech classification. In Sect. 4, we describe our experimental design and results. Section 5 concludes the paper.

2   Related Work

In general, pathological speech classification firstly requires salient feature extraction (as illustrated in Fig. 1). During feature extraction, raw speech signals are typically converted from the time-domain into frequency-domain features (by means of, for example, the Fourier transform). Frequency-domain features are then fed into a classifier. We summarize in Table 1 related work including relevant details on datasets, features, classifier design and resulting classification accuracy.

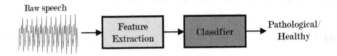

Fig. 1. A general pathological speech classification system

Generative Adversarial Networks (GANs) [9] have been employed in SSL and have been shown capable of contributing considerable improvements in overall classification performance using benchmark image datasets such as MNIST, CIFAR-10 and SHVN. In [25], several new architectural features and training procedures were proposed in order to boost GAN performance in a semi-supervised setting. In [29], SSL incorporating a GAN, specifically a Categorical GAN or CatGAN, was proposed. For the SSL task the GAN's discriminator, a binary classifier, was replaced with a $(K+1)$-class classifier (where K is the number of classes to be classified). This approach demonstrated a significant improvement in accuracy compared to traditional classifiers in image classification tasks. In [20], the proposed GAN-based approach outperformed traditional classifiers at the MNIST classification task. In [13], the proposed GAN-based SSL method

Table 1. Related work in pathological speech classification: features, classifiers and reported accuracy

Reference	Dataset	Features	Classifier	Accuracy
Poorjam et al. (2018) [22]	Data collected by the authors in collaboration with Sage Bionetworks	MFCCs	SVM	88.0%
Moon et al. (2018) [17]	SVD [3]	Jitter, shimmer and MFCCs	MLP	87.4%
Smitha et al. (2018) [28]	Supplied by the Nitte Institute of Speech and Hearing Mangaluru	MFCCs	MLP	95.0%
Shia et al. (2017) [27]	SVD	Wavelet Subband Energy Coefficients	MLP	93.3%
Alhussein et al. (2018) [1]	SVD	Spectrogram (after framing and applying STFT)	CNN	97.5%
Trinh et al. (2019) [31]	SVD	Spectrogram	CNN	99.0%
	SPDD[18]			96.7%

with manifold invariance achieved accuracy gains with CIFAR-10 and SHVN datasets. In [6], the proposed GAN method along with a complementary generator improved the overall performance in image classification tasks. Recently, MarginGAN [8] (based on margin theory) achieved high accuracy compared to other SSL methods. Besides GANs, variational inference generative methods such as Variational Autoencoders (VAE) have also been tested in an SSL context [12]. In [2], the proposed approach using sequence to sequence autoencoders for representation learning achieved a promising accuracy gain with the acoustic scene classification task.

Semi-supervised approaches have been applied in medical imaging. In [4], the authors report a significant improvement in medical imaging segmentation thanks to SSL. In [30], a graph-based SSL approach incorporating a CNN was proposed for breast cancer diagnosis. In [19], an attention-based SSL approach achieves state-of-the-art results on real clinical segmentation datasets. Work to-date in pathological speech classification has typically assumed an adequate corpus of pathological speech data. In our previous work [32], we presented preliminary results where a semi-supervised method was applied to mitigate the data shortage problem. In this paper, we further explore and extend the GAN-based SSL approach by testing against three popular pathological speech datasets.

3   Methodology

In this section, we describe our method for modifying the traditional GAN architecture to fit the task of semi-supervised pathological speech classification.

3.1   Architecture Overview

The original GAN [9] architecture is illustrated in Fig. 2a. A GAN is a generative model taking random noise as input and seeking to generate a real data distribution. A vanilla GAN consists of a discriminator and a generator. The generator takes random noise as input and generates new data samples. The discriminator's objective is to discriminate between real and generated samples (provided by the generator), classifying them as real or fake, respectively. The two networks compete with each other until an equilibrium is reached where the discriminator cannot reliably discriminate between real and fake data.

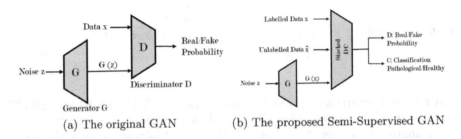

(a) The original GAN   (b) The proposed Semi-Supervised GAN

Fig. 2. Architecture overview

Let D be the discriminator and G be the generator. The minimax game between D and G is modelled mathematically as follows:

$$\min_{G} \max_{D} V(G, D) = E_{x \sim p_{data}(x)}[log D(x)] + E_{z \sim p_z(z)}[log(1 - D(G(z)))] \quad (1)$$

where $E_{x \sim p_{data}(x)}$ is the expected value over all real data samples with a data distribution $p_{data}(x)$, $D(x)$ is the probability that a real data sample is classified as real, $E_{z \sim p_z(z)}$ is the expected value over all noise samples with a prior noise distribution $p_z(z)$, $G(z)$ is the generated output from the generator from input noise z. The objective of the training process is to train D to maximize the probability of classifying generated samples $G(z)$ as fake and data samples x as real and to train G to convince D that generated samples, $G(z)$, are real. In other words, D is trained to maximize the loss function (1) while G is trained to minimize (1).

Semi-supervised GAN. To mitigate the problem of a shortage of training data, unlabelled and labelled data are incorporated into the training process in order to enhance the classification decision boundary (depicted in Fig. 3). By incorporating unlabelled data, the semi-supervised model can shift the decision boundary to better cluster the data distribution [34]. This can be viewed as the model attempting to first cluster the data before subsequently identifying the decision boundary by assuming that unlabelled data points carry the same label as the labelled data region they reside closest to.

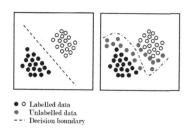

● ○ Labelled data
● Unlabelled data
--- Decision boundary

Fig. 3. Data points in supervised learning with a limited amount of labelled data (left) and in semi-supervised learning with labelled data and unlabelled data (right) [34]

A GAN-based approach for semi-supervised learning (as illustrated in Fig. 2b) incorporates data supplied from the GAN's generator and feeds the latter, along with labelled and unlabelled data, into the discriminator. In this work, we modify the discriminator to not only classify a data sample as real or fake (as in the original GAN formulation) but to also classify that sample as healthy or pathological. Using the same method outlined in [25], we modify the discriminator's architecture by adding an output layer in parallel with the output layer responsible for real/fake classification in order to classify speech data as pathological or healthy. This can be considered as a stacking of a discriminator D (for real/fake discrimination) and a classifier C (for healthy/pathological classification).

As shown in Fig. 5, the weights of the two networks (D and C) are shared across the input layer to the last hidden layer. Following the hidden layer, the output layers of D and C are separated. A detailed description of this implementation is presented in Sect. 4. The shared weight structure ensures that as D learns a feature representation from the unlabelled data, D shares that representation with C and helps C improve its feature learning compared with C being trained on only limited labelled data.

3.2   Loss Functions

We train D to maximize the probability that D classifies both labelled data x and unlabelled data $\tilde{x}$ as real but generated data $G(z)$ as fake. We train C to classify the labelled data as healthy or pathological. We train G to maximize the probability that D will classify generated samples $G(z)$ as real. We derive the loss functions for D, C and G as follows:

$$Loss(D) = -(\mathbb{E}_{x \sim p_l(x)}[logD(x)] + \mathbb{E}_{\tilde{x} \sim p_u(\tilde{x})}[logD(\tilde{x})] \\ + \mathbb{E}_{z \sim p_z(z)}[log(1 - D(G(z)))]) \tag{2}$$

$$Loss(C) = -\mathbb{E}_{(x,y) \sim p_l(x,y)}[ylogC(x)] \tag{3}$$

$$Loss(G) = \mathbb{E}_{z \sim p_z(z)}[log(1 - D(G(z)))] \tag{4}$$

where $p_u(\tilde{x})$ and $p_l(x)$ are unlabelled data and labelled distributions, $p_z(z)$ is the prior Gaussian noise distribution, $\mathbb{E}_{x \sim p_l(x)}$ is the expected value over all labelled data, $\mathbb{E}_{\tilde{x} \sim p_u(\tilde{x})}$ is the expected value over all unlabelled data, $\mathbb{E}_{z \sim p_z(z)}$ is the expected value over all noise samples, $\mathbb{E}_{(x,y) \sim p_l(x,y)}$ is the expected value over all labelled data points (x, y), $G(z)$ is the generated sample from the generator G, D is the probability that the discriminator classifies a data sample as real and $C(x)$ is the pathological/healthy classification result. The minimax game equation for the proposed semi-supervised GAN model is as follows:

$$\min_{G} \max_{D,C} J(G, D, C) = \mathbb{E}_{x \sim p_l(x)}[logD(x)] + \mathbb{E}_{\tilde{x} \sim p_u(\tilde{x})}[logD(\tilde{x})] \\ + \mathbb{E}_{(x,y) \sim p_l(x,y)}[ylogC(x)] \\ + \mathbb{E}_{z \sim p_z(z)}[log(1 - D(G(z)))] \tag{5}$$

4   Experiments and Results

In this section, we describe our experiments applying the approach above to three popular pathological speech datasets. We compare the performance of the GAN-based SSL approach with that of a baseline CNN (that shares the same architecture as the GAN's discriminator in order to ensure results produced by the two approaches are comparable).

4.1   Datasets

The Spanish Parkinson's Disease Dataset (SPDD) [21]. SPDD consists of speech samples from 50 Parkinson's disease patients and 50 healthy controls, 25 men and 25 women per group. All subjects are Colombian native Spanish speakers. Several types of speech recordings are included in the dataset:

- sustained vowels including /a/, /u/, /i/, /e/ and /o/,
- some specific words and phonemes,
- conversational speech.

We use speech data extracted from sustained vowel /a/ recordings at 44100 Hz as labelled data and from other sustained vowels /u/, /i/, /e/ and /o/ as unlabelled data in the experiments described below.

The Saarbrucken Voice Database (SVD) [3]. SVD is a collection of speech samples from more than 2000 people including healthy and pathological speech samples (with 71 different voice pathologies). There are three types of recordings in the dataset:

- sustained vowel sounds (/a/, /u/ and /i/) at normal, high and low pitch,
- sustained vowel sounds (/a/, /u/ and /i/) at rising-falling pitch,
- a conversational sentence in German.

In our work, we make use of a subset of SVD data comprising of 50 pathological speech samples and 53 healthy speech samples from the sustained vowel /a/ as labelled data and sustained vowels /u/ and /i/ at different pitches as unlabelled data.

The Arabic Voice Disorder Dataset (AVPD) [16,18]. AVPD is a collection of 353 normal and disordered speech samples. Types of voice disorders in this dataset are cysts, nodules, paralysis, polyps and sulcus. Three types of speech recordings are included:

- sustained vowel sounds (/a/, /u/ and /i/),
- isolated words including Arabic digits and common words,
- continuous speech.

Similar to SVD and SPDD, we also use sustained vowel /a/ samples as labelled data and sustained vowel /u/ and /i/ samples as unlabelled data.

For all three datasets, we include both healthy and pathological samples in both labelled and unlabelled sets.

4.2 Experimental Design

Speech Spectrogram Extraction Our chosen feature representation is the spectrogram. To extract spectrograms from raw speech, we use the librosa [15] speech processing framework. The Short-time Fourier Transform is calculated with 128 frequency components. The extracted feature matrices (with a shape (128, 96)) are then zero-padded to obtain (128, 128) square matrices.

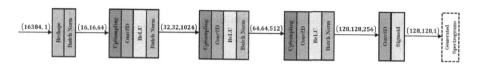

Fig. 4. The generator

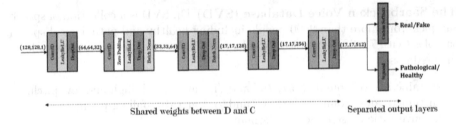

Fig. 5. The stacked discriminator D and classifier C

Semi-supervised GAN. The proposed semi-supervised GAN includes a stacked discriminator/classifier and a generator as shown in Fig. 2b. Our GAN's architecture is inspired by that of the DCGAN [23]. The architectures of the generator and the discriminator are shown in Figs. 4 and 5.

The architecture of the generator is depicted in Fig. 4. The generator's input is a Gaussian noise vector of shape $(16384, 1)$. The latter is reshaped to a square tensor of shape $(16, 16, 64)$. Next, three stages of upsampling are applied to increase the data dimension from $(16, 16, 64)$ to $(128, 128, 256)$. Each stage includes an UpSampling layer followed by a convolutional layer with ReLU activation and a batch normalization layer [10]. We finally apply a convolutional layer with a sigmoid activation function. The output of the generator is a tensor of shape $(128, 128, 1)$.

The architecture of the discriminator is shown in Fig. 5. The input to the discriminator has shape $(128, 128, 1)$. We employ successive 2D convolutional layers with filter numbers of $32, 64, 128, 256$ and 512 respectively. To the output of each convolutional layer, we apply LeakyReLU with an alpha of 0.2, a dropout layer with a rate of 0.25 and a batch normalization layer with a momentum of 0.8. The final output is then flattened and a copy sent in two directions: to a discriminator for classification as fake or real and to a second classifier for pathological/healthy classification. For pathological speech classification, the final output layer is a single neuron with a sigmoid activation function for binary classification. For real/fake discrimination, we create a custom softmax layer to output the probability of data being real.

Baseline CNN. To implement the baseline CNN, we reuse the GAN's discriminator architecture. This ensures results produced by the SSL and baseline approaches are comparable. The baseline is trained only on labelled data.

Training Configuration. For each dataset, we train our models in 100 epochs, with a batch size of 32, with the Adam optimizer[11] and with a learning rate of 0.00002. Across experiments, we reduce the number of labelled spectrogram samples for training from 1000 through 800, 600, 400 and 200 and test on 800 spectrogram samples. We use 20000 unlabelled spectrograms (without healthy/pathological labels) as unlabelled data to train the proposed SSL approach.

4.3   Results

Generative Results. We present, for visual inspection, in Fig. 6 sample spectrograms produced by the generator trained on the SPDD alongside original spectrograms extracted from the dataset. Similar frequency content is observed.

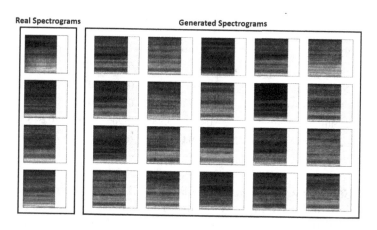

Fig. 6. Original spectrograms (left) and generated spectrograms (right)

Table 2. SPDD classification accuracy

Approach	Number of labelled data samples				
	1000	800	600	400	200
CNN [31]	0.896	0.835	0.851	0.798	0.705
VGG16-based CNN [1]	0.925	0.923	**0.929**	0.873	0.769
Baseline CNN	0.914	0.874	0.855	0.788	0.746
Proposed GAN-based SSL	**0.951**	**0.942**	0.919	**0.890**	**0.833**

Classification Accuracy. Accuracies obtained for the three datasets SPDD, SVD and AVPD are presented in Tables 2, 3 and 4 respectively. We compare the classification accuracy of the proposed semi-supervised GAN approach with that of the baseline CNN. We also compare the accuracy of the proposed approach against two additional classifiers previously proposed in the literature [1,31]. We observe an accuracy gain across all three datasets. The accuracy gains with only 400 and 200 labelled data samples are significant across all three datasets.

Table 3. SVD classification accuracy

Approach	Number of labelled data samples				
	1000	800	600	400	200
CNN [31]	0.976	0.967	0.974	0.942	0.862
VGG16-based CNN [1]	**1.00**	**1.00**	0.993	0.984	0.946
Baseline CNN	1.00	0.998	0.985	0.973	0.939
Proposed GAN-based SSL	**1.00**	**1.00**	**0.999**	**0.998**	**0.960**

Table 4. AVPD classification accuracy

Approach	Number of labelled data samples				
	1000	800	600	400	200
CNN [31]	0.984	0.939	0.939	0.920	0.870
VGG16-based CNN [1]	**0.991**	0.991	0.978	0.963	0.860
Baseline CNN	0.990	0.986	0.966	0.944	0.818
Proposed GAN-based SSL	**0.991**	**0.998**	**0.993**	**0.971**	**0.889**

Ablation Study by Removal of Unlabelled Data. To study the effect of unlabelled data on the training, we remove the unlabelled data in an experiment using the SPDD data to observe any drop in the classification performance. The result of the ablation study is presented in Table 5. We observe a significant drop in the accuracy obtained, especially when training on only 400 and 200 labelled samples and without unlabelled data. This result further validates the effect of unlabelled data on improving the classification performance.

Table 5. SPDD Ablation Study

Proposed GAN-based SSL	Number of labelled data samples				
	1000	800	600	400	200
w/unlabelled	**0.951**	**0.942**	**0.919**	**0.890**	**0.833**
w/o unlabelled	0.934	0.940	0.899	0.866	0.734

5   Conclusion and Future Work

This paper describes a proposed GAN-based semi-supervised approach for pathological speech classification tasks. Results are presented that indicate the approach has the potential to mitigate the labelled data shortage problem faced by certain medical applications of deep learning. A GAN is incorporated into SSL by replacing the former's traditional binary discriminator with a multi-class discriminator that not only classifies a sample as real or fake but also categorizes that sample as healthy or pathological. We test the approach against three commonly used pathological speech datasets: SPDD, SVD and AVPD. Comparing the performance of our GAN-based approach with a baseline CNN and two additional classifiers previously proposed in the literature [1,31], we observe a promising improvement in accuracy when we decrease the number of labelled training samples from 1000 through 800, 600, 400 and 200.

Future work will evaluate the performance of alternative GAN architectures (e.g. infoGAN [5] and marginGAN [8]) in semi-supervised pathological speech classification. Feature matching [25] will be explored as a means to improve discriminator performance. The proposed approach has potential applications not only in pathological speech classification but also across other audio classification tasks.

Acknowledgement. The ADAPT Centre for Digital Content Technology is funded under the SFI Research Centres Programme (Grant 13/RC/2106) and is co-funded under the European Regional Development Fund. Nam H. Trinh is funded by Science Foundation Ireland under grant No. 17/RC/PHD/3488.

References

1. Alhussein, M., Muhammad, G.: Voice pathology detection using deep learning on mobile healthcare framework. IEEE Access **6**, 41034–41041 (2018)
2. Amiriparian, S., Freitag, M., Cummins, N., Schuller, B.: Sequence to sequence autoencoders for unsupervised representation learning from audio. In: Proceedings of of the DCASE 2017 Workshop (2017)
3. Barry, W., Pützer, M.: Saarbrucken voice database. Institute of Phonetics, Universität des Saarlandes (2007). http://www.stimmdatenbank.coli.uni-saarland.de
4. Baur, C., Albarqouni, S., Navab, N.: Semi-supervised deep learning for fully convolutional networks. In: Descoteaux, M., Maier-Hein, L., Franz, A., Jannin, P., Collins, D.L., Duchesne, S. (eds.) MICCAI 2017. LNCS, vol. 10435, pp. 311–319. Springer, Cham (2017). https://doi.org/10.1007/978-3-319-66179-7_36
5. Chen, X., Duan, Y., Houthooft, R., Schulman, J., Sutskever, I., Abbeel, P.: Infogan: interpretable representation learning by information maximizing generative adversarial nets. In: Advances in Neural Information Processing Systems, pp. 2172–2180 (2016)
6. Dai, Z., Yang, Z., Yang, F., Cohen, W.W., Salakhutdinov, R.R.: Good semi-supervised learning that requires a bad GAN. In: Advances in Neural Information Processing Ssystems, pp. 6510–6520 (2017)
7. Deo, R.C.: Machine learning in medicine. Circulation **132**(20), 1920–1930 (2015)
8. Dong, J., Lin, T.: Margingan: adversarial training in semi-supervised learning. In: Advances in Neural Information Processing Systems, pp. 10440–10449 (2019)
9. Goodfellow, I., et al.: Generative adversarial nets. In: Advances in Neural Information Processing Systems, pp. 2672–2680 (2014)
10. Ioffe, S., Szegedy, C.: Batch normalization: accelerating deep network training by reducing internal covariate shift (2015). arXiv preprint arXiv:1502.03167
11. Kingma, D.P., Ba, J.: Adam: a method for stochastic optimization (2014). arXiv preprint arXiv:1412.6980

12. Kingma, D.P., Mohamed, S., Rezende, D.J., Welling, M.: Semi-supervised learning with deep generative models. In: Advances in Neural Information Processing Systems, pp. 3581–3589 (2014)
13. Kumar, A., Sattigeri, P., Fletcher, T.: Semi-supervised learning with GANs: manifold invariance with improved inference. In: Advances in Neural Information Processing Systems, pp. 5534–5544 (2017)
14. Litjens, G., et al.: A survey on deep learning in medical image analysis. Med. Image Anal. **42**, 60–88 (2017)
15. McFee, B., et al.: librosa: audio and music signal analysis in python. In: Proceedings of the 14th Python in Science Conference, vol. 8 (2015)
16. Mesallam, T.A., et al.: Development of the Arabic voice pathology database and its evaluation by using speech features and machine learning algorithms. J. Healthc. Eng. **2017** (2017)
17. Moon, J., Kim, S.: An approach on a combination of higher-order statistics and higher-order differential energy operator for detecting pathological voice with machine learning. In: 2018 International Conference on Information and Communication Technology Convergence (ICTC), pp. 46–51 (2018). https://doi.org/10.1109/ICTC.2018.8539495
18. Muhammad, G., et al.: Voice pathology detection using interlaced derivative pattern on glottal source excitation. Biomed. Signal Process. Control **31**, 156–164 (2017)
19. Nie, D., Gao, Y., Wang, L., Shen, D.: ASDNet: attention based semi-supervised deep networks for medical image segmentation. In: Frangi, A.F., Schnabel, J.A., Davatzikos, C., Alberola-López, C., Fichtinger, G. (eds.) MICCAI 2018. LNCS, vol. 11073, pp. 370–378. Springer, Cham (2018). https://doi.org/10.1007/978-3-030-00937-3_43
20. Odena, A.: Semi-supervised learning with generative adversarial networks (2016). arXiv preprint arXiv:1606.01583
21. Orozco-Arroyave, J.R., Arias-Londoño, J.D., Bonilla, J.F.V., Gonzalez-Rátiva, M.C., Nöth, E.: New Spanish speech corpus database for the analysis of people suffering from parkinson's disease. In: In Proceedings Of the International Conference on Language Resources and Evaluation (LREC), Reykjavik, Iceland, pp. 342–347 (2014)
22. Poorjam, A.H., Little, M.A., Jensen, J.R., Christensen, M.G.: A parametric approach for classification of distortions in pathological voices. In: 2018 IEEE International Conference on Acoustics, Speech and Signal Processing (ICASSP), pp. 286–290. IEEE (2018)
23. Radford, A., Metz, L., Chintala, S.: Unsupervised representation learning with deep convolutional generative adversarial networks (2015). arXiv preprint arXiv:1511.06434
24. Ravì, D., et al.: Deep learning for health informatics. IEEE J. Biomed. Health Inf. **21**(1), 4–21 (2016)
25. Salimans, T., Goodfellow, I., Zaremba, W., Cheung, V., Radford, A., Chen, X.: Improved techniques for training GANs. In: Advances in Neural Information Processing Systems, pp. 2234–2242 (2016)
26. Shen, D., Wu, G., Suk, H.I.: Deep learning in medical image analysis. Ann. Rev. Biomed. Eng. **19**, 221–248 (2017)
27. Shia, S.E., Jayasree, T.: Detection of pathological voices using discrete wavelet transform and artificial neural networks. In: 2017 IEEE International Conference on Intelligent Techniques in Control, Optimization and Signal Processing (INCOS), pp. 1–6 (2017). https://doi.org/10.1109/ITCOSP.2017.8303086

28. Smitha, Shetty, S., Hegde, S., Dodderi, T.: Classification of healthy and pathological voices using mfcc and ann. In: 2018 Second International Conference on Advances in Electronics, Computers and Communications (ICAECC), pp. 1–5 (2018). https://doi.org/10.1109/ICAECC.2018.8479441
29. Springenberg, J.T.: Unsupervised and semi-supervised learning with categorical generative adversarial networks (2015). arXiv preprint arXiv:1511.06390
30. Sun, W., Tseng, T.L.B., Zhang, J., Qian, W.: Enhancing deep convolutional neural network scheme for breast cancer diagnosis with unlabeled data. Comput. Med. Imaging Graph. **57**, 4–9 (2017)
31. Trinh, N., O'Brien, D.: Pathological speech classification using a convolutional neural network. In: IMVIP 2019: Irish Machine Vision & Image Processing. Technological University Dublin, Dublin, Ireland (2019). https://doi.org/10.21427/9dnc-n002
32. Trinh, N., O'Brien, D.: Semi-supervised learning with generative adversarial networks for pathological speech classification. In: 31st Irish Signals and Systems Conference (ISSC2020). Letterkenny, Ireland (Virtual) (2020)
33. Zhu, X., Goldberg, A.B.: Introduction to semi-supervised learning. Synth. Lect. Artif. Intell. Mach. Learn. **3**(1), 1–130 (2009)
34. Zhu, X.J.: Semi-supervised learning literature survey. University of Wisconsin-Madison Department of Computer Sciences, Technical report (2005)

Author Index

Bredin, Hervé   137

Caltagirone, Francesco   23
Carson-Berndsen, Julie   85
Caulier, Alexandre   23
Colotte, Vincent   157
Coria, Juan M.   137
Coucke, Alice   23

d'Ascoli, Stéphane   23
Denzler, Alexander   122
Droua-Hamdani, Ghania   149

Ghanem, Bilal   35
Ghannay, Sahar   137
Goudeseune, Camille   3
Guðjónsson, Ásmundur A.   46

Hasegawa-Johnson, Mark   3

Ingólfsdóttir, Svanhvít L.   46
Ircing, Pavel   58

Jouvet, Denis   157

Kirchhoff, Katrin   3
Knight, Dawn   71
Kulkarni, Ajinkya   157

Lehečka, Jan   58
Lelarge, Marc   23
Levow, Gina-Anne   3

Lloret, Elena   109
Loftsson, Hrafn   46

MacCarthy, Muireann   85
Mazzola, Luca   122
Muralidaran, Vigneshwaran   71

O'Brien, Darragh   169
O'Neill, Emma   85

Pikuliak, Matúš   97
Ponzetto, Simone Paolo   35

Rolston, Leanne   3
Rosset, Sophie   137
Rosso, Paolo   35

Šimko, Marián   97
Šmídl, Luboš   58
Spasić, Irena   71
Švec, Jan   58

Thiaville, Elsa   85
Trinh, Nam H.   169

Ventresque, Anthony   85
Vicente, Marta   109

Waldis, Andreas   122

Young, Robert   85

Printed in the United States
By Bookmasters